Pre-Publication Reviews of

ABOUT THE COPTS

by John H. Watson

"The Church which in one large city alone has 30,000 Sunday-school-teachers has to be taken seriously by Western Christians. Such a Church is the Coptic Church of Egypt. John Watson has spent many years studying this fascinating Church, getting to know its leaders and its people. His writing has made the fruits of this long relation-ship available more widely. I warmly commend *Among the Copts* as a substantial contribution to Ecumenical understanding."

George Carey, Archbishop of Canterbury

"*Among the Copts* is likely to take its place at once as one of the best informed and authoritative books on the contemporary situation in this great Oriental Orthodox Church whose many diaspora communi-ties are to be found today in the USA and Canada, as well as in Europe and Australia. Written with both sympathy and insight, this book will be greatly welcomed by all who have an interest in Eastern Christianity."

Dr Sebastian Brock, Reader in Syriac Studies, University of Oxford

"John Watson has a long record of concern for the Human Rights of the Copts. In the past two decades his journalism, broadcasting and academic research has been directed towards those in the West who are unaware of the long agony of the Coptic Orthodox Church in Egypt. His new work includes up-to-date comment on the situation faced by the Church in Egypt."

Bat Ye'or, author of The Dhimmi: Jews and Christians under Islam

"Fr. John Watson brings to life one of the most ancient churches, whose survival into modern times, despite many waves of persecu-tion, must be regarded as miraculous. It is a church that has not only survived but in the past century has experienced an astonishing renewal which has had an influence on the rest of Christianity."

Jim Forest, author of The Ladder of the Beatitudes
and Praying With Icons

"The section on Iconography in *Among the Copts* will be greatly valued by all who are continuing to explore the venerable and distinguished tradition of this aspect of the Coptic tradition."
Professor Keith Critchlow, author of Order in Space, Into the Hidden Environment, Chartres Maze, *and* Islamic Patterns: an Analytical and Cosmological Approach

"Fr. John in an Episcopalian priest, but his heart and soul are with the Coptic Orthodox church and the Coptic people. His book is a balance between critical examination of Coptic history and original research."
Professor Shawky F. Karas, Southern Connecticut State University

"Dr Watson's long familiarity with Coptic Christian Egypt has enabled him to chart the main themes of Coptic renewal, be it in the domains of monasticism, art and iconography and patristics. Further, his mature judgements have enabled us to understand the importance and the role of recent Coptic Patriarchs, Kyrillos and Shenouda, in the recent history of the Coptic community. He has also taken a special interest in the historical and contemporary presence of the Copts in Jerusalem and the important, but difficult, relationship between Coptic Egypt and the Ethiopian Church."
Dr Anthony O'Mahony, Heythrop College, University of London

"This book is a pleasure and a joy to read. He is a master of his subject."
Professor Fayek M. Ishak, Thunder Bay University, Canada

"The Coptic community worldwide will certainly welcome a new publication by Dr Watson because of his excellent reputation as a fair, thorough and insightful author. Even more, I claim these communities are eager to hear from him. Scholars and students of Coptology, history, political science and religion will all be interested in a fresh look at the interaction between religion and politics in the turbulent Middle East."
Dr Saad Michael Saad, President, Society for Antiquity and Christianity, Claremont, California

"The author has first-hand knowledge of the Copts and when he writes about them, especially in the recent past, he is writing about part of his own life, since he lived with the immigrant Copts in the UK as well as the USA, sharing their aspirations and their suffering."
Rodolph Yanney, Editor of Coptic Church Review, *Editor of* Al Rissalah *(Arabic), President of the Society of Coptic Church Studies*

"Dr Watson's first-hand knowledge of Christianity in Egypt is extensive and his personal library is probably better stocked with publications on this subject than any of the British University Libraries. I have long been in the habit of consulting him on all matters concerning the Copts."
Dr Andrew Palmer, Research Associate at the School of Oriental and African Studies, University of London

"Books providing good, in-depth information about the Copts are rare. Dr Watson focuses in a unique way on the contemporary spiritual life of the church, which has not been done before him. *Among the Copts* will certainly be important for western readers needing to get an understanding of this ancient church."
Dr Cornelis Hulsman, deputy secretary-general of the Foreign Press Association in Egypt

"A scholarly study of Pope Kyrillos the Sixth will be most welcome. He was an outstanding person; a saint and mystic but one who has been presented as naïve. I believe that *Among the Copts* will contribute positively to the understanding of the contemporary Coptic Church."
Youhanna Nessim Youssef, General Secretary Societe d'Archeologie Copte, Research Fellow, University of Melbourne, Australia

AMONG THE COPTS

sussex
ACADEMIC
PRESS

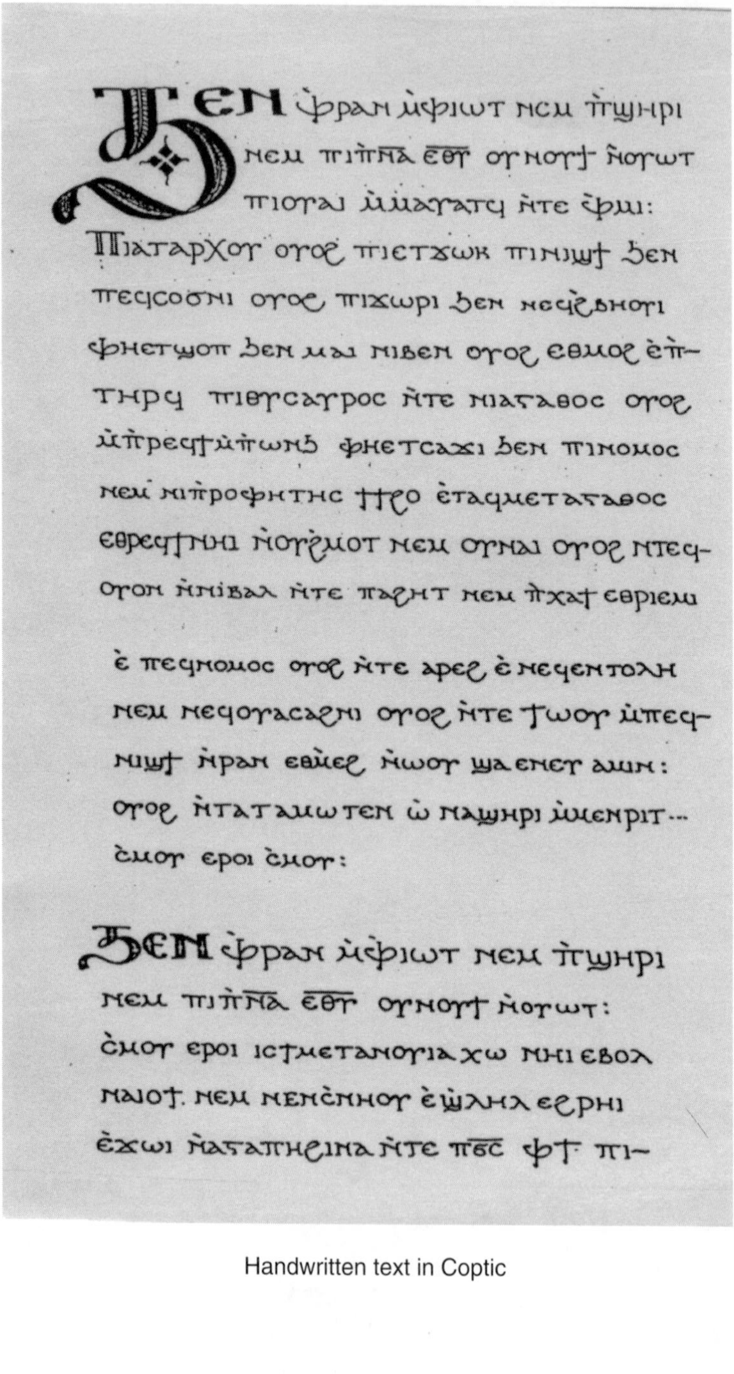

ϧⲉⲛ ⲫ̀ⲣⲁⲛ ⲙ̀ⲫⲓⲱⲧ ⲛⲉⲙ ⲡ̀ϣⲏⲣⲓ
ⲛⲉⲙ ⲡⲓⲡ̀ⲛ̅ⲁ̅ ⲉⲑ̅ⲩ̅ ⲟⲩⲛⲟⲩϯ ⲛ̀ⲟⲩⲱⲧ
ⲡⲓⲟⲩⲁⲓ ⲙ̀ⲙⲁⲩⲁⲧϥ ⲛ̀ⲧⲉ ⲫ̀ⲙⲓ:
Ⲡⲓⲁⲧⲁⲣⲭⲟⲩ ⲟⲩⲟϩ ⲡⲓⲉⲧϫⲱⲕ ⲡⲓⲛⲓϣϯ ϧⲉⲛ
ⲡⲉϥⲥⲟϭⲛⲓ ⲟⲩⲟϩ ⲡⲓϫⲱⲣⲓ ϧⲉⲛ ⲛⲉϥϩ̀ⲃⲏⲟⲩⲓ
ⲫⲏⲉⲧϣⲟⲡ ϧⲉⲛ ⲙⲁⲓ ⲛⲓⲃⲉⲛ ⲟⲩⲟϩ ⲉⲑⲙⲟϩ ⲉ̀ⲡ-
ⲧⲏⲣϥ ⲡⲓⲉⲩⲥⲁⲩⲣⲟⲥ ⲛ̀ⲧⲉ ⲛⲓⲁⲅⲁⲑⲟⲥ ⲟⲩⲟϩ
ⲙ̀ⲡ̀ⲣⲉϥϯⲙ̀ⲡ̀ⲱⲛϧ ⲫⲏⲉⲧⲥⲁϫⲓ ϧⲉⲛ ⲡⲓⲛⲟⲙⲟⲥ
ⲛⲉⲙ ⲛⲓⲡ̀ⲣⲟⲫⲏⲧⲏⲥ ϯϩⲟ ⲉ̀ⲧⲁϥⲙⲉⲧⲁⲅⲁⲑⲟⲥ
ⲉⲑⲣⲉϥϯⲛⲏⲓ ⲛ̀ⲟⲩϩ̀ⲙⲟⲧ ⲛⲉⲙ ⲟⲩⲛⲁⲓ ⲟⲩⲟϩ ⲛ̀ⲧⲉϥ-
ⲟⲩⲱⲛ ⲛ̀ⲛⲓⲃⲁⲗ ⲛ̀ⲧⲉ ⲡⲁϩⲏⲧ ⲛⲉⲙ ⲡ̀ⲭⲁϯ ⲉⲑⲣⲓⲉⲙ

ⲉ̀ ⲡⲉϥⲛⲟⲙⲟⲥ ⲟⲩⲟϩ ⲛ̀ⲧⲉ ⲁⲣⲉϩ ⲉ̀ ⲛⲉϥⲉⲛⲧⲟⲗⲏ
ⲛⲉⲙ ⲛⲉϥⲟⲩⲁⲥⲁϩⲛⲓ ⲟⲩⲟϩ ⲛ̀ⲧⲉ ϯⲱⲟⲩ ⲙ̀ⲡⲉϥ-
ⲛⲓϣϯ ⲛ̀ⲣⲁⲛ ⲉⲑⲙⲉϩ ⲛ̀ⲱⲟⲩ ϣⲁ ⲉⲛⲉϩ ⲁⲙⲏⲛ:
ⲟⲩⲟϩ ⲛ̀ⲧⲁⲧⲁⲙⲱⲧⲉⲛ ⲱ̀ ⲛⲁϣⲏⲣⲓ ⲙ̀ⲙⲉⲛⲣⲓⲧ---
ⲥ̀ⲙⲟⲩ ⲉⲣⲟⲓ ⲥ̀ⲙⲟⲩ:

ϧⲉⲛ ⲫ̀ⲣⲁⲛ ⲙ̀ⲫⲓⲱⲧ ⲛⲉⲙ ⲡ̀ϣⲏⲣⲓ
ⲛⲉⲙ ⲡⲓⲡ̀ⲛ̅ⲁ̅ ⲉⲑ̅ⲩ̅ ⲟⲩⲛⲟⲩϯ ⲛ̀ⲟⲩⲱⲧ:
ⲥ̀ⲙⲟⲩ ⲉⲣⲟⲓ ⲓⲥϯⲙⲉⲧⲁⲛⲟⲓⲁ ⲭⲱ ⲛⲏⲓ ⲉⲃⲟⲗ
ⲛⲁⲓⲟϯ. ⲛⲉⲙ ⲛⲉⲛⲥ̀ⲛⲏⲟⲩ ⲉ̀ϣⲗⲏⲗ ⲉϩⲣⲏⲓ
ⲉ̀ϫⲱⲓ ⲛ̀ⲧⲁⲧⲁⲡⲏϩⲓⲛⲁ ⲛ̀ⲧⲉ ⲡ̅ϭ̅ ⲫ̅ϯ̅ ⲡⲓ-

Handwritten text in Coptic

Among the Copts

—

John H. Watson

sussex
ACADEMIC
PRESS

BRIGHTON • *PORTLAND*

2 4 6 8 10 9 7 5 3 1

First published 2000 in Great Britain by
SUSSEX ACADEMIC PRESS
PO Box 2950
Brighton BN2 5SP

and in the United States of America by
SUSSEX ACADEMIC PRESS
5804 N.E. Hassalo St.
Portland, Oregon 97213-3644

British Library Cataloguing in Publication Data
A CIP catalogue record for this book is available from the British Library.

Library of Congress Cataloging-in-Publication Data
Watson, John H., 1939–
Among the Copts / John Watson.
p. cm.
Includes bibliographical references and index.
ISBN 1–902210–56–5 (alk. paper)
1. Coptic Church—Doctrines. 2. Coptic Church—History. I. Title.
BX136.2 .W38 2000
281'.72—dc21 99-087320

Printed by Bookcraft, Midsomer Norton, Bath
This book is printed on acid-free paper

Contents

Acknowledgements   x

One   Introduction: At the Sources of Christian
        Civilization   1

Two   Copt and Coptic   5

Three   In the State of Angels   13

Four   In Liturgical Time   33

Five   Patriarchs: Fathers of the Fathers   44

Six   Mission: For Africa and the World   73

Seven   The Egyptian Church Struggle   93

Eight   Thinking with the Church   119

Nine   Conclusion: Era of the Martyrs   142

        Appendix   151
        A Coptic Chronology   153
        Further Reading   156
        Bibliography   159
        Index of Names and Subjects   164
        Index of Biblical References   176

Acknowledgements

This book evolved from a series of visits to the Middle East over a period of four decades, frequent sojourns with the Copts in Egypt, and the writing of innumerable academic papers, book reviews and lectures in the past thirty years. I have always been an ecumenist since my period as Chairman of the Theological Colleges Union at Cambridge in the early 1960s, but the great ecumenical passion of my life has been the Coptic Orthodox Church in Egypt and the Diaspora.

The Copts must be the first to be thanked. His Holiness Pope Shenouda the Third has been a kind, warm-hearted host in his residences in Abbasiya and the Wadi Natroun. I am grateful for the hospitality of the monks of St. Antony, St. Bishoi, St. Macarius, St. Paul and the monasteries of the Romans and the Syrians. Father Boula el-Baramousi was an inspiration.

On my visits to the Mariout Desert Abouna Paphnutius entertained me: Mari Mina always reminds me of Ezekiel, "this is the place of my throne and the place of the soles of my feet, where I will dwell" (43:7). Dr. Rodolph Yanney, Professor Isaac Fanous, Dr. Stephane Rene, Dr. Saad M.Saad and Professor Shawky Karas have all befriended me at different times.

In the field of linguistics a number of colleagues have fortunately come to my aid: Dr. Richard Marrash, Nicolas Zoghb, Robert J. Klancko and Dr. Andrew Palmer.

For his encyclopaedic knowledge of all things Coptic I am indebted to Dr. George H. Bebawi of Nottingham University. John Harcourt examined the proofs.

In the arcane discipline of computing, especially index making, Richard Rothwell and Mel Horley were constantly responding to my cries for help.

I am grateful to Anthony Grahame, Editorial Director at Sussex Academic Press, for his calm professional assistance and support.

Thanks, above all, to my wife, Jacquie. She has supported me at every stage of research and writing, and tolerated my absences in Egypt. She also worked on the proofs and the index.

As to mistakes, the usual formula applies: that is, that all those which remain, and all the opinions expressed, are my own.

At Sutton Valence
February, 2000

Chapter One

Introduction:
At the Sources of Christian
Civilization

Christianity is a Middle Eastern religion, in intimate familial relationship with Judaism and Islam. The need for roots is universally felt.
Western civilization has constantly and correctly been drawn back to
the crescent-shaped area of fertile land extending in the East from
historic Mesopotamia, the lands of the Tigris and Euphrates, westward
over Syria to the Mediterranean and southward through modern
Lebanon, Israel–Palestine to the Nile Valley in Egypt. This region
provides the important bridge between Africa, Asia and Europe.
Armies, merchants and pilgrims criss-crossed these lands for centuries.
They continue to do so in the twenty-first century.

The armies of Joshua, Alexander the Great, Julius Caesar, Saladin,
Tamburlaine, Napoleon, Lord Allenby and Moshe Dayan fought here.
The Epic of Gilgamesh, the *Maqaddimah* of Ibn Kaldun, the *Tales From One
Thousand and One Nights*, Farid ud-Din Attar's *The Conference of the Birds*,
the *Incoherence of the Philosophers* by Ibn Sina (Avicenna) and the final
recensions of the Hebrew and Christians Scriptures, with influential
copies of the Qur'an, were all written here. The many rulers of the fertile
lands have included the Greeks, the Romans, the Caliph Haroun al-
Rashid, the Mamluks, and the Ottomans; for a brief period, the French
and the British were mandated to rule some countries; more recently
statesmen like David Ben-Gurion, Colonel Gamal Abd el Nasser and the
Ayatollah Khomeini have dominated the scene. Moses, Jesus and
Muhammad each lived in the Fertile Crescent for all or some of their
lives. For five millennia this region has been, and as recent events have
shown, remains, a most sensitive and deeply significant part of the
world.

Christianity has taken and does take many different forms. The western scholar engaged in the widespread rediscovery of the ancient churches of the Fertile Crescent frequently experiences a feeling of being in contact with the ancient originals of Christianity. There is a sense of returning, perhaps as far as it is possible to reach, to the most primitive models. The worship in these churches conveys the sights and sounds of the mystical, Semitic and antique. From the moment when the Oriental Orthodox priest begins to sing the exquisite Arabic *melisma*, the newcomer is beguiled. The ageless chant hovers in the incense shrouded air. The robes for these timeless liturgies are those of Palestine in late antiquity, or even the robes of pharaonic Egypt. Every move is rooted in archaic and unvarying choreography. The climate of these ancient communions is one of changelessness. All the western rites are sanitized versions of this mysterious drama. In a Middle Eastern church, time vanishes and with bare feet we approach the eerie secrets of the temples, synagogues and catacombs of late antiquity. This can be true in Syria, in the Assyrian Church of the East or in the numerous Armenian and Ethiopian congregations of the area, but the largest and most influential of all the ancient churches is the Coptic Orthodox Church in Egypt.

Alongside Israel–Palestine, Egypt stands out as a central location in the history of Christianity. The Founder of Christianity with Mary and Joseph was a refugee in Egypt. In the first century, Saint Mark the Evangelist baptized the Egyptian Church with his martyrdom. Eusebius, the Father of Church History, recognized Mark as the founder of the Alexandrine Church, and Coptic tradition confirms the saint as their first patriarch. Alexandria ranked side by side with Antioch and Rome, later still beside Constantinople, as one of the chief sees of the early Church. Christianity had penetrated so deeply into Egypt in the first centuries that archaeologists of the modern period have discovered some of the oldest Biblical papyri in the Coptic language, buried for centuries in the sands of Upper Egypt. Some of these Coptic fragments, from the Chester Beatty Library in Dublin, predate the great codices held in the British Museum and the Vatican. They are one representative testament among many to the distinctive Coptic form of Christianity that has remained deeply rooted in the Nile Delta and Valley for the entire period now habitually described as the Common Era. In Coptic Egypt there is an impression of being close to the sources of Christian civilization.

This book intends not only to introduce new acquaintances to Coptic life and culture, but also to invite old companions to reconsider all the central issues of modern Coptic existence. I hope that the serious student of Oriental Orthodoxy will find in these pages a conversation to join; though this book was not written primarily for experts. As far as possible the essential apparatus of scholarship has been assigned to the bibliography at the end of the book. I have tried to provide a straight-forward narrative that will be read without too much difficulty by the non-theologian who is willing to learn about the Copts and is prepared to devote some time and thought to the subject. The intention behind the biographies, reviews, surveys and scenarios that make up this book is always to present stories on the highest possible intellectual level but without technical reference to Coptology or Theology.

The difficulty throughout has been selection. I have attempted to separate and explain the main themes of the Egyptian Orthodox Church in their historical setting, and in the modern world. At the outset, the various groups who seek to secure their authenticity as Copts are intro-duced with an explanation of Coptic language and culture. When Coptic Monasticism is discussed it is examined not only as the most important Egyptian contribution to the Christian world, which it certainly is, but as a living Christian witness, embodied in the life of one of the greatest though least known mystics of the twentieth century. The nature of the Coptic Patriarchate is explored in the biographies of the two most recent holders of the office. The Coptic Orthodox Church has never lived solely for itself and the discussion of Mission in these pages is epitomized in the life of Raphael Wanyama, an African born in the Kenya–Uganda borderlands. He is known to the Copts as Abouna Marcos el-Askiti. I translate this as Father Mark of Scetis. As a Coptic Orthodox priest he defended the authentic theological position of the Copts not only against the Egyptian Government but also against bishops who were Egyptians by birth. At the time of this defense, he was murdered. The biographical outline given here appears for the first time, being the result of original research. It may be expected that this remarkable man will eventually be canonized by the Coptic Orthodox Church. The Liturgy, Iconography, Theology and Martyrology of the Copts are surveyed in this volume. The chapter on the *Egyptian Church Struggle, 1981–1985* is the fruit of daily contact with the primary sources throughout that period. Spiritual and narrative scaffolding supports each topic.

Aziz Atiya, the greatest Coptologist of the twentieth century, liked to present his simplified image of Coptic Orthodox history. The ancient Coptic Church, he said, was like a great and solitary Egyptian temple standing sorrowfully on the edge of the desert. It steadfastly weathered constant sandstorms through the passing centuries. Slowly the detritus of the generations and seasons submerged the temple. The Orthodox Church in Egypt led its lonely life unnoticed on the fringe of Christian civilization, buried in the sands of time and oblivion. The Coptic Orthodox Church, like the same immense temple, has proved itself to be indestructible though battered and much buffeted by the winds of change. As an organism, its potential vitality, though enfeebled by sustained fighting, has survived in a latent form under the weight of accumulated rubble. In the last few decades, with increasing security and liberty from within and support and sympathy from without, its sons have started removing the sands of time from around the edifice, which has shown signs of shining again.

This book portrays the current shining life among the Copts, presented in the historical frame of Atiya's temple.

Chapter Two

Copt and Coptic

Egypt has often been likened to a palimpsest, a parchment on which the old survives beneath the new, as scribes in sequence write upon a fading past. Coptic Christianity is the text that persists below the Arabic and the Arabism of Islam and is itself a superscription on pharaonic Egypt through the Greco-Roman heritage. Kenneth Cragg

Arguing about dictionary definitions can be fun for the aficionados of crosswords, and perhaps a professional pastime for a certain kind of philosopher. Words are slippery and even an apparently simple noun may require several alternative definitions from the lexicographer. The words "Copt" and "Coptic", central to this essay, receive the following treatment in the eighth edition of *The Concise Oxford Dictionary* (1994):

Copt n.	1	a native Egyptian in the Hellenistic and Roman periods.
	2	a native Christian of the independent Egyptian Church.
Coptic n. & adj.– n		The language of the Copts, now used only in the Coptic Church.
– adj.		of or relating to the Copts.

These are serviceable definitions. When Judy Chicago, in her celebrated multimedia tribute to women, *The Dinner Party* (1979), refers to "traditional Coptic designs" in the place she has devoted to Hypatia (AD 370–415), the great Alexandrine philosopher, we may assume that she refers to the designs of Greco-Roman Egypt. When Jeffrey Eugenides, in his middle-American novel *The Virgin Suicides* (1993), alludes to a "Coptic headstone" we may deduce that the grave is that of a member of the Egyptian Christian Diaspora in the United States. But in 1993, when Eugenides was publishing his intense piece of magic realism, the Egyptian Ambassador to The Hague was teasing two western scholars of Egyptian Christianity: "Copts? But, my good sirs, we are all Copts. You know the origin of the word. We are all Egyptians." Egypt has no Christian ambassadors, and the diplomat's good-humoured interpretation falls outside the usual dictionary definitions.

Perhaps the ambassador to the Netherlands was merely echoing one of the pieties of the Egyptian nationalist revival: "We are all Egyptians". Certainly, he was, consciously or unconsciously, providing his own abbreviated gloss on the words of a Copt called Marqus Simaika writing in the newspaper *Al Ahram* in 1926: "All of you are Copts: some of you are Muslim Copts, others are Christian Copts but all of you are descended from the ancient Egyptians." In this vocabulary "Copt" is a synonym for "Egyptian". This usage is far from idiosyncratic and has an interesting history.

Egypt is a wonderland. The world is constant in its passion for the Pharaonic past of the Nile valley. The golden gaze of Tutankhamen (*Tut Ankh Amun*, the name means "in the living image of the hidden one") is a fixed icon in the minds of millions who have not looked at the original; the high cheek bones, full lips and perfect poise of the three thousand year old bust of Nefertiti (*Nofret Ete*, the name means "Beauty is come") remain a defining model of classical elegance; and for fifty-five centuries pilgrims from the ends of the earth have stood in wonder before the Great Pyramid of Cheops and its guardian Sphinx (known in Arabic as *Abu Hol*, "the father of terror"). Any comprehensive list of much-loved Pharaonic wonders would fill several large volumes. Egyptian awareness of this past flowered suddenly at the beginning of this century: Nefertiti was found in Armana in 1912 and Tutankhamen in the Valley of the Kings in 1922. *Pharaonism* was born and proposed that the modern Egyptian spirit was explicable in terms of the Pharaonic tradition, with the Egyptian character growing through the centuries around a Pharaonic heart. Nationalists were happy to argue that the majority of the population were directly descended from Pharaonic Egyptians and were untainted with Arab blood from the more recent Islamization of the country after the seventh century of the Common Era.

Confronted with the rediscovery of so much Pharaonic imagery, Egypt's Christian minority recovered an interest in their past. It was proposed that if all Egyptians had a Pharaonic lineage then they also had a Christian ancestry. A more dangerous and sinister interpretation developed. It was not only suggested that Egypt's Muslims were largely Christians who had converted to Islam, for which there is substantial evidence, but also that the Muslims now lacked the racial purity of the

Copts. Some Copts were eager to apply exclusively to their community the sobriquet "the sons of the pharaohs". The bitterness occasioned by this exclusivity may be judged from the frequently repeated view of the majority in Egypt that the Copts are "not so much the sons of the pharaohs, as the descendants of the slaves of the pharaohs". The Copts are not the masters in Egypt.

The sentence "We are all Copts" on the lips of a Muslim who is also a government envoy may be a proud nationalistic assertion, a conciliatory expression inviting a minority into a more inclusive grouping or a blunt denial of Christian identity. The word Copt remains in contention. The refusal to differentiate "Egyptian" from "Copt" is at best a piece of understandable romanticism. The dictionary rejects it.

The etymology of the term "Copt" is relatively straightforward. The word is derived from the Greek noun *Aigyptos* (Egypt): Its adjective *Aigyptios* was used to refer to the native inhabitants of Egypt and the Nile valley, in distinction from the Hellenes and other foreigners. It is customary for Egyptian Christian commentators to suggest that the Greek is an phonetic corruption of an ancient Egyptian word for Memphis. This was *Hak-Ka-Ptah*, which may be translated into English as the temple of the spirit of Ptah. Ptah was the senior and creator deity of classical Egyptian mythology. After the Conquest of Egypt in AD 641, the Arabs called Egypt *dar al-Qibt*, "the home of the Copts", and the implied corruption from *Aigyptos* to *Gypt* or *Qibt* eventually became Copt in European languages (*Copte* in French and *Kopte* in German). Since the Egyptians of the seventh century were Christians, the words Coptic and Christian became interchangeable in the minds of the Arab invader and subsequently in the reference books of European visitors and invaders. Lord Cromer, British Consul General in Egypt from 1883 to 1906, was an imperialist who liked to have everything cut and dried when dealing with the native people. In his much-quoted phrase: "A Copt is an Egyptian who worships in a church and a Muslim an Egyptian who worships in a mosque."

Egyptian nationalists, secularists and Muslims may have some historical claim to the name, but though the word "Copt" once had no religious connotation, today in common use and dictionary definition it refers to the Christians of Egypt.

The simple equation "Copt equals Egyptian Christian" is further complicated by the proliferation of Christian churches in Egypt in modern times. It was possible in 1997 to visit between twenty and thirty different Protestant congregations in Cairo alone. Most Protestant groups have their roots in the Coptic Orthodox Church. A contemporary sheikh of Al-Azhar, the great Islamic centre of learning, tells an instructive story about Christian divisions in his country: An American missionary with a small staff came to Egypt for a summer mission in the 1960s. The title chosen for the project was "the Jesus Mission". His purpose was to "bring Muslims to Christ", but he soon found that this was a complicated political and legal task. Converting Muslims to Evangelical Christianity was going to be tough, but in the same mission field there were many Copts – obviously nominal adherents of the ancient Church, who needed to be "saved" – and they were ripe for conversion. So the missionary turned his attentions to them. A number of conversions followed. In the following Summer the Jesus Mission experienced some doctrinal debate amongst staff members, and there was a rift over the issue of mission to Muslims which led to the establishment of "the true Jesus Mission". In the third year, theological controversy and questions about the mission to Islam led to the formation of a splinter group calling itself "the truer Jesus Mission". In the fourth year a controversy about predestination led to the fourth division when the "truest Jesus Mission" was born. The sharp, humorous tang of the tale can only be bittersweet. The Muslim teacher recognizes the endemic disease of Christian disunity and its infection of the Egyptian Church. The varieties of Christian expression have their impact upon the use of the term Copt.

Missionaries from North America arrived in Egypt in 1854, at the height of the great period of western missionary expansion, with the intention of converting the population to Christianity. One of their number was met by the Coptic Orthodox Metropolitan of Assyut who asked a simple question: "We have been living with Christ for more than 1800 years, how long have you been living with Him?" The rebuke has not deflected Protestant missionaries from their work, which has been largely focused upon the conversion of Coptic Orthodox Christians to a western form of Christianity. Islam stands mostly untouched by Protestant mission. The American Presbyterian Synod of the Nile became the Coptic Evangelical Church after the Revolution of 1952.

Alongside those Evangelicals who are happy to describe themselves as Copts there is, amongst the diversity of Roman Catholic representation in Egypt, a Coptic Catholic Church with its own Patriarchate which was established in 1895. The Coptic Catholic Church is heir to centuries of contact between Rome and Egypt. At the Council of Florence in the fifteenth century the Abbot of St. Antony's monastery represented the Copts, and in 1741 the Coptic Metropolitan of Jerusalem became a Catholic. The Liturgy of the Coptic Catholics employs traditional Orthodox hymnody in Coptic and Arabic. A spiritual and intellectual authority out of all proportion to its size marks the present Roman Catholic presence in Egypt. This is largely due to the quiet but effective ministry of Dominicans, Franciscans and Jesuits; religious orders active in Egypt for centuries. Two Egyptian-born priests of the twentieth century are models of an exemplary moral and intellectual tendency in Egyptian Catholicism. Father Henri Boulad (b. 1931), a Jesuit educated in France, Lebanon and the USA worked in the slums, in a leper colony, and in pioneering educational projects. In Egypt, Fr. Boulad is best known for giving a regular series of open lectures in Alexandria; and through their publication in French, German and English he has gained an international reputation as one of the significant spiritual figures of this era. Father George Anawati (1905–94) was for fifty years a pioneer in Muslim–Christian Dialogue at the Dominican Institute of Oriental Studies in Abbasiya. Originally a pharmacy graduate at the University of Lyons in France, Fr. Anawati undertook his Dominican studies at Saulchoir, near Paris. As Arabist, Orientalist and philosopher, he earned his doctorate in Montreal, Canada. He worked in Algeria and held honorary doctorates from many universities, including Louvain and Washington, D.C., Anawati was intellectually and spiritually liberated by John XXIII and the Second Vatican Council. He embodied the ecumenical spirit of those open-hearted Christians who, enlightened by the truest and deepest values of faith and reason, attempt to unite humankind in a time of division. Through these Egyptian witnesses, Catholics have earned their identification as Copts.

Coptic Catholics and Coptic Evangelicals appear to graciously affirm a debt to the past when they identify with the ancient *dar al-Qibt*. Other small but influential Christian churches survive in Egypt. The Greek Orthodox (Melkite) Church of Alexandria has its own line of Popes from St. Mark, which only diverges from the Coptic Orthodox list after the Council of Chalcedon in AD 451. The Greek Patriarchate has bishops throughout Africa. The Anglican Communion has a native Egyptian bishop, and this small episcopal body has an excellent reputation for work amongst refugees. The Anglican programme was originally one of support for the native church. The Greeks and Anglicans lay no claim to the name of Copt.

Coptic is the ancient language of Christian Egypt. The Copts are Arabic speaking but retain the Coptic language in their liturgies. Coptic is the result of the evolution of ancient Egyptian, through hieroglyphics, a hieratic script and written demotic writing. The sacred hieroglyphic scripts appeared in public literature and art for centuries; the less formal priestly, hieratic script was developed to deal with more mundane tasks; and the demotic development virtually abandoned pictographs. After the arrival of the Greeks a new system developed. This we know as Coptic: the demotic Egyptian transliterated into the Greek alphabet with seven additional characters to convey additional native Egyptian sounds. Coptic reflects local dialects in Egypt: Bohairic, Lower

(Northern) Egyptian is the language of Church liturgies; Sahidic, Upper (Southern) Egyptian is probably the dialect most studied in academies outside Egypt because of the discovery of manuscripts in Upper Egypt, especially the Nag Hammadi codices found at the Gebel el-Tarif in December 1945. During the Coptic cultural revival, which followed the Pharaonic discoveries at the beginning of this century, the Coptic weekly *al-Watani* proposed that the Copts should reject Arabic as a foreign language and return to their native tongue. Attempts to put flesh and bones on this idea failed, but the notion has always had some champions. The distinguished American papyrologist L. S. B. MacCoull has distinguished between those who wish to study Coptic as "a link with the glorious past" and those who understand that Coptic linguistics could provide "a link with authenticity". The former is overemphasized by Copts and the latter seriously underrated. Dr MacCoull quotes with approval the words of Freeman Dyson: "The smaller and more evanescent the minority, the more precious is their ancient language, the only weapon they have left with which to humble the conqueror's pride and maintain their own identity as a people". As the State of Israel has shown, it requires vast resources not merely to revive an ancient language but more importantly to supplement it with a twentieth-century vocabulary for contemporary objects; from clothing to foodstuffs, from telephones to television to computers. Only through the creation of that vocabulary could the language be used in home, school, shop and office. It is almost impossible to imagine a restored Coptic as a living language. Kenneth Cragg's words most pointedly apply to the Copts as they do to all Christians in the Middle East: "The crux of Arab Christianity might be linguistically expressed; it is bound over to a language that is bound over to Islam."

Political, historical and denominational claims to a specialized use of the word Copt and its cognates deserve the respect and acknowledgement given them here. In the pages that follow a narrower, but sharper focus is applied to the word. In this essay a Copt is a Christian of the native Orthodox Church of Alexandria, following those who seceded from the Byzantine Orthodox Church at the Council of Chalcedon and one who is in communion with the Coptic Orthodox Pope and Patriarch of Alexandria. This Christian has a distinctive view of the person of Christ. It has been called "Monophysite", which may be offensive to a modern Egyptian Christian if it is meant to imply that Christ had only one divine nature into which his humanity was absorbed, but may be welcomed by some Copts if it is allowed to refer to the one nature of God Incarnate, a perfect union of human and divine natures. This is a subject to which we must return. The Copts do not recognize any discontinuity between the Orthodox Church in Egypt before the Council of Chalcedon and the "Monophysite" tradition which followed: Pantaenus, founder of the Catechetical School in Alexandria (d. *circa* 190), Clement of Alexandria, philosopher (*c.*150–215), Antony the Great, the first Christian hermit and "father of monasticism" (*c.*251–356), Athanasius the Apostolic, defender of Nicaea (*c.*296–373), Didymus the Blind, theologian (*c.*313–398), Cyril of Alexandria, the pillar of orthodoxy (d. 444) and Dioscorus, the defender of Alexandrine Christology (*c.*454) were all Copts and even Origen (*c.*185–254) is described as "a true son of Egypt, Coptic to the core" by Aziz Atiya, the greatest Coptologist of the twentieth century. In the present usage, St. Mark was the first Coptic Patriarch of Alexandria and Pope Shenouda the Third is the one hundred and seventeenth. Heraclas the Copt (consecrated as Patriarch in AD 232, d. 248) was the first Christian prelate to bear the title pope, centuries before it was known in Rome. The Copts are the Christian majority in Egypt, but a minority in a state whose official religion is Islam.

Nobody knows how many Copts there are in Egypt. In the official census of 1960, the first to be conducted after the 1952 Revolution, the total population was discovered to be 26 million with a Christian population of 7 per cent, a drop from 8 per cent of the total in 1940. In 1982 the US Department of State's Bureau of Public Affairs calculated that the population of Egypt had risen to 44 million, and 10 per cent were Copts. Other sources in 1985 were claiming that there were six million Copts out of an Egyptian population of 50 million. It is tempting when walking in Tahrir Square, in downtown Cairo, to guess how many Copts are passing by in the swirling multitude. Is it every eighteenth or nineteenth person passed? Is it every sixth or seventh, as some Copts would have us believe? Or is it every tenth or eleventh? It is impossible for the inhabitants of Cairo to distinguish between a Muslim and a Copt. There is no racial difference. Perhaps the closest the majority of Copts come to expressing their identity is through their names, for over 80 per cent still carry pharaonic names. Both Muslim and Christian populations have their fair share of the rich black hair, big brown eyes and warm, glowing skin of Egypt. Given the vagaries of politics and the hazards of census taking, perhaps it is better not to know exactly how many Copts there are.

There are millions of Copts in Egypt and they are often so completely integrated in Egyptian society that their religious identity dissolves into the national one: the same may be said of their Muslim compatriots. An indication of the Coptic presence on the international scene may be given in summary by reference to three typical representatives: a doctor, a lawyer and a teacher. From the middle of the nineteenth century, as a result of improved educational opportunities, a Coptic meritocracy began to assimilate modern western culture to such an extent that they were able to acquire significant weight in medicine and the liberal professions. Some of the beneficiaries of this progress have remained in Egypt. They are generally secular-minded. Others have left Egypt, or drift between home and abroad. Some Copts are highly placed. Professor Sir Magdi Habib Yacoub was born into a Cairene Coptic family in 1935. After graduation at Cairo University he held a number of relatively minor posts in Egypt. Since 1962 he has developed innovations in heart and heart-lung transplants which have given him a place of international pre-eminence in Cardiothoracic Surgery. Boutros Boutros-Ghali, a Copt born in Cairo on 14 November 1922, became the sixth secretary-general of the United Nations on 1 January 1992. At the time of his appointment he had been a Minister of State for Foreign Affairs from October 1977. Between 1949 and 1977, Boutros-Ghali was Professor of International Law at Cairo university: he holds a Ph.D. in international law from the University of Paris. The achievements of Professor Fayek Matta Ishak are modest when compared with those of Magdi Yacoub and Boutros Ghali, but they are typical of the migrant Coptic intellectual. Ishak read English at Cairo University, followed by post-graduate work at Exeter University in the UK and a Ph.D. at Liverpool. He was Professor of English at Lakehead University, Thunder Bay, Canada for a quarter of a century before his retirement. Ishak has produced workman-like English translations of the Coptic Liturgy and Prayer Book.

There is one Egyptian Christian the inclusion of whose name is obligatory in any work that promotes Coptic Studies. He was Professor Aziz Suryal Atiya (1898–1988): Founder-President of the Institute for Coptic Studies in Cairo (1950); Founder of the Middle East Centre, University of Utah (1959); Editor of Middle East Manuscripts, Library of Congress (1970) and first Editor of the *Coptic Encyclopaedia*, which was published posthumously (8 volumes, Macmillan, New York, 1991). No writer has contributed more to the present clearer understanding of the Copts than Aziz Atiya. The chapters on the Copts in his book *The History of Eastern Christianity* (1968) have become landmarks, not only for specialists but also for the general public. It was Atiya who, after many lively debates with the publishers and their readers, had the words "Coptology" and "Coptologist" introduced into the English language.

Since the middle of the nineteenth century the Coptic Orthodox Church has enjoyed a burgeoning renaissance, focused upon monasticism, communal awareness, ecumenical consciousness, missionary endeavour, religious education and a sense of vocation as a suffering church. The Coptic Revival has attracted international attention. The thematic presentation of Coptic Orthodoxy, which follows, is designed to provide a comprehensive introduction to the Copts at the beginning of a new millennium.

Chapter Three

In the State of Angels

And Jesus answering said unto them, The children of this world marry, and are given in marriage: But they which shall be accounted worthy to obtain that world, and the resurrection from the dead, neither marry, nor are given in marriage: neither can they die any more: for they are equal unto the angels; and are the children of God, being the children of the resurrection.   (Luke 20: 34–36)

There is an unusual passage in one of the essays of Nobel prize-winner Sir William Golding where he is being shown around the scenes of the American Civil War by a professor who was himself born in the South. The day began well enough with the Southerner urbane and objective, describing all the battles and engagements. The day wore on. With each passing hour, the professor became more and more emotional. Finally they came to the place of the Surrender. The professor broke: "Oh, shucks," he cried out, trod on the accelerator and drove away. Places evoke persons and histories. T. S. Eliot spoke of "significant soil". Coptic Egypt has such "significant soil", most of it monastic.

The Copts believe that the establishment of their altars was foreseen in the Old Testament. The Coptic Orthodox Monastery of the Blessed Virgin Mary, Al-Muharraq in Assyut Province, lies exactly in the middle of Egypt on any standard map. Copts see this as a literal fulfilment of the prophecy in Isaiah 19: 19 "In that day there will be an altar to the Lord in the midst of the land of Egypt." The location has a larger claim to fame. There are many traditions of varying antiquity and authenticity concerning the flight of the Holy Family to Egypt – the most ancient account is that found in St. Matthew's Gospel 2: 13–23. In Coptic tradition the Holy Family came down into Egypt by the Mediterranean coastal road. Joseph, Mary and the baby Jesus made a circuitous detour across the Nile Delta before proceeding due south, past the environs of modern Cairo. They then took to the river and went further south into

Upper Egypt. In Coptic judgement Al-Muharraq is the site of the home of the Holy Family in Egypt. Here, Joseph built a small house of bricks with a palm-leaf roof. The Holy Family remained in the locality for three years, six months and ten days. When they prepared to return to Nazareth, the Blessed Virgin asked Jesus to honour the place, and he blessed the spot. Egyptian Christian Tradition says that Christ returned over thirty years later, after His resurrection from the dead, to confirm the house as "the first church in the world".

As a pilgrim centre, the monastery of Al-Muharraq is still thriving. It has many modern buildings, a Theological College in its outer courtyard, a primary school nearby and new guests houses for the many pilgrims following the Holy Family. One hundred monks of the last decade have taken their vows in the confines of this ancient place as Saint Pachomius (*c.*290–346), the founder of coenobite (communal) monasticism did long ago. Pachomius ruled over two convents for women and nine monasteries for men in this district. Copts who live around Al-Muharraq today refer to the location as the "second Jerusalem" or the "second Mount of Olives". The visit of the Holy Family has endowed the soil with immense spiritual significance. Historically, the monastery has been a place of martyrdom, especially during the Arian controversy in the fourth century and at the time of the Arab invasion in the seventh century, though monks have also been killed here in the last decade by Islamic extremists.

When the Holy Family crossed the Nile, en route to Al-Muharraq, they saw the Desert of Scetis from afar and the Blessed Virgin Mary blessed the area. Scetis lies in the north-eastern corner of the great Sahara and just south of Cairo over two hundred miles to the north of Al-Muharraq. It is one of the hallowed grounds of Coptic history. Today it is called the Wadi Natroun and is not far off the modern toll-road running between Cairo and Alexandria.

The larger region of the Natroun was divided into three important centres of monasticism in Late Antiquity: the Nitrian Hills; the district "of the cells", known as Cellia; and the Wilderness of Scetis. This wilderness stretches from North to South in the Wadi Natroun and slopes slightly eastwards. It contains four important monasteries – from west to north-east – Deir al-Baramus, Deir as-Surian, Deir Anba Bishoi and *Abu Makar*. Scetis has been a notable monastic centre since the fourth century of our era, when Abba Macarius the Great (the Egyptian) lived there (*circa* AD 300–390), and is associated with the lives and sayings of numerous Desert Fathers.

The name Scetis has come to signify not only a place, but also a retreat from the dictates of the world, and an engagement with the demands of spiritual conflict and asceticism. Derwas Chitty, in his pioneering book

The Desert a City, describes Scetis as a "citadel, with a stark abased remoteness [three of its surviving monasteries are set below sea-level], that even a motor-road from Alexandria to Cairo, passing within sight along the low scarp to the north, cannot really destroy." This is a romantic view from fifty years ago. Today the monasteries of the Wadi Natroun are bustling centres of pilgrimage, tourism and agricultural development, invaded almost daily by busloads of visitors. Nevertheless, the essential fact remains that the Wadi Natroun has a positive place in the story of Christian Spirituality.

The senior Coptic bishop, the Patriarch or Pope, has built a residence at the Monastery of St. Bishoi where he spends a part of each week. For some years he was under house arrest there (1981–5). The foundation of this monastery is intimately associated with the life of its patron. The uncorrupted relics of St. Bishoi (fl. 390) are the focus of a great deal of devotion at the end of the twentieth century, with the relics of Ephraim the Syrian (c.306–373). Syrian Orthodox monks, as its name suggests, occupied the neighbouring Monastery of the Syrians (Deir as-Surian) in the past. It has a reputation for being progressive. The present patriarch was once a monk there. Both monasteries have many monks. The oldest, friendliest and most beautiful monastery in the Wadi Natroun is Deir al-Baramus deriving from a community *circa* 340. The atmosphere of authentic spirituality on this sacred ground is almost palpable. For thirty-five years (1935–70) an Ethiopian ascetic Abouna Abd al-Masih lived in a cave a mile or two from the monastery walls. The fourth surviving monastery of Scetis is the Monastery of St. Macarius. It has been the model for the revival of the other three monasteries since 1969. In that year Pope Kyrillos sent a dozen monks under the direction of Father Matta El Meskeen to renew the monastic life there.

Matta El-Meskeen (Matthew the Poor Man) is an important figure in recent Coptic history and in the chronicle of the Monastery of St. Macarius, which is one of the greatest religious houses in the world. Matta was born in Benha Kaliobia in 1919. He graduated in Pharmacy from Cairo University in 1944. In 1948 he left his profession and entered the Monastery of St. Samuel, roughly half way between Beni Suef and Minya in Middle Egypt. In the late 1950s Matta began one of the critical revolutionary monastic experiments of modern times. He moved out into the Wadi El Rayan, a desolate valley of the Western Desert 124 miles South West of Cairo. For twelve years he lived a solitary ascetic life in the spirit of the ancient Desert Fathers. By 1960 seven other monks joined him. The community expanded to twelve by 1964. These twelve monks were sent to the Wadi Natroun in 1969.

In the Wadi El Rayan the twelve had lived very simply under the strict direction of their spiritual father, Matta El-Meskeen. The valley was entirely cut off from the outside world. For twelve years they read no newspapers and heard no radio. They lived in ground caves, not unlike those in Cappadocia or Qumran. Some caves extended into the hillside and were covered in Coptic writings on plastered walls from early monastic settlements in the fourth century. The modern monks took turns to bake bread once a week. Water was carried on a donkey in petrol cans from an oasis. They were literally dispossessed. Wild gazelles ran across the sand dunes, but the monks were vegetarians. They grew tomatoes, radishes and other fruits and vegetables. The hermits met once a week on Saturday night for the raising of incense. Matta would share his spiritual thoughts, garnered from the meditation and silence of the last week. He usually spoke without notes for three or four hours. At the break of day on Sunday they celebrated the Divine Liturgy and received Holy Communion. They then shared their weekly communal meal before returning to their desert cells in the sand dunes. In Matta's words they, "delivered their past egos to the country of death".

When these twelve monks were sent to the Desert of Scetis they found six old monks presiding over ruins. The monastery of St. Macarius the Great (*c*.300–390) had been a focal point of monasticism. The prayers of St. John the Short, St. Moses the Black, St. Pimen and many other Coptic leaders, had hallowed it in ancient times. Although constantly occupied by monks from the fourth century onwards, in the middle of the twentieth century it had fallen upon bad times. Father Matthew the Poor Man and his companions set out to completely reform and reconstruct the monastery. The scale of the achievement is staggering.

Within a decade their new buildings covered an area six times larger than that of the old monastery. In 1971 the number of monks increased to thirty and by 1981 there were eighty. Today there are over a hundred. Their agricultural project is huge. The monks have reclaimed and cultivated large areas of desert. There are herds of cows and sheep. A poultry farm provides eggs for city shops in Cairo and Alexandria. The monastery's milk is taken to international hotels in the capital city every day. In 1977 and 1980 a Japanese academic, Takao Yamagata, visited the monastery and noticed that the melon planting season in September was the busiest farming season of the year, so the monks had to pray before three in the morning to be in the fields by 5 a.m. The monastery employs and trains young people in agriculture and allied trades. Workers are paid according to length of service and in addition receive free food, accommodation and medical care. In recognition of the extraordinary achievements of the monastery known in Egypt as *Abu Makar*, President Anwar Sadat donated two thousand hectares of desert land to the monks and a fleet of tractors to work the land he had given. A new well was drilled to obtain sub-soil water. The monastery has a superb printing press. Matta's books and articles are distributed throughout the world. The monks also edit *St. Mark*, a monthly periodical of spirituality, published in Arabic and English. Tapes of Father Matta's talks are circulated in Egypt and the Coptic Diaspora. The Monastery has good relations with the National Democratic Party, the ruling political party in Egypt for many years. The political opinions of Abouna Matta El Meskeen, calling for the complete separation of State and Religion, are widely respected. He has also warned the Copts about the tendency of minorities to turn in upon themselves and to despise others. Most of the monks at St. Macarius have been conscripts in the Egyptian armed forces.

The administrative, agricultural and institutional revolution at St. Macarius has particular importance for the Copts, not least because of the attempts to copy it at St. Bishoi monastery just down the road, but the transformation in the Wadi Natroun seems far from the model proposed in the Wadi El Rayan. Matta has been described as a radical Socialist, even a Communist, in the past. He did not easily accept the patriarchal command to move from the isolation and silence of the Wadi El Ryan to the bustling establishment at *Abu Makar*. Matta El Meskeen is a marginal figure, a prophetic critic of the institution, a master of authentic desert spirituality. Yet, elsewhere in the Wadi Natroun he has been criticized for being too close to the ruling political party. The practical activities at the monastery have tended to undermine Matta's more serious reputation for creating an interior change. Most of the original band of monks in the Wadi El Rayan when asked what directed them to the hermit life said that it was reading Matta's book on *The Life of Prayer*. When asked about the direction of Coptic monasticism monks of St. Macarius are most likely to talk of the need to ensure that the practical works of the monastery, which are many, are truly transfigured into one spiritual activity. Labour is to become an uninterrupted praise of the Triune God, a witness to the Incarnation and a means of fraternal love.

International interest in the monastery of St. Macarius and its spiritual father is not focused upon farming and printing. Attention is given because these monks are said to live, like earlier desert fathers, in the state of angels. Matta El Meskeen has said that the Monastery has only one rule. That is Love. Love without condition or limit, such as has been shown to us on the Cross. It is fitting to remember that Matta has had nearly fifty years' experience of monastic life. He is a spiritual guide well versed in the tensions and peculiarities of religious practice. The only condition for admission to the monastery is "that the aspirant should have felt his heart stirred by love for God, even if but a single time". This emphasis upon love is an unending theme at *Abu Makar*. Love for God; love for the Fellowship; love for the Christian Church; love for Theology and Spirituality.

There is integrity, a wholeness of life within the community of monks at St. Macarius. The pattern of daily life is such that the monks can only meet together to pray and to eat the midday meal in the Refectory. During the meal, the sayings of the Fathers are read. On Sunday evening they meet for a period of intercessory prayer, offering to God their spiritual and material needs. In accordance with what Matta believes to be the tradition of the Desert Fathers, the monks have only one celebration of the Divine Liturgy a week. It begins at two o'clock on Sunday morning and lasts for about five or six hours. It is followed by an Agape meal, a re-enactment of the common religious meal, which was in use in the early Church, apparently in close relation to the Eucharist. The Mass, a term which is occasionally used by Copts, cannot be the prayer of an individual priest for the Church, or even the prayer of a part of the Community. It is the prayer of the Community through which the monks of the monastery are transformed from an ordinary human gathering of Coptic Christians into the mystical Body of Jesus Christ.

Although the monks of the Wadi Natroun are powerful exemplars of the way of St. Pachomius, living the coenobitic life, Matta teaches that the most effectual development of the monastic vocation is to be found in the solitary life. He has lived as a solitary for much of his life, and is even now frequently away from his monastic cell. As a young man, Father Matta had approached Abouna Abd al-Masih el Habashi, the most extraordinary Christian hermit of the Egyptian Desert in the twentieth century, and asked to live with him. *El Habashi* (the Ethiopian) at first refused to allow Matta to come anywhere near his cave. Then, after only a week of seeing from a distance how the Egyptian lived an exemplary eremetical life, the great Ethiopian mystic allowed Matta to join him. Matta lived with the legendary Abd al-Masih for a year. Their cell was dug from a hillside not far from the monastery of the Romans. For the true ascetic, the cave for two in the Wadi Natroun was crowded and, on the advice of the Ethiopian mystic, Matta left to live the same "angelic life" in the more isolated Wadi El Rayan. At St. Macarius, Matta still teaches his monks that the eremetical life – a major form of religious being – must be lived out in the open desert. They have prepared a number of caves. Most had to be cut out of the hillside not far from the monastery. When a monk shows sufficient aptitude to live in this way the spiritual father advises him to go out into the desert. The communal and solitary forms of Coptic monasticism exist in tandem throughout the monasteries of the Wadi Natroun, but to examine a most remarkable recent life embracing both types of monastic expression it is necessary to move from the sacred soil of Scetis in the Western Desert out into the Eastern Desert near the Red Sea, to the *terra firma* of the first Coptic hermit.

The monastery of St. Antony the Great (*c.*251–356) is hidden away in the barren cliffs of the Qalalah mountains on the edge of the Wadi Arabah. It is about 300 hundred kilometres – a six-hour drive – from Cairo and some thirty kilometres from the Red Sea coast. The significant soil of the Wadi Arabah is a barren flatland of sandstone layers over-shadowed by rocks and mountains. It is the most important site in the history of Monasticism. Antony lived here. Saint Paul of Thebes lived nearby, and in the fifth century it was known as "the mountain of cells" because of the thousands of monks who lived in this inhospitable land-scape at that time.

Antony was the proto-hermit and, in spite of his Greek name, he was a Copt who spoke only Coptic, even when in conversation with the learned theologian and spiritual master Athanasius (*c.*296–373) who was his biographer. The *Life of Antony* by Athanasius is the foremost work in the ever-widening field of Christian biography. It was appar-ently written, possibly in Coptic, at the request of monks who wanted a perfect model of the ascetic life. The *Vita Antonii* has been translated into many languages and has probably contributed more than any other work to the establishment of Christian monasticism. It tells the well-known story of Antony's visit to the village church, after his parents' death. How it happened that the Gospel was being read, and he heard the Lord saying "If you would be perfect, go and sell all that you have and give to the poor and come and follow me". Antony sold his farm, kept a small sum for the maintenance of his sister, and placed himself under the direction of a holy man. He eventually retired to a mountain near the Red Sea where he became renowned as a saint and seer. On his deathbed in January 356 at the ripe age of 105 he gave Athanasius his most valued possessions – an old sheepskin coat and a cloak on which he had slept. Antony was a holy nomad who could not think in institu-tional terms. Solitary prayer and fasting, with many other ascetic feats separating him from all that is safe and social, were his paths to holi-ness. He occupies a place on the fringe of organized religion. The Church has sanitized him, but a pagan, in late antiquity or even today, can look at the Life of Antony and see a wise man, a guru and a visionary. He is a model of self-sufficiency. The first hagiography was devoted to an outsider. Antony not only dramatized the Gospel's call to absolute obedience, but represented an issue at the heart of the Christian Gospel – the danger, as Paul put it of being "conformed to this world" (Romans 12: 2). Antony, the man of God, confronted the Church and its members with a radical redefinition of Christian identity and purpose. The man on the boundary of church life appealed to many in the centre. He came to symbolize the type of the monk – *the one on his own* – which became for many an ideal portrait of the human being, as he should be. If the life of Antony is extraordinary, it is much more extra-ordinary that a life modelled so closely upon it should have been lived so very recently in the twentieth century, and in the monastery that bears the name of Antony.

Abba Justus was a Coptic monk in Egypt. Of his external life there is little to tell. He was born in the province of Assyut in Upper Egypt in 1910. His name "in the world" was Naguib Shah-hat. For twenty-nine years he lived with his parents in the township of Zarabi Dir ul-Mahraf, close to the monastery of the Holy Family, called Al-Muharraq. Naguib followed his father into the family tailoring business. He worked hard but his deepest interests were not in commerce. Even as a young layman Naguib was widely known for his piety. In later years many were to comment upon his beautiful public reading of the Scriptures. As a child he studied Arabic and Coptic. The parish priest chose Naguib as a reader at the Divine Liturgy. It was no surprise when he left home in 1939 and entered the famous monastery of St. Paul the Hermit near the Red Sea. At the age of 31, Naguib transferred to the nearby monastery of St. Antony. He was professed as a monk on 17 November 1941. Naguib became Justus. He remained faithful to his monastic vocation for the next thirty-five years. He was not ordained as a priest. He did not leave the monastery. He held no position in the hierarchy, but he established a reputation as a healer, clairvoyant and ascetic. He died on 17 December 1976 and was buried in the graveyard. In 1987 the Coptic Patriarch consented to the request of the brethren of Saint Antony's monastery and allowed reinterment of the Abba's uncorrupted body in one of the monastery's seven churches. It is an extraordinary place with an atmosphere of overpowering mystery and terror. A local cult attaches to the earthly remains of a man widely perceived as a saint.

It is historically precise to apply the honorific "Abba" to the monk Justus. The term "Abba" is often translated as "father", but it alludes to a spiritual paternity and not to priesthood. Abba Justus represents for us a living tradition which reaches right back to the time of the Desert Fathers, men of spiritual authority who were recognized as spiritual fathers. Their words and examples were accepted absolutely as God-given. Abba Justus enjoyed such authority.

It is often said that the collected tales and sayings of the desert fathers make it possible for a modern reader to make contact with early Coptic Egypt across time and space: the gap between fourth century Egypt and the English-speaking reader, one and a half millennia later, is signifi-cantly narrowed. This is only partly true. The gulf that separates us from the Abba of late antiquity is very deep and wide. If that gulf is bridged at all it is by the very small number of Coptic monks, within the larger Coptic Orthodox monastic revival, who continue to live the same life even in the twentieth century. There is a world of difference between the interiorized desert of modern spirituality and the real wilderness of the desert fathers. The spiritual emptiness of the vast secular city is not the immense physical emptiness of the true wasteland. A compromise between the church and the world has been made in the international urban community, and this is certainly as true in Cairo or Alexandria as it is in London or New York, but in the desert there is no reciprocity between the desert father and the Adversary.

The Abba of the fourth century lived within an apocalypse. He lived in the Endtime. He embraced a life of extreme asceticism and physical privation. For most of the time he lived in silence. He neither wrote nor read books, but occasionally left "a saying". The Abba was not famous, even in his homeland, but lived his life hidden from the world and from the institutionalized church. We call the modern monk Justus "Abba" because he lived this same life for over three decades, but he lived it in our time. The legacy of Abba Justus was an unwritten but miraculous parable of seclusion, simplicity, poverty, fasting, silence and humility. Justus wrote upon the desert sands with his life. The wilderness of Egypt is the icon of alienation: silent, waterless, disconnected, treeless, feature-less, separated and different. The human enters the picture in the anticipation of being swallowed up by the fearful void. But it is exactly there in the wasteland that the Coptic monk rises to the heights of sanctity and achieves the glorification of man.

Justus left the comfort of his family home and went out into the desert to meet the implacable hostility of an especially strange milieu. Uniquely, the desert demands submission or grants conquest through confrontation. No record remains of his struggle to discern the difference between the authentic and inauthentic in the world of the spirit. The record does show that he eventually acquired, and expressed in his relationships, such a depth of holiness, that those who might criticize him most called him an angel, though it is also recorded that, like all truly-trained ascetics, he made no show of his inner life, standing most often before God in the secret of his shabby cell.

The desert is a place where some are overcome by illusions, and others are overwhelmed by dreams of self-importance. Some are swallowed up by mere monasticism, and others are permanently lost in the routines of regimented religiosity. Some take the city, their ambitions and passions with them into the desert, to live masked but unchanged lives. Others are possessed by the demons they went out to suppress. Abba Justus seems to have been one of those who discovered that the desert is a place where desire is purified and where it is possible to learn to be truly free. Freedom was learnt by the desert fathers as they made the dead wilderness blossom with the beauty of their lives. Abba Justus learnt this life of freedom by surrendering completely to a time-tested physical environment, which in his life yielded its own spiritual fruit. This is perhaps what Thomas Merton had in mind when he said that "it is essential to experience all the times and moods of one good place." There is no ultimate contradiction between the particular and the universal in religion, but for the individual it is the particular that counts first. For Abba Justus it was the monastery, a place of struggle and suffering, but also a place of glory.

Poverty is one of the three primary vows of monasticism in most traditions. Christian Theology is a reflection upon the absolute gift, the complete and voluntary poverty and the unqualified love, which characterizes the life of the Holy Trinity. For the life of the Holy Trinity is an unending chain, cycle or concatenation of voluntary poverty. This *kenosis*, self-emptying, on the part of God in creation, incarnation and inspiration is the paradigm of the desert vocation of Abba Justus. The Church has rarely expressed evangelical poverty unless it has been forced to do so by revolution or oppression. "Expediency" has always had more dogmatic status than "emptiness". Even among the Copts and also in a desert monastery, monasticism involves little more than a formal recognition of the uncertain virtue implicit in a life of poverty. Justus was an exception. His witness is immeasurably strengthened by his refusal ever to carry money on his person. Justus expressed the progressive "de-selfing" of Christian spirituality by possessing nothing. He would not even carry the small monthly allowance granted to all monks by the monastery. One of the brothers kept the money for him and just before Justus's death the entire amount was handed to the abbot. The money was used to buy some carpets for the monastery chapels.

Justus always dressed in the same robe, appearing in it for long years after it was worn out and colourless with age. His cap had also lost all its pigment with the passage of time. His shoes dated back to his time in the world and were rarely worn. In the desert's cold winter evenings he wrapped himself in a moth-eaten blanket. A wealthy woman who had heard about the holy man visited St. Antony's to see the Abba for herself. When the two met the monk's scruffy robe, mangy appearance and lack of social refinement disgusted her. Her face and her manner clearly expressed her revulsion at the sight of the Abba. Some hours later the rich lady saw Abba Justus in the church. He effused light, which seemed to emanate from his body, and she smelt the fragrance of beautiful incense coming from him. In the liturgy he was transfigured. After the service she waited for the tattered little monk to apologize to him and confess her fault. Justus fled. She never saw him again.

The intensity of the Abba's inward life instantly conveyed itself to some other visitors to Saint Antony's. A millionaire from the Maghrib once came up to the monastery from his private yacht in the Gulf of Suez. The traveller, who was well educated and a seeker of curiosities, saw the poor monk and immediately instructed one of his companions, who was an accomplished artist, to make a drawing of Justus. The monk sat. He was silent. The millionaire watched. The charcoal drawing was quickly completed. Without instruction and making no comment the monk walked away. The millionaire told the artist, "I possess millions but he is the richest man in the world". The millionaire and the monk had not met before and did not meet again. It was later recorded in Algeria that the rich man believed that he had seen one of the individual versions of the inexhaustible image of the Son of Man who asked his disciples "And why are you anxious about clothing?" (Matt. 6: 28), and who lived as a poor man who had "nowhere to lay his head" (Matt. 8: 20).

Even his cell was not his own. It had no door. Anyone could wander in and out. It comprised two rooms built of clay. It was roofed with palms and had no windows. The floors of both rooms were bare, though coloured by the dust and ashes of the wood burnt there in winter. The furniture consisted of an old mat and a pitcher for water. There was no bed, mattress or pillow. There were no chairs, no plates or cups. Everything was kept on the open floor. He liked to have dried tomatoes or dates to hand and occasionally pomegranates, carobs and oranges. He would sometimes distribute these to guests of the monastery as they passed his cell. The books for the Divine Office and the Psalter were kept in a corner.

Justus did not think of the cell as his home. He wandered around the monastery at any time of the day or night. Like an animal, he would sleep when he needed sleep, without regard for the time. Abba Arsenius in ancient times used to say that one hour's sleep is enough for a monk if he is a good fighter. Nobody ever saw Justus stretched out upon the ground. He would rest with his back against something solid, or sleep in a kneeling or sitting position with his head down between his knees. He lived without recognising the time or place for sleeping, and the monks would find him in the cloisters, under the trees or beside walls, whether in the blistering heat of the desert summer or the chill of the wasteland's winter. At times he was found in the cold with the flesh clinging to his bones. Towards the end of his life he would usually sleep under a tree. In his earliest years he had slept up in the trees as an ascetic discipline. In the winter there are some days when the Wadi Arabah is intensely cold, and Justus would gather a few sticks of firewood from the gardens and take them into his cell where he would burn them on the floor and rub his hands above the flames. His room was simply another place in the monastery. It was the same as any other place in the house of his pilgrimage. His cell was torn down after the Abba's death and a guest house now marks the spot. The poverty of Justus expresses those same dimensions of divine humility and self-sacrifice discerned at first in the processes of Creation and Incarnation. Outside Theology and Spirituality the poverty makes no sense.

One day a doctor was visiting the monastery of Saint Antony and saw Abba Justus about to eat his main meal. The medical man was alarmed. Did the monk eat something more substantial on other days? Was Justus fasting? It was discovered that the crude mixture of gruel, dried _mulukhiyyah_ leaves and onions, which Justus made into a type of loaf, was his staple diet. (_Mulukhiyyah_ is a leafy summer vegetable that is extremely popular throughout the Middle East. Only the leaves are edible. They are usually available fresh, dry or frozen). Since the time of the early desert fathers, fasting has been linked with the virtue of poverty and the attainment of holiness. Abba Poemen, "the Shepherd" (_c._450), used to say, "Poverty, hardship, austerity and fasting are the instruments of the solitary life. It is written, "When these three men are together, Noah, Job, and Daniel, there am I, says the Lord." Noah represents poverty, Job suffering and Daniel discernment. So, if these three works are found in man, the Lord dwells in him." Justus lived consciously in this tradition.

Justus was a vegetarian and invariably took his ration of uncooked meat and fed it to the cats who would often wait patiently before his cell in anticipation of their feast. The monk's only known luxury food was boiled beans: _Fool Baladi Sa'idi_ are white, medium-sized beans, traditionally from Upper Egypt, and hardly rate as a delicacy in most cuisine. Justus usually ate his frugal meals quite alone. He would fast for many days. During lesser fasts he was content with spring water and dried bread, which was ordinarily thrown to the sheep. It was his daily custom to give some of his food to the workmen who came to assist in building, excavation and repairs at the historic location.

Nobody can remember his eating a complete meal and one monk quotes the proverb, "Not even the sun has seen him eat." Visitors to the monastery would often try to press some victuals on the monks. Justus always replied by thanking God for the gifts and would say, "I have eaten and I have drunk." Fasting has received some serious attention in modern Christian thought. It is viewed at first as a form of prayer or devotion through bodily discipline. Fasting emphasizes the wholeness of the individual Christian's commitment to the spiritual life; body and "soul" are engaged together. The physical discipline involved in the struggle against the most common contemporary sin of gluttony emphasizes the intensity of the prayer in the religious life. Fasting may also be understood as an outward expression of our hunger for God.

Fasting may assert the goodness of creation by temporarily surrendering the pleasure of enjoying some of its most obvious fruits. Fasting can be perceived as a purity ritual. To have the right intention when fasting is very important indeed. Some have approached fasting as part of the *imitatio Christi*- following Jesus of Nazareth in his way of fasting – and this would be central to their understanding of discipleship.

There is a need to protect the Christian notion of fasting against all implications of magic and of masochism. It is quite common to hear Copts boasting about the fasting involved in their tradition. It sounds hollow when it comes from someone abstaining from dairy products whilst over-indulging with a ton of "permitted" foods. It is equally common to hear such people claim that they have acquired a "debt of grace" by fasting and that they experience genuine faints and physical discomfort. These doctrines of fasting as a form of "indulgence" or "propitiation", involving some acquisition of grace, are not Orthodox. They are extremely common. It may be the case that Abba Justus was never so close to the ideal of Abba Antony as he was when he was fasting. Certainly, we may not expect either of them to be guilty of the elementary faults mentioned above but neither should we attribute to them recent theological interpretations. For these two desert fathers, fasting was an ascetic achievement or feat. According to Saint Athanasius, Antony often prayed that he might be a martyr but, even after a visit to Alexandria during the persecution of Christians, this was not granted to him. Asceticism was his martyrdom:

> When finally the persecution ended Antony departed and withdrew once again to the cell, and was there daily being martyred by his conscience, and doing battle in the contests of the faith. He subjected himself to even greater and more strenuous asceticism, for he was always fasting, and he had clothing with hair on the interior and skin on the exterior that he kept until he died.

The lives of the desert fathers remind us continually of the mental discipline which is necessary to understand and overcome evil desires and thoughts. But the most severe physical austerities of fasting, exposure to heat and cold, total abstention from all sexual activity, and controlled deficiency of sleep always seem to accompany the intellectual and psychological disciplines. It is in this sense that Justus mirrors Antony who used to say, "If he is able to, a monk ought to tell his elders confidently how many steps he takes and how many drops of water he drinks in his cell, in case he is in error about it." Justus lived by such accountability.

Coptic liturgical tradition is noisy. Vocal participation in the Liturgy is loud and long. The Coptic hymns are bouncy and catchy, and frequently taken up by the entire congregation. One or more deacons will play hand cymbals to accompany the vigorous music. This lively devotion is the common and communal aspect of Coptic worship. It continues even in the desert monasteries, where the monastic offices are robust and direct. But there exists alongside the liturgical work of the Copts a contemplative aspect, which is severe and forbidding to the outsider. For those few who realise the balance between Coptic liturgy and stillness the perfect expression of devotion may have been found: oriental tradition and occidental aspirations meet here.

Justus was devoted to the liturgical life. It is reported that he was always the first to arrive in chapel and the last to leave. He invariably entered in silence, barefoot and head bowed. He would go straight to the front of the sanctuary and prostrate himself before the altar, dedicating himself on each occasion to the task of performing the worship. Then he would stand in his allotted place.

In the regular night vigils, at the Divine Liturgy or in the recitation of the divine office, he would stand in silence, not joining his voice to those of his brothers. He lived the solitary life within the community. Sometimes he would squat in silence but mostly he stood. Some monks recall his habit of going to the lectern and standing for hours, even whilst a service was taking place, silently reading the Coptic version of the Gospels or the Book of Hours. He would clutch a lighted candle to read more easily. Meeting him for the first time, many took him for an illiterate peasant. Nothing could be further from the truth. He was a master of the Coptic language. He loved to read the Gospel aloud in Coptic. He read with a soft, deep voice and with great emotion. One of the senior monks says, perhaps in forgivable exaggeration, "No ordinary mortal can describe this wonderful angelic voice which would draw the attention of everyone present." His reading of Coptic was clear and precise. Whenever he read out the words for "The Lord" in Coptic he would repeat them gently but firmly three times in adoration of the Holy Trinity. He loved the Coptic language so much that just before his death he asked for a book of the Lenten prophecies and read it in his cell. His reading of the Gospel was the only time when the monks would ever hear his voice, and apart from that ministry he lived in sacred silence. From the first days of his monastic life until its end, Abba Justus put on the mantle of silence. In time his silence became so famous that people travelled into the desert asking for "the monk-saint Justus the silent". This usage followed the tradition of a fourteenth-century monk *Marqus Al-Antuni* who was known to the Bedouin as "the silent monk."

Silence is, of course, important for every monk but Justus was an outstanding and austere witness for silence. The mysterious phrase in the Revelation to John the Theologian, 8: 1, "There was silence in Heaven for about half an hour" has never received definitive elucidation but, at the very least, it suggests awe and devotion in the presence of God which was the essence of the Abba's life.

It says much for the treatment of individual monks in the Wadi Arabah that Justus was allowed to be a solitary and lead the eremitic life whilst living in a community. Many monks have felt that only solitaries can attain the absolute ascetic ideal, and a strategy has developed to deal with such vocations. There are five degrees of initiation involved. First, a monk must live well within the community. As a beginner in the solitary life he will then be allowed to observe silence at his work. Thirdly, he is permitted to spend some weeks in the monastery, only emerging from his cell for the Divine Liturgy once a week. The fourth stage is life in a cave outside the monastery. It is said that the final, and ultimate, stage of the life is to become an itinerant anchorite, living in caves but known only to God. The present Coptic patriarch, a solitary in the past, has said that there are no monks living the fifth degree at present. Justus lived out the ideal of spiritual silence whilst physically in the monastery.

At the centre of the vocation of a monk–ascetic lies the need to achieve the state of sacred silence in which the heart and mind are free and feed upon the perception of God as Trinity. The individual hermit may create problems for the community and for himself, but the sacred silence itself is valued even by the most sceptical of the monastic community. Abba Isidore of Pelusia (c.350) said, "To live without speaking is better than to speak without living. For the monk in the former state who lives rightly does good even by his silence, but the latter does no good even when he speaks. When words and life correspond to one another they are together the whole of philosophy." In his own eyes and in that of his community Abba Justus was always a monk among monks. He did not ask for or want any special attention. But his life of silence, paradoxically, cried out to some of his brethren and to a noisy church. It is not difficult to find young Coptic monks, within the episcopate, who dismiss the Abba's silence, saying that he had nothing to say and so it was best that he was silent. He is often described as "simple" and "uneducated".

Silence is a reproach to the institutionalized church, which so easily accommodates itself to secularism or materialism. The establishment seems to its critics to have lost the pristine vision of the Judaean wilderness. In every report about Abba Justus, written or oral, the word "silence" occurs again and again. One of those younger monks who admired Justus has said, "He did not respond to the words of those around him, but he heard the word of Him who dwells within." The same admirer claims that Justus brought back a lost tradition to the monastery and says that some of the monks slowly became sensitive to the view that Justus was one of those "who were living in the world but were not of the world" and that this did not imply rejection of the brethren. It is rather a question of priorities. Abba Justus exemplifies, for his fellow ascetics, a life that has a centre and a foundation. First things first: "I cannot be with God and man in the same moment", Justus would quote, "therefore it is better that I be with God."

Now, at the beginning of the twenty-first century, the desert monasteries of Egypt are places of activity; far too much activity for some of the monks who answered the desert call to live in silence and separation. The Wadi Natroun in Egypt's Western desert is at times not unlike a vast agricultural and industrial estate. It is a time of building and business in the Western Desert of Egypt. Tourism has also had a dramatic effect upon Coptic monasticism, though the two Red Sea monasteries are perhaps less affected by commercialism. When Abba Justus joined the monastery, "work" was part of the religious life of the house. It could be very boring and routine but it has always been understood that labour is one of the tested paths to holiness. In the fifth century someone asked Abba Arsenius, "How is it that we, with all our education and our wide knowledge get nowhere, while these Egyptian peasants acquire so many virtues?" Abba Arsenius replied, "We indeed get nothing from our secular education, but these Egyptian peasants acquire the virtues by hard work."

The monks who worked with him say that Justus sanctified the labour of the monastery with his work. He threw himself into the seasonal activities of the monastery. Though the Wadi Arabah is rocky, the monks of St. Antony have planted palms, olive trees and vines for many centuries. Since the beginning of the religious settlement heavy, rich soil has been moved from the Nile Valley across the desert on the backs of camels. Justus liked to work on the olive harvest and would follow the younger monks under the olive trees, collecting the olives in his long gown. At different times in his monastic life, Justus worked on the olive millstone, used to break the olives before pressing. He was also skilled at the olive press. He was not shy of back-breaking labouring in the extensive monastery gardens. He liked to carry heavy loads even towards the end of his days.

Work was a time when the Abba would smile and laugh, though he generally retained his silence. There was especial joy for him in the making and baking of bread. Bread is so ordinary, but bread in the wilderness is resonant with evangelical significance. Of course, it is "the staff of life", "the support of life"; but the Christian cannot lose sight of the fact that even the most ordinary bread may, by its nature, be invested with another meaning. Bread from Melchizedek in Genesis; the Unleavened Bread of the Exodus; the bread of the Presence; the bread for the five thousand in the gospel; the bread of the Last Supper; the Bread of Life come down from heaven; Bread of the Eucharist broken for our salvation; Bread from the raven for Saint Paul of Thebes and Saint Antony the Great. This chain of reference only hints at the need for the monk to attend to the ovens of the monastery.

The community has a supply of water. If it had no water there would be no monastery in the Wadi Arabah. The spring of Saint Antony supplies the entire monastic congregation and guests with enough water for daily use. Located in the southern part of the monastic compound, the spring flows from a natural tunnel deep in the mountain and provides about 100 cubic metres per day. The temperature is constant at 23^0 C. and, in spite of a small percentage of phosphorus, it is a sweet and excellent drinking water. The monks say that those who drink from the spring will return to the Wadi Arabah. The visitor easily yields to the fancy. Until the day of his death, Justus daily carried large pitchers of water from the spring down into the monastery. He liked to offer drinks of the water. Like all long-time residents in the desert, he regarded the spring as a miracle of divine providence. Water-carrying was a sanctified and sanctifying movement. All work was a participation in the divine activities of creating and sustaining.

Justus was not a priest. Once in a while he would enter the sanctuary as an acolyte standing alongside a priest. He would put on all the priestly vestments held out before him. He would vest himself in alb, stole, cowl and girdle. Some of the vestments were those reserved solely for the episcopate. He would take them too. The monks said nothing. Some have recorded that they felt that he endowed the vestments and liturgy with his extraordinary, convincing sanctity.

Hierarchical ceremonial and formalism at times overwhelm Orthodoxy. The externals can appear to be excess baggage in a monastery. Spiritually the liturgy is too often weakened by the fact that ambitious men become monks solely because it is the only route to the episcopate. Justus in the sanctuary, wearing the hierarchical robes, is Christ's troubadour and *jongleur*, a "fool for Christ". The folly achieved at the cost of personal dignity is that type of holy idiocy and spiritual infancy that mocks all ecclesiastical pretentiousness. That the tradition of the holy fool has been detected in Syria, Egypt, Russia, France, America and Ireland is testimony to the need for such a witness within the ecclesiastical structures. But it would be misleading to understand Justus's folly as anything so trivial and ill conceived as an attack upon an ambitious leadership. His folly is spiritual and radical, bringing us to the threshold of paradox and mystery. On several occasions he was in chapel at the moment of the Holy Communion. He placed his hand in his pocket then raised it to his mouth. Nobody could see anything.

One of those present writes: "All we could see was that he was eating something. He would not enter the sanctuary and join those receiving Holy Communion. He hid before the icons and ate. The fathers of the monastery were convinced that he was already in the realm of the anchorite saints."

It would be wrong to suggest that this was in any sense a denial of the sacrament of the altar. It is rather a mystical sign from Christ's fool, pointing an often forbiddingly sacramental church to the spiritual fulfilment and heart of the liturgy in the sanctification of the people of God: "the holy for the holies."

We have seen that the sacred silence of the solitary was the overruling ascetic accomplishment in the life of Justus. When he broke the silence, which was extremely rare, he had only one question to ask, "What time is it now?" His posthumous fame rests partly upon his use of this question. Justus asked the question, at one time or another, over a period of many years, to everyone at the monastery. The abbot of the monastery was very annoyed one night when woken by Justus asking him, "What time is it now?" When the abbot turned back angrily to his bed he found, to his astonishment, a large venomous scorpion on his pillow. After killing it he returned safely to sleep. Justus often welcomed visitors with genuine warmth. Some recall how he sat with them in silence. Some would press around him with trivial and prying questions. His response was always the same, "What time is it now?" He was never tired of asking the same question many times in the same day.

"What time is it now?" The monks thought that he knew the time. He knew it by the sun, but he also knew it when there were clouds. When given the wrong time, he would immediately give the correct time. He did not own a watch.

Justus was deeply imbued in the traditions of the Fathers whom he read in Coptic and in later Arabic forms. His mind was set in a Patristic cast, indebted, as most of that literature is, to Platonism. He read beautifully in chapel and carried books to his cell. We may surmise that the question, "What time is it now" has a subtle sub-text and invites us to distinguish between two uses of the word "time". In the genius of the Greek language this usage is designated by two words, *chronos* which indicates the continuous flux of time, the measurable time of the clock, determined by the movement of the earth around the sun, and *kairos* which points out a significant moment of time, a unique moment in the temporal process in which something is especially fulfilled and accomplished. It is *kairos*, which is alluded to in the first words attributed to Jesus in the synoptic tradition. Mark 1: 15 "The time is fulfilled"; the *kairos* is accomplished. *Kairos* is focused upon a unique event in time – the appearance of the Messiah, the central event of history and the moment providence prepared during the long passage of ordinary time. The answer to the question "What time is it now?" is that it is "the right time". It is the time of Christ, the one right time, the fulfilment of time in his appearance in Galilee, at the end of time and at each "time" when we acknowledge his coming to us. Abba Justus was a prophet of the possibility of *kairos*, which lies in the present moment of *chronos*. He told us that at each moment when we allow the eternal to break into the temporal there is the moment of *kairos*. "What time is it now?" The monk who asks the question is a disclaimer. He knows the answer to his question but is content to give a false impression of himself, pretending ignorance and folly so that others will engage in the spiritual struggle required to find the answer.

The enigmatic, absurd, disquieting and persistent question of the Abba stands. It troubles our self-satisfied certainty that we are not threatened and that everything continues to remain the same: "What time is it now?"

It is repeatedly remarked that Abba Justus has been the most important inspiration in the revival of the religious life amongst women, because he is the perfect contemporary example of the classic ideal of Coptic monasticism. Contemplative and active convents are playing a significant role in the Coptic revival. It is a world that is closed to men. It is hardly surprising that Pope Kyrillos gave special encouragement to the establishment of contemplative communities, though socially active and consecrated women have always found popular and official recognition much more difficult. Women do not have a prominent role in the Coptic Orthodox Church. In two decades, it has been impossible to obtain an interview with a nun in Egypt, but the Coptologist is fortunate that the essential narrative of modern Coptic nuns has been written by a Dutch scholar, Pieternella van Doorn-Harder. Devotion to Abba Justus is a widespread feature of conventual life in modern Egypt. He is a model of holiness.

The monasteries of Al-Muharraq, blessed by the visit of the infant Jesus; of St. Antony, sanctified by the life of Abba Justus; of St. Macarius, consecrated by the sacrificial labours of Fr. Matta and his brethren; like all the great religious houses of modern Egypt, resonate with the virtues of poverty, chastity, obedience and stability. But the modern mind, sometimes uncertain of the value of what it thinks of as a retreat to the cloister, will delight in the discovery of great sanctity in the sacred soil of Cairo, the mother of cities, not in a monastery but on a mountain of refuse.

Cairo is the largest city of Africa and the Middle East with an annual population increase of some million souls. For half a century the Mokkatam Hills of Cairo have been the home of the *Zebaleen*, the garbage collectors of the city. More than 95 per cent of this entirely Christian community collect most of Cairo's garbage, a vital service in the absence of municipal facilities. The garbage is collected in trucks and carts drawn by donkeys. Fathers and sons work together from house to house. Mothers and daughters sort through everything brought home. Through the labours of the *Zebaleen*, Cairo has the highest ratio of recycled material in Africa and the Middle East: approximately 80 per cent of the garbage brought in to Mokkatam goes out as a usable material. The goats and pigs have an extraordinary diet from the other 20 per cent. The streets often stink. The piles of garbage are an offence to every sense. It is a metropolitan hell, far from the sanctity of the desert, but there is no hint of self-pity. The *Zebaleen* are enterprising and cheerful though as reticent as any monks, and suspicious of outsiders. They dislike being treated as another oriental curiosity.

In the adult learning centre, materials based firmly on the system of Paulo Freire, in his books *Cultural Action for Freedom* and the *Pedagogy of the Oppressed*, are much in evidence. "The preferential option for the poor" means here, tragically, as almost everywhere else where Freire is honoured, self-help.

The pride of the *Zebaleen* is not their badly needed public service with the metropolitan garbage, which is after all indispensable for the great city of Cairo, or that politicians and development agencies admire their highly organized recycling operation. The pride of the *Zebaleen* is their buildings. Beside the mounds of garbage there stand a superbly equipped hospital, partly a result of Norwegian aid, and an immaculate primary school, both are resolutely Christian. The children in the school are an instant reminder of Egyptian, and Coptic, continuity. The visitor looks into the faces and the large, beautiful eyes, staring soulfully back, are those of the second-century mysterious Fayum portraits. The faces of Mokkatam are the faces of the ancient Egyptians. The spiritual treasure of the *Zebaleen* is their children. The building programme is personal and spiritual. For the *Zebaleen*, all growth must be not only outward but also inward. Their forbidding life is devoid of self-pity and the physical expression of their human dignity and religious faith is nearby. Taking the hand of the visitor, they lead him up the hillside. Not far from their school is the great cathedral of the Blessed Virgin, blasted and dug from the mountainside. Entering the great cave, the Coptic *Zebaleen* remove their shoes and stand barefoot before the true glory of their God, as Moses before the burning bush. The intensity of their devotion is a rebuke to comfortable, western agnosticism. In the harshest imaginable environment the Copts have once again defined their own "significant soil".

Chapter Four

In Liturgical Time

You can only pray when you find yourself in the presence of God in a state of quietness and inner peace which transcends the notion of time. Here I don't mean our objectively measurable time, but our subjective experience of the passing of time around us and the certainty that we ourselves are timeless. Metropolitan Anthony of Sourozh

Worship is at the centre of the Coptic experience, and the Copts have a favourite story about the Divine Liturgy of Saint Basil the Great. It concerns a priest who was especially devoted to the Liturgy as the summation of Christian life. When he was the celebrant at the Eucharist he was focused entirely upon the holy work of the altar. He recited every phrase of the ancient text with absolute conviction. He accomplished the performance of the liturgical drama according to the precise rubrics he had learnt from childhood. One day, coming to the words " Our Lord lifted up his sacred eyes", he raised his head slightly and lifted his eyes. A deep silence prevailed. The priest gazed upwards. Minutes passed. The priest continued to stare aloft in silence. Time passed. The congregation stood silently behind the priest, attending to the central actor in the sanctuary. A long time passed. Then the priest slowly lowered his eyes. He continued to pray aloud. His voice was deep and firm. It seemed as if he was unaware of the passing of time. After the liturgy, one of the deacons who had been in the sanctuary approached the priest to discuss the incident. Was he unwell? Had his memory failed? The priest was confused and refused to reply, but the deacon pressed him for an answer. Finally, the priest explained that when he looked up, he saw no ceiling only the blue of the sky dotted with clouds. A bright, shining ladder reached from the altar into the distant spaces of the sky above. He looked at the sky, as it seemed to him, for just a second or so, no more, and then went on with the liturgy.

Liturgical time is different from Time. The supernatural touches the natural as a tangent touches a circle. The temporal expresses the eternal. Here, more than anywhere, is the Coptic genius: the expression of the inexpressible. Coptic Orthodoxy requires no other justification than its liturgy, which is a mysterious amalgam of music, drama and the visual arts, and is completely self-authenticating. Many foreigners have found that the language of the liturgy is universal. The liturgical domain is in itself a parallel world existing outside time. It is heaven upon the earth. The experience of the priest standing in rapturous silence may appear to be quite extraordinary to the occidental mind, but in the Coptic encounter with the mystical it is commonplace. If the outsider knows nothing of Coptic Culture, Theology, Mission and History but knows the Liturgy then the outsider knows everything that is important. The Liturgy is the heart of the encounter between human and human, between human and divine. The Liturgy is, in a mystical sense, all that there is. Whilst it is true that a priest must always be present for this sacrament, it is more important that the Liturgy is understood as the self-defining action of all the people of God.

Statistics rarely signify virtue, but, before we step into the Coptic sanctuary, it is worth reflecting that Kyrillos VI, the 116th Coptic Pope from 1959 to 1971, celebrated the Divine Liturgy on not less than 12,500 occasions. He attended the Eucharist over one thousand times before his ordination. In sum, he stood as a priest in the sanctuary for over 50,000 hours, as a layman over 4,000. He celebrated the Mass for the equivalent of more than seven thousands days, the equivalent of 297 weeks or more than five years. Years spent standing before God at an altar.

The stage for the Christian drama is the *Haikal*. The Arabic word for sanctuary applies to the area behind the screen or iconostasis and the altar itself. As we approach the holy place, we see that white ostrich eggs are hanging from their ropes, which reach up into the roof in front of the *Haikal*. Ostrich eggs are the symbols of loyal mindfulness. The ostrich buries her eggs in the sand. She then stays at a distance from them with her eyes fixed on that spot. The church stands watching the place of New Life; the *Haikal*. The sanctuary is the place of death and resurrection. The icon screen and the wall behind the altar are decorated with icons. The saints are looking down on us.

Preparatory prayers have been said the night before and since sunrise someone has been prayerfully awaiting the Mass. The psalms are sung. The altar and the sacred vessels of the Liturgy must only be used once a day: another priest may repeat the liturgy on one of the neighbouring altars but not here and not with these utensils on this day. On the altar is the book of the gospels, a hand cross and a fan for keeping flies and insects from touching the chalice. We are reminded that we are in the Middle East. Some larger fans stand around the sanctuary, adding to the oriental sensitivity of the *Haikal*. Four candles stand at the altar corners.

The priest is standing at the entrance of the sanctuary. He faces the people. He holds the bottle of wine in his left hand and smells it. He must ensure that it is fresh and pure wine. In modern times he must also ensure that the wine of the Eucharist is unfermented grape juice. In ancient times, the Copts used the fermented juice of the grape, but as a concession to Islam and its teetotalism the Copts abandoned apostolic practice. Some authorities state that the wine may be the fermented juice of raisins. Some Coptic priests have used the Cypriot wine commonly used in other churches. Middle Eastern Christians are sensitive to Muslim criticism of alcohol.

The priest or an authorized person baked the holy bread, leavened but not salted. It must be used today. The small and rather flat round loaves are stamped with a cross surrounded by twelve smaller crosses, symbolising the Lord and the twelve disciples. There is an inscription marked by the wooden stamp used in the preparation. The inscription is the Trisagion: *Agios O Theos, Agios Ischyros, Agios Athanatos*, "Holy God, Holy and strong. Holy and immortal". Coptic tradition traces this hymn to the singing of Nicodemus and Joseph of Arimathea at the entombment of Christ. The loaves are pierced five times around the central cross, symbolising the nails, crown of thorns and spear used on Calvary in the passion of Christ. This central configuration of the bread is called the *Spadikon*. To be chosen for the Eucharist the bread must be the finest, fully rounded, without blemish, with the correct number of holes and with each hole clear and unblocked. It is to be like the whole and unblemished Passover lamb of Exodus 12: 5. The chosen loaf is called *Hamal*, the Lamb of God. The priest chooses the bread with his arms crossed over each other, the right hand on top, as Jacob blessed the sons of Joseph in Genesis 48. The priest says: "May the Lord choose for Himself a lamb without blemish". Now the priest places the *Hamal* on the napkin in his left hand. He wets his right thumb with wine and makes the sign of the cross upon the elected *Hamal*. Now the celebrant has water from a stone pitcher poured into his cupped right hand and, as Christ was baptized in the River Jordan, so at each Eucharist the *Hamal* is baptized as the celebrant's hand passes carefully over the chosen Lamb of God. The prayer which the priest offers refers to the liturgical sacrifice about to take place. It is for the remission of sins.

The priest wraps the *Hamal* in the napkin, covers both with the hand cross and enters the sanctuary, making a procession "of the Lamb" around the altar. The celebrants – priest and assistants – are barefoot in the sanctuary. Woollen sanctuary slippers may be available, but shoes or sandals are not worn. The vesture is white, signifying purity and chastity. The robe reaches down to the feet and its long sleeves are embroidered with Crosses. An amice – Arabic *tailasama* – is worn over the head as a shawl. It creates a distinct sense of the Semitic provenance of this Mass. The Liturgy is sung. The priest sings as he makes the sign of the cross three times over both bread and wine. All participants have been fasting.

The chalice is prepared upon the altar. It is placed on the Ark, a cube with paintings of the Last Supper, Our Lady, angels and the patron saint of the church painted on four sides. It will hold the chalice until the Communion. The chalice is covered with a napkin. The paten, a flat silver dish is prepared for the *Hamal*. Two half-hoops of silver have been joined together at right angles. When they are placed over the paten, they form a canopy to prevent the cover from touching the *Hamal* and defiling it.

The priest holds the end of the *prospherine*, a fair linen cloth, and a deacon holds the other end. In their white clothes and moving the *prospherine* above the altar in a gently flapping movement, they are the angels who appeared at the tomb of Christ (John 20). The *prospherine* comes down gently upon the altar. Now it symbolizes the stone laid on the tomb of Christ. The tomb is "sealed" with a smaller napkin.

The censer and incense box have already been used in the preparatory prayers. They will have a vital role in the Liturgy, symbolising the cleansing and sanctification of the building, the holy gifts and the people. With the incense smoke the prayers of the faithful rise to the heavens. The priest blesses the incense as it is offered to him. He censes the altar and the people. His hands are bathed in the smoke of the censer so that they will be purified in preparation to hold the holy gifts of the altar. He then censes the bread and wine, touching both to symbolize the spices, which Nicodemus placed on the body of the Lord at the time of his burial.

A stone ewer and basin have been prepared to wash the priest's hands before he touches the *Hamal*. The cruet of the holy Myron, the oil of chrism, prepared infrequently and with elaborate patriarchal ritual, is standing there. The *artophorion* may have been prepared. It is a small silver box for the conveyance of part of the precious Body and Blood to those who need Communion but cannot attend the Liturgy.

For hours of intense devotion the Liturgy floats on a sea of prayer and Scripture. A distinctive feature is the four lessons from the New Testament. Excerpts from Paul, the general epistles and Acts precede the Gospel. The litanies of intercession encompass everything and everybody: the faithful departed, the sick, travellers by land, sea and air; the great river Nile, the fish of Egypt, the natural world and its creatures who run, swim and fly; the priests, prelates and rulers of the Copts. All are brought into the sanctuary. The liturgical language of the Copts is the Bohairic (North Egyptian) dialect. In addition, Arabic has been used for centuries. Translations into European languages have proved to be culturally and spiritually unavailing, their poverty only too apparent to the discerning ear and mind. This is the Coptic *art of arts*, uniquely of the Nile.

The Liturgy of the Faithful leads to the Kiss of peace. Neighbour places closed hands into the open hands of neighbour. They touch. The hands are kissed. Peace passes on.

The great Anaphora, or prayer of consecration, is the climax of the worship. Here the holy gifts of bread and wine become the Body and Blood of Christ and are shared by the people. The Anaphora may be that of St. Cyril, in Lent. The normal Anaphora is that of St. Basil the Great. The third possibility is that the Anaphora of St. Gregory Nazianzen will be used. For those who have faith the effect is always the same: that which is bread and wine is blessed, sanctified, purified and changed so that it is for those who believe the Body and Blood of Jesus Christ. In no other Christian tradition is the matter expressed more starkly than here among the Copts. Before his communion the priest makes his moving profession of faith: "This is in truth the Body and Blood of Emmanuel our God". The people respond: "Amen. I believe". These mysterious utterances are physically enshrouded in clouds of incense. Before their departure the communicants give thanks for that which "Eye has not seen, nor ear heard, neither have entered into the heart of man, the things which God hath prepared for them that love him" (1 Cor. 2: 9).

Water is cast upon the congregation at the blessing, bringing the purifying and refreshing blessing of God through the hands of the priest who collects the water in the palm of his hand and throws it on the people. Worship is a celebration of the traditional senses: animation, touch, speech, taste, sight, auditory and olfactory senses.

Music and Coptic Orthodoxy are inseparable. There is no point where worship ends and music begins. The Divine Liturgy is sung in its entirety. Many of the melodies have the captivating quality associated with all great music. Some of the music is microtonal: the range of intervals can be narrow – a semitone or smaller. Coptic musicologists regard unison singing as an expression of spiritual purity, thus all hymns are performed without harmony. A cantor with a male choir of robed deacons leads the singing. Some cantors are blind, and have received special training because it is believed that they have a unique musical and spiritual "insight" which is essential for this music. Miniature cymbals and triangles with studied syncopation accompany some chants. The congregation plays an indispensable role in the sung versicles and responses: the liturgy is the work of the entire congregation.

Ragheb Moftah, the leading Coptic musicologist, has established that

Coptic music is one of the most ancient forms of liturgical music. It has been preserved by oral tradition. The modern nationalist school of Coptic musicians regard church music as an important key to the mystery of Pharaonic music, seeing their music as the authentic successor of the ancient music of Egypt. Copts love to sing and their performances of the Liturgy in small churches, monasteries and cathedrals is of a uniformly high standard, often rising to great spiritual heights and done with tremendous energy and ardour. The romantic assessment of the British musicologist Ernest Newlandsmith is suggestive: "Coptic music is a great music, one of the wonders of the world. If a Caruso, filled with the Spirit of God, were to sing some of the Coptic themes in the form of an oratorio, it would be enough to re-kindle Christendom." Newlandsmith spent many years in Egypt reducing Coptic chant to western musical notation. Ragheb Moftah has recorded the central corpus of Coptic music on tape and record.

The purest forms of Coptic music were handed down from generation to generation in isolated monasteries and secluded country churches. Thanks largely to Moftah and Newlandsmith this musical tradition is now much more accessible and in regular use. Those who are prepared to spend hours near the *Haikal* appreciate the impact of Coptic music. It covers a great range of human emotions. The music of a Requiem is filled with pathos, and is said to be derived from the Pharaonic liturgy attending the death of an heir to the throne. The modern Coptic version wrenches at the emotions, dragging the eyes and heart to the open coffin in the centre of the church. Other rugged and rhythmical hymns greet the patriarch or bishop on their entry into a church. Hymns of praise to the Father of Light lift the eyes upward into the vault above the sanctuary. Other hymns, like *She-re Ma-ri-a* – the Coptic *Ave Maria* – teach the people important lessons, in this case relating to the *Theotokos* who bore the Saviour in shame and humility, but has been exalted as Queen of Heaven, and much-loved protectress of all Copts.

Coptic music ranges from sighs to exclamations. It is never the accompaniment of the text. The words and the music are one. The Coptic Liturgy is uniquely Egyptian, and vanishes when it leaves the Nile, unless recreated in its entirety by exiled Copts who were raised in the tradition. An American or German "Copt" is a contradiction in terms. The Coptic Liturgy is a unity of sublime Coptic literature, with some Arabic, of transcendental theatre, of matchless music and meaning. Anyone may attempt total immersion into Coptic culture, hoping to achieve a bridge between two worlds, but it is essential to remember that Coptic Orthodoxy has its own "language" like Islam. It cannot be translated. Of course, all liturgies in all places have a constant reference back to their prototype in Palestine but as the Book of Common Prayer of 1662 is Classical English so the Coptic Liturgy is quintessentially Egyptian. Our hearing confirms the mysterious otherness of Coptic worship. Seeing is, perhaps, an easier exercise.

Icons can be seen; looked through, as spiritual windows to a world beyond; entered through the eyes of mind and spirit. Icons are a wonderful aspect of modern Coptic worship. It has not always been so.

The Copts have faced iconoclasm during Islamic expansion and Protestant intrusion. Although Islam is aniconic in outlook it is correct to refer to iconoclasm since this literally refers to the "smashing of icons". That is what happened. The first major campaign took place when the Ummayad Caliph Yazid the Second promulgated an Edict in 721 ordering the destruction of all Christian pictures in his dominions. Wholesale destruction followed. A number of sources claim that the Caliph was under the influence of a Jewish necromancer who had cured Yazid of a serious illness. According to Lord Norfolk, there is evidence that the same malign personality impressed the Byzantine Emperor Leo III (717–741), who applied similar pressure in the Christian Empire.

Sporadic movements of iconoclasm took place in Egypt and Syria over the centuries. Otto Meinardus says that Islam prevented the Copts from creating their indigenous rich iconography. A more serious factor must be the absence of any Coptic theologian to compare with St. John of Damascus who has left his mark upon theological history, in part by defending the holy icons. Ironically, John wrote in Palestine under the protection of Islam, and in isolation from Byzantium.

In popular devotion, icons remained at the heart of Coptic devotion. There were many miraculous icons. Abba Mina's mother was granted fertility after praying before an icon. Abba Mercurius was cured of leprosy when venerating the icon of the Theotokos at Tmai. In the ninth century there were accounts of all the icons at Abu Makar in the Wadi Natroun weeping because of the persecution and suffering of the Copts. Icons bled, as in the case of the icon seen by Syrian and Coptic monks in the Wadi Natroun during the reign of Abba Christodoulus (c.1077). Many icons emanated light: there was a notable instance at St. Victor's, Gizah near Cairo. There are innumerable examples of the importance of icons in over a thousand years of Coptic piety, but the greatest acts of iconoclasm were instigated within the Church itself.

In 1854 Kyrillos the Fourth, called the Reformer, was enthroned as the 110th Patriarch. He assumed the patriarchal office with a definite programme that included the establishment of schools in Cairo, the raising of educational standards amongst the clergy and the importing of modern printing presses. Two years of his pontificate were spent in Ethiopia on a mission of political reconciliation. This was all admirable.

But he was also responsible for an iconoclasm greater than the Bolshevik destruction of Russian icons. Kyrillos believed his people to be theologically primitive and guilty of idolatry. English missionaries from a conservative Fundamentalist organization had educated him, and Kyrillos prohibited the exposition of icons in his cathedral. Coptic icons were publicly burned in the streets before the bemused Muslim population. In Cairo and Assyut priceless works of early and mediaeval art were destroyed. This denial of Orthodoxy was supported by some Copts, and still has supporters today.

In 1954, exactly a century after the attack upon icons by Kyrillos, a department of Coptic Art was established at the Coptic Institute in Cairo. Sacred art at the time was in thrall to western, Italianate art forms, but in one of the wonders of providence, the renewal of Coptic art was to involve the union of Pharaonic, Coptic and Byzantine traditions in what has become a major evolutionary step in the history of iconography.

Isaac Fanous Yussef was appointed the first professor of Coptic art and archaeology at the Cairo Institute. His initial task was to awaken Coptic artistic awareness. Isaac was steeped in the hieratic techniques of dynastic Egypt. He had trained as an architect, earned a tertiary diploma in Sculpture in Paris and a French government degree in art education. In the late forties and early fifties, although still primarily a sculptor, Fanous was working in fresco, and mosaic whilst experimenting with a contemporary Coptic style. He received his doctorate in Paris for work in iconography. In 1965, a grant from the World Council of Churches allowed Dr Fanous to return to France to investigate the restoration of icons at the Louvre. At the same time he was to study Byzantine and Russian iconography at the St. Sergius Institute in Paris and at the *Foyer Internationale des etudiants*.

Leonid Ouspensky (1902–87), a Russian Orthodox émigré in France and author of the principal modern treatise on icons, initiated a revival in iconography in places where the theological depth and artistic beauty of the icon had been forgotten. Paul Evdokimov (1901–70), who left St. Petersburg after the Russian Revolution, also taught theology and philosophy in Paris. He affirmed the essential orthodoxy of the Platonic maxim: "Beauty is the splendour of truth". Evdokimov wrote of that divine-human beauty "that will save the world", as Dostoevsky had expected. For him the spirit of Orthodoxy is a *philokalic* spirit: the *Philokalia* ("love of beauty") is an anthology of writings on mystical theology. Evdokimov taught that all truthful iconography is similarly mystical, theological and beautiful. The Russian teachers focused upon the iconographic mystery in which wood and paint is transformed so that it becomes spirit bearing. It is said that the entire theological approach of Evdokimov and Ouspensky was in complete harmony with the spirit and ethos of Orthodox life. They communicated this spirit to students from all over the world, teaching them the theology of icons, the art of iconography and the restoration of icons. Fanous studied with Leonid Ouspensky for two years and on other occasions with Paul Edvokimov. It was this immersion in an assured theological tradition that made Isaac one of the most profoundly Orthodox of Copts. Ouspensky initially wished to keep his Egyptian iconographer in Paris, painting in the Russian style. The Russian master eventually relented and supported the intention of Fanous to establish a new Coptic school of iconography, which would not paint Russian icons in Egypt but would learn to speak again the ancient language of the Copts in art.

Orthodox Iconography had once been given noble expression in the most famous of all Coptic icons at the Middle Egyptian monastery of Bawit in the seventh century. This eloquent spiritual statement, now in the Louvre, shows the full-length figures of Christ and St. Mena – not the national saint of the Diocletian persecution, but the Abbott of the Bawit Monastery – the right arm of Jesus is around the Abbott's shoulder, his hand resting in an embrace of protection, acceptance and familiarity. It is one of the world's great religious images; an expressive declaration concerning Christ's relationship with his disciples. An hour spent with this icon is never wasted.

Iconography continued to flourish in most countries of the Mediterranean from the end of the eighth century, following the triumph of orthodoxy, which asserted the centrality of icons for Christian orthodoxy at the Second Council of Nicaea on 13 October, 787, but there was no equivalent expansion in Egypt. The few old Coptic icons, like the Bawit icon in the Louvre, are well known. The monastery of St. Antony has wall paintings from the thirteenth century. In 1991 French scholars uncovered a ninth-century fresco, revealing a strong, blue image of the Blessed Virgin, in the Monastery of the Syrians in the Wadi Natroun. The church of St. Mercurios in the monastery of Abu El Sefein in Old Cairo has remarkable icons of the fifteenth century. A modest number of Coptic icons date from the eighteenth and nineteenth centuries – notably the works of Yohanna the Armenian, Ibrahim the Scribe (*el Nasikh*), the el-Gohari brothers, Ibrahim and Girguis, and Eustathius the Greek (*al Rumi*) – but there are very few Coptic icons from the seventh to the eighteenth century. Linda Langen of the Netherlands Institute has suggested that this intriguing absence of Coptic icons for a thousand years is accounted for by the fact that many icons were burnt in the preparatory ceremonies associated with the Holy Myron – the patriarchal oil used in the sacraments – but iconoclasm or simple indifference in an Islamic environment are more likely explanations.

Certainly, at the beginning of the twentieth century with a burgeoning revival amongst the Copts, their iconography was clearly awaiting a new champion. From Leonid Ouspensky and Paul Evdokimov in Paris, through Isaac Fanous, a further development has taken place in Egypt.

Isaac Fanous Yussef has given the Copts a resource of orthodox theology and spirituality, which is second to none in the Christian world. The icons of Fanous are extensively used in devotion. At St. Mary's, Heliopolis, Ard El Golf District, he has created the Sistine Chapel of Coptic Orthodoxy. It is a staggering achievement, with at least 70 large icons in the nave and more in the sanctuary. In between two visits – the first in 1989 and the second in 1994 – some icons had been worn away by kissing and touching. The icon of St. Stephen the Protomartyr in particular had vanished on the lips of the faithful.

The spiritual master Fanous is meeting a devotional need. One of his students, Dr Jackie Ascott, has written: "The true iconographer is engaged in a work of spiritual expression and the Icon is related very closely to the Spirituality of the icon painter himself. His own depth of spiritual life and experience will inevitably affect the icons he paints." This valuable observation echoes the words of Evagrius the Solitary in the *Philokalia*: "If you are a theologian, you will pray truly. And if you pray truly you are a theologian." It would be accurate to rewrite this for our discussion: "If you are an iconographer, you will pray truly. And if you pray truly through you artistic techniques then you are an iconographer". We should not hesitate to describe Isaac Fanous as a major theologian of Orthodoxy. His work, now preserved across the world in churches and private collections, will endure. Isaac Fanous is fortunate in the quality of his disciples, including his assistant in Cairo Ashraf Fayek Mikhail, Jackie Ascott in Cyprus and one of the greatest younger iconographers and spiritual masters of contemporary Orthodoxy, Dr Stephane Rene of the Royal College of Art and Prince of Wales's Institute in London. St. Andre Rublev in fourteenth-century Russia was surrounded by hierarchs, theologians and patriarchs whose names now mean nothing. His icon of the Hospitality of Abraham speaks to and for the prayerful every day, as it has for six hundred years. The Coptic legacy of Isaac Fanous Yussef is as great a wonder. Its future in the history of spirituality is guaranteed. The only comparable development is found in the work of Photis Kontoglou (1895–1965) who not only wrote the first Greek manual of iconography in two centuries but was the only modern Greek artist to fully comprehend the vital role that painting ought to play in Orthodoxy today. His role was theological, revelatory, dogmatic and didactic. At his funeral it was said that he not only fulfilled the role of an artist, but also the role of a confessor. As much can be said of Isaac Fanous Yussef. This great Coptic Master of iconography stands alongside Abouna Matta El-Meskeen as a giant of theology and spirituality.

The Coptic Liturgy, the holy icons, the ancient music and the primeval ritual draw the worshipper into the mystery of Liturgical Time. The icon is transfigured matter. The music elevates speech to spiritual conversation. The perfected ritual of sacred theatre articulates human longing for eternal life. Here we may see, hear and touch the vision of the redeemed universe. In this most tactile of religious encounters the Copts test and make manifest the Mystery of the grace of our Lord Jesus Christ, the love of God the Father and the communion of the Holy Spirit. One God.

Chapter Five

Patriarchs:
Fathers of the Fathers

Your bishop's office, which exists for the good of the whole community, was never obtained by his own efforts, nor by any other mere human agency, still less in any spirit of self-glorification; but it was conferred upon him by the love of God the Father and the Lord Jesus Christ. Ignatius of Antioch, d. *circa* 107

In the Coptic tradition, the Church is not the Patriarch. Copts often say that the only pyramids they recognize are those of the pharaohs. There is no ecclesiastical pyramid with a broad base of laity and the Pope at the pinnacle. The whole Orthodox People of God are the Coptic Orthodox Church. It has been a tradition that a priest is ordained to serve a congregation who have nominated him and already believe him to be worthy, that a bishop is appointed by the people of the diocese and that a large representative electorate is involved in the selection of a short list of three for patriarch. In the 1960s the appointment of Amba Mina El Makari as Metropolitan of Girga was opposed by the faithful and he remained outside his diocese for two years. The Coptic laity are said to have an intuition about who is fit to be their episcopal father. The spiritual and mystical concept "baba", "papas", "father" or "pope" appeared first in Egypt. A bishop of a diocese must be a father: the patriarch is a "baba" for all the Copts and a "father of the fathers" (Papa Abba). That is the ideal.

In Coptic Church history, there have been many ways of selecting a patriarch. Annianus (d. 83) was the second Patriarch. According to the tenth-century Coptic Bishop Severus Ibn al-Muqaffa, Annianus was chosen by all the faithful to replace St. Mark the Evangelist, the first patriarch. After the death of Annianus "the orthodox people assembled together and took a man named Abilius and elected him patriarch".

Most scholars would agree that in the majority of elections the orthodox people have appointed the patriarch, though it is often suggested that there is a serious misuse of historical evidence from time to time to support virtually any current practice.

Sometimes a patriarch nominated his successor. Theonas (d. 300), the sixteenth Coptic patriarch, spoke to his people from his deathbed: "You are not orphans, but this Peter is your father and he shall be patriarch after me." This method would not be acceptable today, though definite attempts have been made by the living to have posthumous influence on the next election. The present patriarch has packed the bench of bishops with unelected nominees, often general bishops, co-adjutors or suffragans, to insure the continuity of his particular party line. (There are more than eighty canonically recognized bishops in the Coptic Church; the ruling patriarch has consecrated over seventy of these.) The two most recent patriarchs have appointed a number of "general" bishops with defined work in administration, social services, diplomacy and youth services. They have often been regarded as bishops in training for the Patriarchate. In the last papal election two "general" bishops were in the final altar ballot. One was elected. That is the closest that the modern church has come to papal nomination by a predecessor.

Copts in the 1990s were inordinately proud of the altar lot as a means of election. In fact, the lot has been seldom used in Coptic history. We first read of the use of a lot in the eighth century, but very rarely since. Modern use of the altar lot for the elections of Kyrillos the Sixth (1959) and Shenouda the Third (1971) was correctly regarded as innovative, though warmly welcomed by most of the constituency. The election process for the last two patriarchs is interesting and worth examining. A list of candidates was proposed in the first round, and through a careful process of consultation, both public and private, three candidates emerged. The Holy Synod, the Coptic Community Council (*Majlis Milli*) and other elected Copts were involved in the operation of finding a monk of lifelong celibacy who was of legitimate birth in a first marriage, at least fifty years old and Egyptian by birth. He must be known for his holiness of life. A series of vigils and services were held throughout Egypt before the lot was taken. At the final stage in the election, the names of the three candidates were placed upon the altar in a small box. A fourth scroll was added. It carried the inscription "Jesus Christ the Good Shepherd". Finally, a child with a blindfold drew the name. If the fourth scroll had emerged it would have been an indication than none of the three was acceptable and the operation would have been repeated until there was a favourable outcome. No such problem arose in 1959 or 1971. The Copts need to interpret the election of their Patriarch as an act of Divine providence. The altar lot helps to impress this sentiment upon the whole Church and upon the nation, where the Pope is regarded as the approved civic representative of the Copts.

In Islamic lands, Turkey as much as Egypt, the government is involved in the electoral process of Christian leaders. Islamic control of elections was once quite common. Past experience even led Mohammed Heikal, sometime editor of *Al Ahram*, the most influential daily newspaper in the Arab world, to suggest that the last Papal election was rigged and that Shenouda (elected 1971) was President Sadat's nominee. However unlikely that may seem, it is true that for the Egyptian National Democratic Party in Government, there is an important relationship at stake when the Copts choose a Pope. Since the Egyptian Revolution in the 1950s the Copts have generally stood solidly behind the government. Kyrillos the Sixth joined the Government in condemning US involvement in Vietnam. Like President Gamal Abd el Nasser, the patriarch supported the emergent and unaligned nations, deploring the effects of British and French Colonial action in Africa. In April and May 1955 Nasser was one of the principal actors on the stage of the Bandung Conference, a large gathering in which the newly independent nations of Afro-Asia came together to debate their future role in the world: the emerging role of Egypt under Nasser was an inspiration to a Church now looking out of Egypt into Africa. The Copts were ready to join Arab Socialism in its attack upon Imperialism in general and gave full support to Nasser's nationalization of the Suez Canal. On the international ecumenical stage the Copts led attacks on Zionism. When the Coptic community supports the government it helps the stability of the nation. The most that can be said about the situation in the years since the Free Officers" Organization coup on 23 July 1952 is that Kyrillos, in the aftermath of the Revolution and in the heady Nasser period, and Shenouda, in the more difficult Sadat and Mubarak years, have been proud nationalists, rather than puppets of the Government. The Copts, as we shall see in a later chapter, have a theological agenda in the field of international relations.

In private conversation, the Copts will always make it clear that the greatest struggles in Coptic Church history have not been those involving the State but those within the Coptic Orthodox Church itself. For most Copts living in Egypt there is no direct involvement in the church as an institution. They have an almost pathological hatred of clericalization in the Church, and see Orthodoxy as a model of Christian collaboration. For most of its history, until quite recent developments, the future of the Egyptian Church has largely been determined by devout laity, not by clergy. Many Copts deplore the modern creation of a professional clerical class, believing Orthodoxy to be most clearly the church of all the baptized. For these Copts the defining moment of modern Orthodoxy came during the reforming Patriarchate of Kyrillos the Fourth (1854–61) when the Coptic Enlightenment of the nineteenth century saw the emergence of the idea of community councils to deal with *personal status* laws for the Christian minority in Egypt. By the end of the century this development had grown into a full scale Coptic Community Council or *Majlis Milli* (5 February 1874). Throughout its existence, which was assumed by most Copts to be an expression of the real theological and spiritual importance of the laity, the organization of the *Majlis Milli* has been the object of many disputes between the laity, the clergy and the patriarch. Copts have a range of views about the relations between the three. There is an extreme right-wing, strongly represented in the Holy Synod of bishops, who appear to be looking for a Coptic Vatican with an absolute monarchy whose spiritual and administrative roles are interwoven so closely that the one is absorbed by the other. On the left wing are those who appeal to the *Majlis Milli* as the ultimate authority, in a Church which is essentially a church of the laity with the clergy as true servants of the Copts. Many see the *Majlis Milli* as an important brake on patriarchal excesses. Practically and theologically it is vitally important for the *Majlis Milli* to maintain its role in the papal elections. The presidential decree of 3 November 1957 gives the *Majlis Milli*, in conjunction with the Holy Synod, the power to appoint the bishop who is to be the patriarchal *locum tenens* following the death of the pope. A search committee of eighteen is formed, and nine of these are from the *Majlis Milli* itself. The electoral committee of seven is to conduct the voting and three of these are to be from the *Majlis Milli*. This decree created unease for those who in 1957, and even more today, would like a patriarchal election made by an episcopal college: a Coptic equivalent of the College of Cardinals in Rome. There is tension between the Holy Synod and the *Majlis Milli*.

Every Coptic Pope is involved with the *Majlis Milli*, the Egyptian Government and the Holy Synod. He must respect popular opinion and national political aspirations. He is conscious of the surviving power of the old Coptic ruling classes in the law, economics, education and the secular establishment. A Coptic intelligentsia observes the Pope with the critical eyes and ears of an informed audience observing a performer in the concert hall. They do not regard the patriarch as the Coptic leader in Egypt, a position quietly and unobtrusively held by some Copts like Dr Boutros Boutros-Ghali operating within Government circles. Within the Church itself, experienced bishops have seen the rise and departure of other patriarchs. They are jealous of their rights and have a sceptical eye. The backdrop to this vast, moving cast is the immense green of Islamic Revival, the greatest power for social change or destruction in the Middle East, and not only in the region but in the world. It is an environment that encourages intrigue and there is plenty of it. The real struggle for the patriarch himself must be how to remain a man of prayer and spiritual discipline whilst assailed from every side with the demand to make political decisions. The second half of the twentieth century offers two contrasting styles for the role of Coptic Pope.

The visitor to the Copts today is impressed by the vast array of post-cards, posters and icons of Pope Kyrillos the Sixth on sale in church bookstalls. There are highly coloured collages of Abba Kyrillos with his patron Saint Mina and the camels of that saint's tradition. Church shops sell postcards of the patriarch having a calming effect upon the imperial lions in Ethiopia, during a very rare visit outside Egypt. Portrayals of the holy man, with an obvious messianic reference, show him seated upon a donkey in the Mariout desert. Disconcerting portraits of him as a long-haired ascetic and hermit, before his days as Coptic Pope, remind us of his reputation as a solitary and a mystic. There are portfolios of press photos of Abba Kyrillos with Nasser, Hailie Selassie, Sadat, Eugene Carson Blake, Ecumenical Patriarch Athenogoras and a parallel collection with Grand Muftis and Sheikhs of Al Azhar. It seems that no opportunity to point a camera at the holy man was ever missed. Even more unusual, and slightly disturbing from a western viewpoint, are those photographs which show Pope Kyrillos after his death, but still seated upon the patriarchal throne of Saint Mark: large electric fans cool his body as the patriarch receives the final, tearful farewells of the faithful.

Photographic collections enliven the pages of numerous monographs and books devoted to the study of the life and miracles of the Coptic "Pope Kyrillos the Sixth, the Most Holy Pope and Patriarch of the great city of Alexandria and of all the land of Egypt, of Jerusalem the Holy City, of Nubia, Abyssinia and Pentapolis, and all the preaching of Saint Mark". A student of the Coptic Orthodox Church quickly discovers that the iconographic presence is an accurate reflection of the impact of this solitary monk upon the Egyptian Church. The Church in Egypt at the beginning of the twenty-first century is the church created during the primacy of Abba Kyrillos.

It is often the case that those who establish a reputation for lives of inner depth and strength have quite simple outer lives. It is particularly true of Abba Kyrillos. His life is a model of outward stability: sixty-eight years spent exclusively in Northern Africa and almost entirely in Egypt: over three hidden decades as a monk and solitary. Even when he rose to the senior bishopric in the Coptic Orthodox Church, Kyrillos was faithful to his inner life. His quietist temperament and pietism disap-pointed some Copts. They saw that he preferred to be absorbed in prayer and contemplation. It was not easy to distract him from this absorption. Not only had a monk become Patriarch, the Patriarch remained a monk.

Pope Kyrillos was born Azer Yussef Atta on 2 August 1902. He was raised, the second of three sons, in the small village of Toukh El-Nassarah in the Delta Province of Gharbiyah. His father was a Coptic deacon, outstanding cantor and a calligrapher. Worship, Bible-reading, prayer and the veneration of the saints were primary experiences for Azer.

One of the Coptic Orthodox monasteries had its dependency in Toukh al-Nassarah, and a frequent visitor to the family home was one of the monks. Abouna Tadros came from the earliest monastic settlement in the Desert of Scetis. The cloister is commonly known as al-Baramus, the monastery of the Romans. According to the hagiographic traditions that later surrounded the boy, it was at this time that the idea of a monastic vocation was formed in Azer's heart.

As a young boy, Azer attended the primary school at Damanhur. He completed his secondary education in Alexandria and obtained employment with Thomas Cook and Son (Egypt) Ltd. He had good English and did well in the firm. The Australian manager and many British customers appreciated Azer's straightforward manner. He was soon promoted. His day began earlier than the working day at Thomas Cook. The office opened at 9.00 a.m. Long before that Azer was attending the daily liturgy in his parish church.

A portrait of this time shows a fine looking young man with a dapper moustache. He is wearing, at a jaunty angle, the flat-topped conical red hat with a tassel, which is known to us either as a *fez* or *tarboosh*. It was the badge of the white-collar worker in the Ottoman Empire. Azer has something of the look of a dandy. His hagiographers tell us that he was already absorbed in a private life of asceticism and solitariness, keeping his bedroom as a monastic cell. Azer soon wished to go into the desert to be a monk. Many obstacles were placed in his path but when everyone realized that he was not going to change his mind they gave their approval. On 27 July 1927 he was ordered to report to the monastery.

Azer was assigned to work in the kitchen. He was known for his baking of the monastery's bread and especially for the preparation of the *Corban*, the bread of the Eucharist. The making of bread became for him a sign of his constant need for spiritual food. At this early stage in his monastic vocation, and in his later thinking, the Eucharist was the focal point of the religious life.

On 25 February 1928 Azer was ordained a monk and became Abouna Mina el-Baramousi (Father Mina of the Roman Monastery). He was appointed an assistant to the Librarian, the savant Abouna Abd al-

Masih ibn Salib el-Baramousi. The monasteries of the Western Desert are not especially noted for scholarship. Most great Coptic scholars are laymen and work in the cities. Abouna Abd al-Masih ibn Salib was the exception rather than the rule. He was an eminent scholar who was famous for his linguistic skills, having the Christian scholar's traditional knowledge of Hebrew, Greek and Latin. Arabic was his first, bread-and-butter language. He also worked in English and French. In the dialects of Sahidic and Bohairic Coptic he was accomplished and in Syriac an acknowledged expert. Mina gave himself to the study of Patristics, his special interest being the works of Mar Ishaq Al-Suryani (Saint Isaac of Nineveh, also known as *the Syrian*). The monk Mina made a set of hand-copied texts of St. Isaac and bound them into hardback for the monastic library.

After a further three years of routine and hidden monastic poverty, chastity and obedience, the monk Mina was ordained priest at St. Mark's, Alexandria. The Coptic Pope John XIX had established a theo-logical college for monastics and Father Mina became a reluctant student in the new patriarchal institution at Helwan near Cairo. It was his home for two years and he acquitted himself well as a scholar. Even as a theological student he insisted upon the daily celebration of the Eucharist. The only upset in Mina's life as a priest and monk came when the Patriarch suggested that he should be a bishop. Mina retreated to the ancient White monastery of St. Shenouda the Archimandrite near Sohag in Upper Egypt. There was some friction until the Patriarch accepted the priest's explanation that he intended to seek permission from his brethren to become a hermit.

About two and a half kilometres to the northwest of the Monastery of the Romans there stands the Rock of Abouna Sarabamoun, named after a monk of the monastery. The rock is a permanent reminder of the many Coptic monks who have lived the eremitic life throughout the centuries: the eponymous monk was extremely well known for his asceticism. Sarabamoun had died just before Abouna Mina's arrival in the Wadi Natroun. The empty limestone cave was a challenge to Mina. After his return from Upper Egypt he was completely convinced of his vocation to the solitary life. At first the fathers of the monastery resisted his requests to become a hermit. They turned to the celebrated monastic Abouna Abd al-Malik al-Masudi. He had been a monk for forty years but he had not found it necessary to go outside the community, and he was Mina's spiritual director. Surely it was enough to be a monk in the choir? The aged Abba would not condemn his protégé. Everyone was silent, but the eloquent silence of the great spiritual director was enough to tip the balance in favour of Abba Mina.

After some preparation within the community, Father Mina retired to the desert cave. He was thirty years old. The move can now be seen as a part of a major revival of anchorite asceticism in Egypt. In the desert, miles away from urban civilization and sufficiently distant from communal monasticism, the future Patriarch met Father Abd al-Masih *el-Habashi* (the Ethiopian), "the prophet of the desert", who inhabited a cave near the monastery for thirty-five years from 1935 to 1970. The anchorite tradition is still alive in the Western Desert in 2000. It owes most to the inspiration of the Ethiopian but also to our subject Father Mina *al-Muttawahad* (the Solitary) al-Baramusi, who became a Patriarch. This modern development of the eremitic life is the most important contribution of the Copts to universal Christian self-understanding at the end of the twentieth century and for the new millennium. It is an authentic expression of Christian discipleship. Abd al-Masih the Ethiopian, his contemporaries in the Western Desert, and those who followed their example, did not solicit the accord of Coptic society. Even the approval of the current hierarchy was not essential for them. We know of some who ran away into the desert. These solitaries were free men, who had, in Thomas Merton's phrase, "become free by paying the price of freedom". Their extreme asceticism is the necessary outward expression of this freedom. Their intercession and supplication are the selfless reasons for the solitariness. Freedom with and for God, leading to freedom for the other, is the meaning of the solitary life.

Abouna Mina was not a solitary for very many years. Abouna Abd al-Masih was. The Egyptian priest wished to rebuild the Shrine of St. Mina the Wonder Worker, and live the eremitic life in the Mariout desert. Permission was refused. From 1936 to 1942, Mina moved to the Gebel al-Guyushi (the Mokkatam Mountains) to the east of Old Cairo. His monastic cell was one of the deserted Napoleonic windmills, erected during the brief but influential French control of Egypt from 1798 to 1804. Mina converted a part of the building into a chapel for his daily Mass.

The six years at the windmill and the following years of ministry in Old Cairo are very important for the story of Mina the Solitary. Abouna Mina was compelled to move out of the windmill during the Second World War. According to Otto Meinardus, the British forced this move because they thought that the priest was a spy. Father Mina moved down into Old Cairo and built a church dedicated to St. Mina. It was at this time that he was made responsible for the Monastery of St. Samuel at al-Qalamun, which belongs to the Fayoum group of monasteries. The Fayoum is a large oasis about eighty-five kilometres Southwest of Cairo and has a long Coptic tradition. Mina travelled to the monastery every month during the period of his appointment as archpriest. He felt bound to the monastery. He also built a centre to house Coptic University students next to the church in Old Cairo. For over two decades Abouna Mina established a powerful reputation as spiritual director and healer who was devoted to the solitary and contemplative life in the midst of the old city. He celebrated the Liturgy every day, often with a large congregation of students from Cairo University.

On 19 April 1959, a small child was led to the altar in St. Mark's cathedral and selected the name of Abouna Mina from a chalice. Chance, according to the Apostolic practice of Acts 1: 26, but seen by many as an act of Divine Providence, was the final act in the election of Father Mina as Pope Kyrillos the Sixth, the 116th patriarch of the See of Saint Mark. It is often related that the monk could not bear to read the appointed Gospel passage at his consecration as patriarch because it began with the words "I am the good shepherd" (St. John 10: 11). He began with his own gloss, which was not in the missal: "Our Lord Jesus Christ said, 'I am the Good Shepherd'". It is an expression of the man and of his understanding of the patriarchal ministry.

Abba Kyrillos held the position of Patriarch from 1959 to 1971. In this period he showed himself to be a man of considerable political insight. He personally determined his succession. He settled innumerable problems of internal Coptic politics. He retained his reputation as an ascetic, celebrated the Eucharist every day and established his renown as a healer. During his Patriarchate repeated apparitions of the Blessed Virgin Mary were reported at Zeitoun in Cairo. These appearances received international attention.

Kyrillos the Sixth died on 9 March 1971. Since his death the reports of his healing powers have increased. His tomb is a pilgrim centre. Amongst the world's wonders the widely travelled experience the large black marble sarcophagus as a place of presence and disclosure. Although not yet glorified by the Holy Synod, his icons are used in prayer and worship. His quietist spirit has been favourably compared with some modern Coptic political activity. His reputation amongst Muslims, Christians and even sceptical secularists is unsullied and bright.

There is no full-scale biographical and theological study of Pope Kyrillos. When it is produced, it will examine a number of issues, which are central concerns in Coptic life. These may be briefly surveyed here.

Kyrillos was first and foremost a priest who celebrated the Eucharist daily. He was also a monk. "Priest-monk" is not always a useful description of either one who has given himself to the sacerdotal life or to one who has joined a monastery as a monk. The priesthood has often been little more than a process in the progress of an ambitious man to a political and ecclessial role in the episcopate. Monastic life is a necessity for a monk seeking the episcopate in the Eastern churches. The abuse of the system may not be universal, but it is certainly transparent in many cases. A man who has devoted his life to the attainment of episcopal office may sit lightly to his priestly or monastic obligations. It was not so with Kyrillos who for forty years stood before the altar almost every day. It was the central action of his life. He was deeply convinced of the strength gained from the Eucharistic elements. This daily devotion to Christ in the Eucharist is especially noteworthy, continuing, as it did, throughout the twelve hectic years of his Patriarchate.

He was a monk, but Kyrillos did not spend much of his life in a cloister. Although dedicated to the monastic life in the monastery of the Romans, he probably spent less than three years within the community. For two years he studied at Helwan. For just over two years he spent most weekdays in the desert cave at the Rock of Sarabamoun. For six years he was at the old windmill in the Mokkatam hills. For a period of about seventeen years he lived in one room in Old Cairo, leaving only to fulfil his duties at the monastery of St. Samuel. For twelve years he was patriarch and, though he made retreats in the desert, he was occupied for much of his time in Cairo. Thirty-nine of his forty-two years of monastic profession were spent away from the monastic community. But when Edward Wakin remarked so pointedly that Kyrillos the patriarch had remained Mina the monk he was drawing attention to the primary emphasis in the man's life. Kyrillos was a man of remarkable religious insights who somehow reached a bureaucratic position in an ecclesiastical structure, where he disappointed many because he had no mind or heart for administration. It is rarely appreciated how distracting the religious establishment can become, or to what extent being a priest or bishop can be so easily reduced to little more than an ecclesiastical career.

Kyrillos as a monk was a living testimony to the supernatural dimension of the Christian vocation. He was not a monastic preacher of negativism and withdrawal, who had no meeting place with the problems of our age. But for Kyrillos, as for all mystics, the only Christian society of importance was spiritual and extramundane: the Mystical Body of Christ on the Earth. Kyrillos experienced the life of that mystical community and represented its society before his church and community. His life with Christ in the Eucharist may perhaps be described, though with ungrudging recognition of our linguistic and theological poverty, as "the true church". The true church is that place where all men are truly equal because subject to only one charismatic authority of wisdom, experience and love under God. By this expression, we mean to imply that the denominational structures are not free, but limiting and very often deeply unchristian. It may be said that, within a hierarchical structure, Kyrillos knew the freedom for which so many have craved in the varying movements of psychological personalism, or by their opposition to the herd instinct of modern times.

At the height of his earthly eminence, Kyrillos presided over the elaborate ceremonies, which accompanied the return of the relics of St. Mark to Egypt. The great national hero President Gamal Abd el Nasser accompanied Hailie Selassie, the Emperor of Ethiopia to the celebrations. At the end of the day Kyrillos called his deacon to one side. "Did you see all these great ceremonies, my son?" The puzzled assistant replied that he had of course seen all that had taken place. He had stood all day beside his master. Kyrillos repeated the question and received the same answer. Then the patriarch overwhelmed his deacon when he said, "All these ceremonies, my son, are not equal to one day spent in the solitude of the windmill above Old Cairo."

Kyrillos as a monk was known as *al-Muttawahad* – the Solitary. His instinct that only a monastic revival and a parallel renewal of the eremitic life would rescue the Copts from their anxieties has been entirely justified. It can be appreciated in the context of Coptic history whose greatest spiritual directors were all monks: when the monasteries are strong, the Copts are strong. At the same time, the monasteries have sometimes been a retreat in the worst sense and they have depended completely upon the secret lives of their finest hermits, like Abouna Abd al-Masih el-Habashi. A life of Eucharistic devotion and prayer was the answer Kyrillos gave to the Coptic situation, the Coptic problem and the Coptic anxiety in Egypt.

When the press interviewed Kyrillos soon after his consecration as Patriarch, he answered all the tricky questions about Coptic anxieties with an admonition; "It is better not to speak, rather to pray". Many Copts were disappointed. Politics is part of the patriarch's job. They wanted to enlarge his definition of prayer. But no patriarch can please all Copts, and it is common to hear hostile criticisms of the present patriarch because of his supposed political activism. Shenouda is often unfavourably compared with Kyrillos, but this may indicate no more than a misunderstanding of both men.

Kyrillos knew what was possible. He understood Coptic anxieties. He also felt that he knew how far to press Nasser and the government. Mohamed Heikal says that Nasser and Kyrillos admired each other and that Kyrillos, "always anxious to avoid a confrontation", made use of this relationship to resolve the problems of the Coptic community. When challenged by an American journalist about the future of the Copts, Kyrillos replied in the third person and reported of the Coptic Patriarch: "His great ambition is to see the church in a spiritual revival that resembles the early days of the Apostolic Fathers. As a hermit, he has had very deep experience with prayer and a great faith that prayer will lead the church to this great revival. He is trying to encourage all Coptic congregations to develop this experience with prayer."

Kyrillos was by every account a healer. Entire volumes are devoted to this aspect of his life and to reports of healing associated with his tomb, pictures, icons and after-death appearances. Many of the miracles have been subject to professional medical scrutiny, and there is every reason to believe that they are genuine. Many hundreds of miracles have been reported. Although the Coptic Orthodox Church does not carry out the kind of investigations associated with Lourdes or Fatima, the present patriarch has pointed out that prayers and actions of healing are a normal part of the Church's ministry. Physical and spiritual healing are essential elements in the contemporary Coptic Christian experience. It would be wrong to suggest otherwise. Miracles are normal in a belief system that acknowledges the reality of God's continuous action in the world.

No doubt, the ministry of Kyrillos as a healer and as a priest at the altar will always be central to his biography. In the dangerous arena of ecclesiastical politics he will also be remembered as a man of peace with a remedy. Abba Kyrillos loved the Ethiopian Orthodox Church. History may record that his greatest act of healing was that effected when he healed the fracture between the sister churches of Egypt and Ethiopia.

For many centuries the Coptic Pope exercised control over Ethiopia by appointing an Egyptian as chief bishop or *Abuna*, not to be confused with the use of the more general term *Abouna* or Father used elsewhere. At times there were long interregnums when the Ethiopian Orthodox Church was left without an *Abuna*, but it was usual for a Coptic Orthodox monk from Egypt to be made available to rule over the Church in Abyssinia. From the Egyptian point of view, it was a canonically formalized arrangement, and they experienced no difficulty in the notion of an émigré bishop wielding great power over a clergy and people whose language, culture and psychology he rarely understood. The imposition of an outsider was never whole-heartedly accepted. The Ethiopians are a proud people who recognize their own cultural history as being at least equal to that of Egypt. The Egyptian Copts have sometimes harboured the unpleasant notion that they alone have preserved the ethnic, racial purity of the Pharaohs. The Copts share with many other peoples some ill-defined misgivings about black people. For centuries this incipient and unacknowledged racism was at the very least a part of the Ethiopian–Egyptian Christian problem. It often seemed strange to the Ethiopians that bishops who crumbled before the might of Islam in the Nile valley were so aggressive and assertive when dealing with black Christians in the Orthodox Empire on the shores of Lake Tana.

The conquest of Egypt by the Caliphs weakened the claims of the Copts over Ethiopia. The Patriarchate in Egypt moved to Cairo. At times the House of Islam stood between the northern and southern houses of Coptic Christianity. To some it seemed that Ethiopia was a great Christian kingdom where the Abuna and his flock could walk with their heads held high, whilst the Copts were an oppressed *dhimmi* people under Islam. Through the centuries, hundreds of thousands of Egyptian Christians converted to Islam. The history of ambivalent relations between Copt and Ethiopian is very long and rarely edifying. Acrimony always surrounded the comparison made between the apparent freedoms of the Empire and the Islamic State. The Ethiopian Orthodox Church found that it was always numerically much stronger than the Church in Egypt.

By the beginning of the twentieth century the situation had became completely untenable, but the Synod in Egypt was unwilling to release control over the Ethiopian Orthodox Church. The turning point was the Italian occupation of Ethiopia, which almost resulted in the incorporation of the Abyssinian episcopate and people into the Roman Catholic Church. In 1941 His Imperial Majesty Hailie Selassie returned from exile and was reinstated in Addis Ababa. His agenda included the establishment of an Ethiopian Orthodox Church, which was absolutely free of Egyptian influence. The 1942 Holy Synod in Egypt rejected his application for a form of autocephaly, or self-government. When the Egyptian Synod again refused any real autocephaly in 1945, the Emperor and the Ethiopian Church threatened to sever all relations with the See of St. Mark. A degree of freedom was suggested but this was not enough for Ethiopia. On 22 October 1950 the reigning Abuna died. He was to be the last Egyptian Copt to hold the office. The Church in Egypt was itself subject to deep divisions at the time, and the situation was temporarily allowed to drift.

When Pope Kyrillos arrived on the scene, he moved quickly. He was enthroned on 10 May 1959. Barely six weeks later he had come to a complete accord with the Emperor Hailie Selassie and the Ethiopian Orthodox Church. Kyrillos signed a pact with them on 29 June 1959. In it he elevated the Abuna in Addis Ababa to the dignity of Patriarch-Catholicos. It was further agreed that any future choice of Abuna was to be made from the Ethiopian monks by the Ethiopians in accordance with the established Alexandrine tradition. The Copts agreed that they would not establish any bishoprics or titles in the Diaspora without first consulting the Ethiopian Church. An agreement since abandoned by the Church in Egypt.

Kyrillos raised the Ethiopian metropolitan Basilios to the new Catholicate. After Basilios's death in 1971 the bishop of Harar, Amba

Theophilos, was consecrated Patriarch-Catholicos with the approval of the See of Alexandria. As far as the Emperor and the Ethiopian Orthodox Church were concerned a completely autocephalous and autonomous church came into being in 1959. The Marxist military government in 1976 deposed Abuna Theophilos. He received the martyr's crown sometime before 1979, during his imprisonment.

The bonds between the sister churches were strengthened when Abba Kyrillos paid a pastoral visit to Ethiopia in October 1960. The encounter between Coptic Pope and Ethiopian Emperor was particularly important. They got on well together and saw that the new arrangements could be helpful to both churches. The Emperor of Ethiopia was a prime mover in international non-aligned conferences and in continental African congresses, some of which met in Ethiopia. He thought that this secular development ought to have its ecclesiastical equivalent. Hailie Selassie had seen a great deal of the Western churches which were not Roman Catholic and he had been impressed with their deep theological learning, their ability to work together without loss of local tradition and above all their willingness to face the problems of tomorrow's world. In the great university, which he built in Addis Ababa, there was a theological college. It was the emperor's intention that this seminary should become the principal theological centre for Copts, Armenians, Ethiopians, Syrians and Oriental Orthodox Indians. Addis Ababa was the obvious place for such a centre. The Ethiopian Church alone was in a Christian country. The Armenians were much harassed and hemmed in at that time in the USSR. The Indians were a very small minority in an enormous secular state. The Syrians were locked in Ba'athist Syria, and the Copts were subject to demographic and religious pressure from Islam. The Emperor wished Ethiopia to lead the Oriental Orthodox family of churches.

Hailie Selassie decided to invite all the patriarchs of the non-Chalcedonian or Oriental Orthodox churches to meet in Addis Ababa in January 1965. These churches shared a distinctive Oriental Orthodox tradition. They had doctrinal and historical links but they had never met as a family, and even those who had met in groups of two or three had not done so for many centuries. The Emperor's idea was idealistic and, as it turned out, realistic. Nobody refused the invitation.

Abba Kyrillos was the senior of six patriarchs who attended the 1965 Addis Ababa Conference from January 15 to the 21. The proceedings of the Conference and the resolutions adopted indicate that the meeting was far in advance of its time. Very little action has been taken to convert resolutions on paper to performance in the world. Most of the leading participants are now dead. There are few tangible results from 1965, but the convergence of needs and expressions of solidarity are now recognized as historically important for the churches involved.

In one area there was conspicuous success. Abba Kyrillos had noticed from time to time that certain Copts had been able to obtain the dissolution of a marriage simply by appealing to the Syrian Patriarch. These Copts had "converted" to the sister-church of Antioch where they had immediately received a dissolution. Kyrillos met Mar Ignatius Yacub the Third and they agreed a common policy. The joint Coptic–Syrian declaration of 1965 stresses the doctrinal unity of the two churches and accepts a common pastoral practice.

Pope Kyrillos remained deeply attached to the Ethiopians and other Oriental Orthodox. If he had lived longer the tragic experience of the Ethiopian Orthodox Church under Marxism and its aftermath, especially in Eritrea, would have been a source of great sorrow to him. Hailie Selassie outlived Kyrillos by over a decade, but he was dethroned on 12 September 1984. He was brutally murdered. An important era in church history also came to an end. Ethiopia entered a dark period of persecution under an atheist dictatorship. Since the fall of the Communist dictator Mengistu, the Ethiopian Orthodox Church has struggled to overcome her many problems, which are internal, social, economical and ecumenical. The complexities of Ethiopian–Coptic ecclesiastical politics require their own volume. Western churches have generally sympathized with Ethiopia.

The Ethiopian Orthodox Church occupies a special place in any projected scenario of the future of Christianity. She has a significant geographical position. It is increasingly recognized that the survival and expansion of Christianity in the twenty-first century lies with the churches of the developing world. The enormous numerical strength of the Ethiopian Orthodox Church places her alongside the ecclesial communions of Russia and Greece. She is one of the big Orthodox churches. The openness of the Ethiopian Church to other Christians indicates a new confidence and maturity. She has faced modern martyrdom and has survived. The ancient liturgical tradition, with sacred dance, drums and sistrums, is also suggestive of the role the Ethiopians might have in the continuing growth of an African Christianity. Ethiopian tradition is desirably distinct from the culture of the European churches, and from the Arab culture to which the Copts are so firmly bound.

Kyrillos the healer was perhaps at his best when applying a salve to the wounded body of his own Church at home in Egypt. There was much need for a curative ministry. The election of a new patriarch had been delayed for over two years. The clerical Holy Synod, which was generally conservative and anxious to reassert its authority, wished to return to the canonical procedure of appointing a patriarch from amongst the monks. The *Majlis Milli* or Coptic Community Council wished to appoint a diocesan bishop. They felt that the Coptic community in general and the Coptic Orthodox Church in particular needed someone who had political and administrative experience.

The three patriarchs immediately before Kyrillos were chosen from amongst the bishops. Conservative elements in the monasteries and parishes blamed many of the difficulties experienced by the church upon the fact that the Copts had ignored the canons by failing to elect a monk. The Holy Synod agreed that all three of the previous patriarchs have been bad for the Church. The election of Kyrillos the Sixth marked a triumph for the clerical traditionalists, but the new patriarch accepted the notion that experience was important. He was ready to take advice.

The *Majlis Milli* existed to take part in the administration of Coptic affairs. It was made up of laymen. It had not been a success and had been seriously weakened by the Egyptian Revolution. Nasser's regime stripped the Community Council of its jurisdiction over marriage, divorce and alimony. These were now referred to state courts. Education was nationalized, depriving the *Majlis Milli* of its role in the administration of Coptic schools. A Ministry of Social Affairs cared for the work of benevolent societies, weakening the role of the *Majlis Milli* as a social security agency.

The administration of *wapfs* remained the province of the Coptic Community Council. *Wapfs* are the endowments and trusts (property and investments of various kinds) held for the monasteries, colleges and churches. The properties involved had accumulated for centuries: one Ottoman sultan alone gave the Copts one thousand *feddans* (acres) of rich arable land in the Nile Delta. This chocolate coloured soil bore abundant harvests for the church. The *wapfs* should have been administered for the benefit of the Church, but the relations between the Community Council on the one hand and the Patriarch and Holy Synod on the other had rarely been harmonious.

Upon the succession of Kyrillos the Sixth, the Community Council were anxious to save their control of the *wapfs*, and the patriarch wished to avoid the chaos and confusion of the past. By the 19 July 1960 he had secured a decree from President Nasser which provided for a joint board called the Council of Coptic *Wapfs*. This Council was formed under the Patriarch and comprised six bishops carefully balanced by six members of the old *Majlis Milli* . This change was effected with consultation and was not in the least autocratic in implementation. The Holy Synod and the old *Majlis Milli* were now working together in a Council where nobody could claim superiority because everyone was a "new boy"; though the continuity was obvious to everyone. This little administrative sleight of hand was in fact typical of the religious insight of Kyrillos.

Whenever administrative difficulties arose within the Coptic community, Kyrillos intervened personally, acquiring state support by presidential decree. Although it would be wrong to suggest that the *Majlis Milli* or the *wapfs* were of major importance to Kyrillos, he was pleased if he could resolve difficulties with a careful piece of legislation, supported by presidential decree. Kyrillos had his own pressing spiritual priorities. There were also more urgent national political problems. Conflict between the patriarch and the *Majlis Milli*, which has often seemed endemic, was put to one side, only to emerge in the next Patriarchate.

There is a popular apocryphal story about Kyrillos and Nasser which tells how an Islamic terrorist, wishing to discredit the Copts, disguised himself as a Coptic Orthodox bishop. The impostor went to the audience chamber at the Presidential palace and waited to murder the leader of the revolution. Kyrillos the clairvoyant foresaw the assassination. He rushed to Nasser's palace, identified the man as an impostor and saved the president's life. The story is an idealistic expression of the supposed relationship between president and patriarch and by extension between the Copts and the State in Egypt. It bears little relation to reality. The Copts have borne centuries of deadly, daily discrimination. Kyrillos must have spent a great deal of time hearing all about the daily irritations and frustrations associated with petty discrimination against Copts. As Patriarch he was called to absorb and express the heritage of heroic defiance in the face of repression from nominal Muslims, but he was also to embody the Coptic search for survival. In April 1959, just after the patriarchal election, Nasser attempted to coerce Kyrillos into a public visit to the presidential residence. The Patriarch would not be compelled. The President sent a government representative to the Patriarchate. Kyrillos responded with two bishops. When Nasser's Coptic-puppet in the government attempted his own pressure, the patriarch told him not to try to "take care" of the Church. "God elected me, not Nasser. The Church is my problem, not yours."

Kyrillos knew where to draw the line and the second of these stories is far more reliable than the first. It reflects the reality of the Coptic experience. One visiting politician gets two bishops in response. Eventually, in his own time, Kyrillos went to visit Nasser. President Nasser did not return the patriarchal visit for many years.

There was, in the relations between Nasser and Kyrillos, as between the Copts and the State, an element of cat-and-mouse with a modicum of calculated diplomacy and more than a little risk. Kyrillos was a fervent Egyptian nationalist who supported the *Wafd* party in the years after the First World War when British control in Egypt was weakening. *Al-Wafd al-Misri*, or the Egyptian Delegation, was a nationalist independence party, led by the charismatic Sa'ad Zaghlul, considered to be the *za'im al-umma*, the forbidding national leader. Many politically motivated Copts participated actively in the nationalist movement and some of them rose to national prominence in the *Wafd*. Like most Copts of his age, Kyrillos would have heard Sa'ad Zaghlul speak to the *Wafd* and the nation about a Coptic-Muslim brotherhood. Much later, the new Constitution of the Republic of Egypt on 16 January 1956 clearly stated "Islam is the religion of the state and Arabic its official language", but Kyrillos was amongst those who distinguished between Faith and Nation.

When Nasser made his only speech at a Coptic cathedral the president defined his position: "We are all Egyptians. Islam recognizes Christians as brothers in religion and brothers in God. God calls for love, and we will not tolerate any more fanatics who create obstacles and problems for the people in their revolution." The warning on that occasion was meant not for the Copts but for the Muslim Brotherhood. Nasser sent six leaders of the Brotherhood to the gallows in 1954, just months after the Revolution. (Executions of members of the Brotherhood followed in 1966, 1974, 1977 and 1981. A number of Muslim activists have been executed in Mubarak's presidency.)

Gamal Abd el Nasser smiled on Kyrillos and on the Copts: the British writer Bruce Chatwin once gave Nasser the perceptive nickname "the Smiler". Certainly, Nasser knew that the Copts posed no threat to him. They welcomed his words. Patriarch and President saw eye-to-eye on the question of "fanatics" because the only extremists asserting their rights in Egypt were Muslim believers. It was largely thanks to the passivity and piety of Kyrillos that there were no Coptic activists or "fanatics". It is the formidable spiritual strength of the Copts, and their social and political weakness, that they have been able, for centuries, to accept the role of second-class citizens in their own country.

Modern militant Islam expects serious and sincere Copts to aspire to a Muslim state, which will guarantee economic and social justice for all. Too much in Egypt is owned by too few. Modern Islam also expects the Copts to vote for a conservative morality. Too much in Egyptian culture is dominated by the false values of an American materialism that debases women and is devoid of all ethical standards. Militant Islam sees the political and economic involvement of America in the Middle East as a simple matter of the pursuit of Oil without Virtue. Such thoughts were common in the time of Kyrillos. He must have considered them. We have no evidence of his willingness to speak out. He turned first to the Church. The daily celebration of the Divine Liturgy, was always his first consideration.

In his concern for the Church, Kyrillos set out to secure the papal succession. He appointed three general bishops. Samuel, a gifted administrator who knew how to manage public relations was appointed to Social, ecumenical and foreign affairs. Shenouda, an exceptional instructor was given the portfolio for Coptic Education. Gregorios, a well-qualified academic, was to lead research and higher education. If general bishops could become patriarch then one of these would be an obvious candidate. Matta El-Meskeen was not raised to the purple but received the care of monastic renewal. If the patriarchal election was confined to monks then Matta would be the heir apparent. Kyrillos knew that they represented, in different ways, the aspirations of a new generation of Copts. We have noticed that the arguments surrounding the patriarchal election focused in part upon the choice, monk or bishop? The anxiety about a monk's lack of administrative experience remained. Kyrillos took the significant and innovative step of appointing Gregorios, Samuel and Shenouda without territorial dioceses. When he died, bishops without a diocese but with experience would be available for election. It is impossible to know if Kyrillos knew what forces he was unleashing when he raised these four monks to positions of such importance. It is not difficult to find Copts who believe that Kyrillos hoped that Samuel would become patriarch. When the Pope died, Abouna Matta el Meskeen, Amba Shenouda and Amba Samuel from Social services were all nominated to take his place. Samuel is dead. The remaining three are now in their seventies. They have little contact. It is the considered view of no less a commentator than Mohammed Heikal that Kyrillos regretted promoting the cause of these four ambitious men. It is hopeless to speculate. Their elevation determined the kind of Church Kyrillos would leave behind. Their several appointments were the most important political decisions made by Abba Kyrillos.

The most significant event in the patriarchate of Abba Kyrillos had nothing to do with church politics. It was an act of grace. It was a miracle for which no natural explanation is possible. From 2 April 1968 until 29 May 1971 nightly crowds of up to a quarter of a million Christians, Muslims and Jews witnessed apparitions of the Blessed Virgin Mary in a Cairo suburb.

The apparitions occurred in the aftermath of the June War of 1967 when Israeli planes swept over Cairo in broad daylight, terrifying the children on their way to school. Over fifteen thousand Egyptian soldiers had been killed in battle, thousands more were wounded and thousands more were prisoners of war. One million Palestinians were displaced. The Suez Canal was blocked. Egyptian oil in Sinai was in enemy hands. Jehan Sadat, widow of the President, has said that in 1967 "Faith was the only resort for most Egyptians". When the Virgin Mary appeared in

Cairo early in 1968, the front page of *Al-Ahram* carried a report that inter-
preted the appearances as a message from the Blessed Virgin: "I know
that you can no longer come and see me in Jerusalem. I have come back
to Cairo again to see you"

When the visions continued, a Papal Committee was formed
comprising three bishops and a larger number of doctors of various
medical specializations. This group made a study of the apparitions and
of the numerous miraculous events associated with them. The members
spent many nights watching, noting and examining. They presented
their findings to Kyrillos who declared that the appearances were
genuine. He reminded the faithful that the Coptic Church in Zeitoun
stood on a road through which the Holy Family had passed during the
Flight into Egypt.

The ecumenical and international dimension of the Zeitoun phenomenon was important for Kyrillos. The Eastern Orthodox and Roman
Catholics united with the Oriental Orthodox in devotions at Zeitoun. In
their liturgical worship, the Copts express their love and devotion for
the *Theotokos*, the God-bearer, and, although the Copts are separated
from Rome by the unbridgeable gulfs of Papal infallibility and the
doctrine of Mary's immaculate conception, it was important at Zeitoun
to express Christian solidarity in relation to Mary. She is the common
Mother of Copts and Catholics. In Coptic devotion she stands at the
head of the rank of apostolic witnesses to the faith that the Son of God
was conceived in her virginal womb by the power of the Holy Spirit.
The Summer Fast of the Theotokos is a major event for the Copts. This
is during the same season as the Western Feast of the Assumption. The
light of Zeitoun fell upon the divided Christians, reminding them of the
fundamentals of unity and confirming the Coptic Orthodox profession
of the doctrine of the Council of Ephesus which proclaims the Blessed
Virgin as the true Mother of God.

For Kyrillos the ministry of the Virgin of Zeitoun was much more
than a confirmation of the steadfastness of the Copts during the long
centuries of discrimination, persecution and martyrdom. The appearances were an evangelical challenge to the Copts and to all Christians.
They were authentic appearances of Mary because they directed the
observers to look beyond her and above her to Christ. The Church at
Zeitoun looked to Mary, who brought forth Christ, so that through the
Church today Christ might also be born and increase in the hearts of
all Christians. In her authentic vocation Mary still carries Christ to the
world. God-bearer. *Theotokos*. The title represents a claim upon all
Christians who carry Christ before the watching world. In one sense
the designation *Theotokos* encompasses the demand and description of
priestly or patriarchal service. The appearances of Our Lady of Zeitoun

in Egypt are widely regarded as a seal of approval upon the ministry of Abba Kyrillos.

Pope Kyrillos the Sixth died on 9 March 1971. Shenouda the Third was consecrated as the 117th Coptic Pope and Patriarch on 14 November 1971. The combined reigns of these two patriarchs have marked the height of the great Coptic renaissance.

Nazir Gayed, the future Patriarch Shenouda, was born on 3 August 1923 in the important Coptic centre of Assyut in Upper Egypt. The family were devout Copts. Early pictures indicate a comfortable, middle-class background with Nazir wearing the *tarboosh*, that badge of Ottoman conformity and respectability we was in the earliest portraits of Kyrillos. Shenouda's mother died soon after his birth, leaving a family of three boys and five girls. His father, Gayed Roufail, died a few years later. An older brother, Raphael, and his wife raised the child. Because of Raphael's work the family were required to move around Egypt. Nazir received a sound primary and secondary education in the Coptic School at Damanhur, the American School of Banha and the Iman Secondary School in Shoubra, Cairo. The Iman (Faith) Schools were founded by Fr. Guirgis Boutros (1892–1967) and played a major part in the nurture of young Copts. In 1961 President Nasser national-ized all the educational institutions in Egypt and so deprived the Copts of a vital resource. Nazir Gayed had already matriculated in 1943.

In his twenties Nazir graduated from the Faculty of History in Cairo University. He completed his National Service as an officer in the Egyptian Army. He became a teacher in a high school and devoted his evenings to study at the Theological Seminary. Some modest financial support came from journalism. He has been a wordsmith for all of his adult life, producing an uneven output of many millions of words. He was known as a poet. His academic achievement as a seminarian resulted in a unique appointment straight from the student body to the Faculty in 1949. Nazir Gayed was twenty-six years of age. He carried a substantial teaching load but made time for post-graduate studies in Archaeology and Classical Arabic at Cairo University.

Pope Shenouda has retained his scholarly interests throughout his life and is valued as a Christian apologist. He has written many books. The world of Pope Shenouda the theologian is one of Black and White. This can be accounted for, at least in part, by the context of Coptic Orthodox Theology. A discussion of Coptic Theology will be found later in this volume (see pp. 119–41). Sufficient to say here that there is in all modern Coptic thought a visceral sense of the overwhelming presence of Islam.

The Coptic Orthodox Church is a conservative body. It is unable to address, and is generally unaware of, the questions, which are the primary premises of theological discourse and investigation in Western Churches. Orthodoxy, as seen by Pope Shenouda, is the bearer of the authentic apostolic tradition. He seeks to make a permanent distinction between the fundamental and the secondary: to know the difference between "how I feel" and "what the Church has always taught". His approaches to homosexuality and feminism are both brutal and forgiving. Submission guarantees mercy.

Whilst teaching in the Theological schools of Cairo in the late forties and early fifties, Nazir Gayed experienced a sharp summons to the monastic life. The refined rule of Amba Theophilus Es-Souriani was appealing to university graduates and Nazir entered the Monastery of the Syrians in July 1954. The monastic revival continues to attract graduates in all monasteries. The monastic experience was central for Nazir. As Father Antonious Es-Souriani he received a further vocation to the life of a hermit and between 1954 and 1962 lived in a desert cave for extended periods. The infiltration of educated young men into the monasteries and subsequently into the hierarchy was crucial for the impending reforms in the Egyptian Church. The weakness of this development is that too many young men in the last two decades of the twentieth century have become bishops too quickly. A dramatic rise in the number of dioceses means that many young men have been consecrated bishops after a very short time as monks. Some Copts must now join monasteries with the expectation of becoming bishops, treating the life of a monk as a means rather than an end. The presence of ambitious monks is always denied, but the desire for advancement, preferment and power is so universal that it is impossible to believe that these are absent from Coptic Orthodoxy.

It is striking that two monks with a preference for the solitary life largely initiated the recent Coptic renaissance: Kyrillos the Sixth and Shenouda the Third. In the future study of the long history of Coptic monasticism it is likely to emerge that one of the most influential figures did not live in the Patristic period but in the deeply-troubled and materialistic twentieth century. He is, of course, Abouna Abd al-Masih the Ethiopian. It is startling that Kyrillos and Shenouda were both called from the solitary life to the treadmill of ecclesiastical administration. Since 1985, His Holiness Pope Shenouda has occasionally referred back to the eremitic experience as the most important in his personal life. His cave is now in the middle of an armed forces battle-training site. In 1994, a western visitor standing with the patriarch looking out into the Desert towards that site was conscious of Shenouda's wistful hankering after his lost past as a humble Coptic hermit.

It was Abba Kyrillos who called Fr. Antonious from the desert in September 1962 and ordained him as bishop for Education. The new

Bishop Shenouda was also to hold the post of Dean of the Theological College. His responsibilities included the oversight of the Sunday Schools which are the central organs for lay education in the Coptic Orthodox Church. He had been actively involved in the Sunday School movement in Shoubra since his late teens. The combined effect of the revived theological schools and Sunday Schools had been to create what amounts virtually to a cultural and intellectual renaissance among the Copts. It has had political overtones. The present liturgical strength and spiritual authority of the Coptic Orthodox Church derives more directly from the unequivocally mystical insights of Pope Kyrillos. "A monk is one who regards himself as linked with every man, through always seeing himself in each", wrote Evagrius, the desert monk and spiritual writer of the fourth century. This is especially true of these two popes whose combined influence reaches out from the desert into every area of Church life.

The Coptic Pope occupies a unique place in Egyptian public life. Shenouda is an effective spokesman and representative for the millions of poor, inarticulate Copts who regard him as a folk hero. Apologists for the Pope will say that he only speaks out when others are silenced. Like his predecessors he has continually to be aware of the potentiality which exists, especially in the House of Islam, for the annihilation of Christianity. Since his house arrest in the 1980s Shenouda has chosen the path of conciliation and works with many moderate Muslims who are his friends and allies. This does not prevent him from being a realist. He was deeply effected by the murder of Farag Foda, the prominent liberal Muslim writer who was shot dead by Muslim extremists on 8 June 1992. In a discussion immediately after Foda's death, Pope Shenouda emphasized the need he felt to seek out and cultivate "moderate Muslims", as he likes to call them. Foda had a personal logo on his notepaper incorporating a cross and a crescent as a public testimony to his belief in the equality of Christians and Muslims. It was a statement not lost on Shenouda. One of the patriarch's central themes is that of patriotism. Again and again, he will refer to "Egypt our Mother". He has rejected the support of international groups supporting minority rights and is resentful of the suggestion that the Copts are like the Kurds in Iraq. He says that minorities are not numerical. The Copts are woven into the woof and warp of Egyptian history. In the reception room of the patriarchal residence in Abassiya, Cairo the same cross and crescent logo is fixed permanently to Pope Shenouda's wall.

Shenouda revolutionized the Coptic Orthodox Church. In the early years of his patriarchal ministry the Church adopted a forward-looking policy. Major issues were directly confronted. The first of these concerned the basic human right of freedom of belief. In Egypt this meant the basic right to move freely from Islam to Christianity, rather than in the opposite direction only. No progress has ever been made in this area. Another sensitive issue was that of the alleged discrimination against Copts seeking posts in Government and Administration. A recurring problem was the use of the *Shari'a*, Islamic law based upon the Qur'an.

The problem that initially brought Shenouda into confrontation with President Anwar Sadat was church building and repair. The legal foundation for the Egyptian state's control of church property is the Ottoman Hamayouni Decree of 1856, amplified in 1934 and a valid part of civil law, though presently under review by President Mubarak. The law requires a presidential decree to build or repair a church. This had been settled privately by Kyrillos with Nasser. With Shenouda as Pope, building was increasing. It was inevitable that some Coptic churches were built without presidential permission. It was, perhaps, equally inevitable that these churches should be subject to arson attacks by Muslim extremists. Communal tensions eventually led to the detention of Pope Shenouda from 5 September 1981 until 6 January 1985, the subject of separate study in this volume.

His Holiness has many critics in his own Church, despite the Coptic tendency to treat clergy with exaggerated deference. Ironically, most of the Pope's problems arise from the improved education and status of the clergy, for which he has worked so hard. The infiltration of educated young men into the monasteries and the hierarchy was crucial for essential reforms in the Church. A handful of recently consecrated and seriously inexperienced Coptic bishops who sojourned only briefly in a desert monastery behave with haughty and arrogant disdain for lay people. They are wise enough to avoid this behaviour in the sight of the patriarch. Away from the patriarch their conduct is lordly. Although sociological study of this phenomenon is difficult, and much "evidence" anecdotal, it is quite clear that someone at the centre of the Church is sensitive to the situation. This may be deduced by reading the sub-text of two revealing articles from *Al Kiraza*, the Coptic Church weekly edited by the Pope Shenouda himself.

In *Al Kiraza* of 17 September 1994 two quite bizarre, unsigned articles appeared. One was concerned with what it described ironically as the "Sin of the Mercedes" and the other attacked the "Protestant attitude of some Orthodox" in their behaviour towards the clergy. The first article noted that Copts had been criticising bishops for being issued with a Mercedes Benz as the episcopal car. The piece is about 750 words long in its English translation, and gives a list of practical and pastoral reasons for owning an automobile. It accuses critics of being influenced by Socialism "where the poor revolted against anyone who seemed to be rich". The context of this article is one in which some bishops of Middle Egypt and the Delta are, by virtue of their mobility, virtually unknown in their dioceses where they spend little time. They are constantly on the road. It is also possible that some Egyptian Christians are seriously concerned about the environment, for Cairo must be one of the most polluted cities on earth. But the Copts referred to in the article are not really concerned about the ownership of a Mercedes Benz. The real issue is the manner of some bishops. They conduct themselves as "princes of the church", enthroned in the back of the motor. A western observer was appalled in 1989 to see a woman dragged across the forecourt of the Coptic patriarchate in Cairo because her hand was stuck in the door of a Mercedes Benz. She had been attempting to kiss the hand of a bishop who was trying to push her out of the way. The Mercedes Benz is an outward and visible sign of an inward and spiritual problem. The tradition of ordaining bishops and priests chosen by the people has virtually been abandoned. The general conduct of the *nouveau eparche* is probably without parallel in the Christian world, and some of them seem determined to impose a monarchical system on the Copts. It is often noted that there is a radical difference between those bishops appointed by Pope Shenouda and those he inherited from Pope Kyrillos or earlier patriarchs. Only one monk of the monastery of Saint Macarius has been ordained a bishop during the reign of the present patriarch.

The second article of 1994 from *Al Kiraza* attacks Copts who do not offer traditional forms of respect to the clergy. The article uses the word "Protestant" as a form of abuse to describe these defaulters. Copts, we are told, kiss the hands of priests, call them "Father" (Abouna), kneel down in front of bishops, call them "Master" (*Sayedna*) and always ask for a blessing. Copts who do not do these things are branded as "Protestants". More seriously, the article says that Orthodox "cannot say anything in public against the hierarchy" and warns that Orthodox would not read the writings of those who criticize the Coptic tradition. The article reflects a situation where there is a loyal but questioning opposition within the Church. It is lay. It is directed against the increasing clericalization among the Copts in the last three decades.

The process of general clericalization in the Coptic Church was examined by Fadel Sidarouss in his dissertation *Eglise Copte et Monde Moderne* and elaborated by Pieternella van Doorn-Harder in her *Contemporary Coptic Nuns*. It is a process in which ordained men and consecrated women have come to control every aspect of Coptic Orthodox life. Opponents of this development will list a number of complaints: General bishops have been made to control social and welfare work and have usurped the role of the laity. Recently (*Roz El Youssef*, 13 March

1995), a new church regulation centralized church welfare work under a central Papal Committee. Bishops have created new rites of initiation for nuns and consecrated virgins, without regard to Tradition. Seminaries, with rare exceptions, exclude lay theologians, though these have been the norm in the past. In the 1940s the Sunday School Schools Committee was administered by the laity with one priest. In the 1950s the committee was made up mostly by priests. In the 1990s it is controlled solely by bishops. The prophetic, anti-clerical tradition of the desert monasteries has been absorbed by the institution. Many modern monks are apparently lacking in the traditional virtue of stability. They travel extensively on church business and may occasionally be encountered on the streets of Paris, Amsterdam, Frankfurt and London.

On 2 October 1995 the International Edition of *Al Ahram* interviewed Shenouda about what it described as "the polarization of the laity and clergy" in the Coptic Church. The elections to the *Majlis Milli* were imminent. Shenouda complained about those who wished to control the Coptic community because they were governed by "liberal and secular thinking". The Pope defined "the Church" as those who were ordained, rather like the quaint old Victorian expression where the younger son "went into the Church". Shenouda saw people standing for the Coptic Community Council who had no relation to the Church. "All they know about Christianity is that they have a Christian name." Some weeks later, after the elections, the Pope revealed that he was less than happy with the outcome. In the popular newspaper *Al Ahrar* (20 October 1995) he outlined how much the importance of the *Majlis Milli* had diminished over the last century. With constant reference to "the Church" as those who are ordained, he said that he would not allow the new Council to take over any functions in the Church "even if the Church needs to excommunicate all the members of the of the *Majlis Milli*". Any member of the Council who wished to serve the Church could get ordained. Shenouda can appear to be uncompromising, but this is often because he is so poorly advised. His mind is frequently in the desert. His advisers on the throne.

Although it invariably seems that Pope Shenouda, operating as a shrewd effective autocrat, holds all the reins of power, he is fact at the mercy of forces that he has himself unleashed. He has created an enormous bureaucracy, where men of ambition mistake authoritarianism for efficiency. His problems are rarely voiced abroad, but an extremely damaging article in the government-sponsored English Language paper *Egypt Today* (April 1995) claimed that Shenouda had unjustly dismissed 67 clergymen during his papacy, and that Church funds had been misappropriated by the Pope's nephew. The council of despair from one victim was, "All we can do is keep raising our voices and wait until the next pope." Shenouda is ill served by his supporters like Maurice Sadek (*Roz Al Youssef*, 24 April 1995) who, against all Coptic faith and practice, claimed for Shenouda "the right of Infallibility in religious dogma". The Pope's position is impossible. Ill-advised, besieged by sycophants, attacked by a church-within-the-church, a physical target for Islamic Fundamentalists and a constant scapegoat for hostile elements in the Egyptian media, the Pope rides a tiger, even if he has a German automobile. His greatest tragedy is that he has no friends, only flatterers.

Anyone familiar with the paintings of the Orientalist artist John Frederick Lewis (1805–75) will know his *Courtyard of the House of the Coptic Patriarch* (1864) which is full of activity: the dictating of letters, the groups of suppliants and the bustle of visitors. The juxtaposition of one race or creed with another is a recurring theme in paintings by Lewis. The suggestion is that the issues dealt with are not only spiritual or theological. They are also economic, social and ethnic. The Patriarch is solving problems and actively in a "helping" role. Shenouda's residence is as hectic today. He tries to be accessible. On any one morning there may be foreign visitors, immigrant Copts, monks, nuns, priests, politicians, diplomats and bishops, and, at times, the sick seeking a blessing. Abba Shenouda's involvement is clearly that of a spiritual father. Others may try to protect him, but he is open to as many people as possible. It is an Orientalist court, but it is a friendly and open one. The Pope can be watched as he seeks to find solutions to problems that are removed from the conventionally ecclesiastical. It is an environment which is far from the teacher's study, lecturer's podium or the hermit's cave. Vocation rules out personal preference.

The adulation accorded to a Coptic Pope in his public appearances is of another order, involving large crowds. Shenouda is frequently mobbed. He is a modern superstar for poor Copts without secular or political intentions. Any Coptic Pope will remain the focus of surviving Coptic communal identity. In his powerful modern novel *Turabuha Za'faran* (City of Saffron), the Coptic novelist Edwar al-Kharrat (b. 1926) portrays an Easter Sunday after the Liturgy in Alexandria:

> The crowd pressed around him, becoming thicker by the minute, every head craned upwards. People were saying to one another joyfully, "Our Father! Our Father!" Then there was one shout of jubilation from all the people together, men, women and children: "Bless us, Father! Bless us! Bless us!" Finally the lean, spare dark face appeared, almost transparent in its purity, through the narrow, topmost window. The shouts and calls increased, people ecstatic now; the thin hand stretched out, far above the people's heads . . . It was an ill face, dried-out, but radiant; the face of an old man; the last face he would have. Then there was a fleeting, twinkling

glance; he murmured some words of benediction which were drowned in the passionate calls and entreaties from the crowded square below.

We may assume that the patriarch in the novel is Abba Johannes the Nineteenth who reigned from 1928 to 1942. In the 1990s the scene is repeated every week in Cairo or Alexandria. The present Pope is a short heavy man. He has a fine head and photogenic face. His voice is rich and he has a warm smile. He has much more rapport with crowds and seems to enjoy the squash. His eyes shift everywhere in the crowd and beyond. Patriarchal hospitality is justifiably renowned.

Pope Shenouda the Third cannot be pigeonholed. He is to varying degrees a teacher, journalist, theologian, solitary, politician or pastor but for him there is only one whole life. Meeting him on a daily basis involves an awareness of the integrity that characterizes this solitary life. His life is of one piece, of wholeness, a seamless garment. His personal naivety and lack of private judgement complement his sternly moralistic and harshly dogmatic Orthodoxy. This stubborn but impressive integrity lifts the unashamedly Egyptian to the universal and Christian. It seems likely that Pope Shenouda sees himself not as one who is served by inferiors but as one who serves all the people of God. Elevation first to the episcopate then to the patriarchate was a disaster for him, a martyrdom. He is required to see it as the work of Divine Providence. He is a man with impossible ideals.

Chapter Six

Mission: For Africa and the World

God sends his Son. It is not enough to give man a new philosophy or a better religion. A Man comes to men. Every man bears an image. His body and his life become visible. A man is not a bare word, a thought or a will. He is above all and always a man, a form, an image, and a brother. Dietrich Bonhoeffer

The Copts are secure in the following affirmations: the early disciple John Mark, himself from Libya in North Africa, was the first official missionary to Africa, although there were Egyptians in Jerusalem at Pentecost (Acts 2: 10); the same Mark, now the Evangelist, gave the world the first written Gospel which bears his name, and he is the first apostle, bishop, martyr, pope and patriarch of the Copts; after Saint Mark's martyrdom in AD 68, the Gospel was heard from his followers throughout the known world.

The early centuries of the Christian era were a time of missionary expansion. Cyrenaica and modern Libya were probably evangelized in the time of St. Mark, and the Coptic patriarch of the twenty-first century still includes the name "Pentapolis", which signifies these regions, in his title. In sub-apostolic times, Coptic missions were to continue, near to Egypt and far away. A significant tradition records Switzerland's debt to the Copts. St. Moritz, the fashionable winter sports centre and spa, is named after a Copt, the leader of the Theban Legion that attended the Roman assault against the Gauls in AD 287. When the Roman general ordered the army to offer sacrifices to the gods after defeating the Gauls, the Theban Legion withdrew and refused to participate in the pagan rites. They were Christians from Upper Egypt. Tradition records the words of Maurice to the Roman commander: "We are your soldiers, but we are also servants of the true God. We owe you military service and obedience, but we cannot renounce Him who is our Creator and Master, and also yours even though you reject him. We have taken an oath to God before we took one to you. You can place no confidence in our second oath if we violate the first." Maurice and the Theban Legion were martyred. Swiss evidence for some form of Coptic mission is nation-wide. Zurich, the country's largest city, lies over one hundred kilometres to the north of St. Moritz, some twenty kilometres from the German border, and its official seal carries the icon of three Copts, remembered because of their missionary endeavours in this part of Switzerland.

In the century following the martyrdom of the Theban Legion, St. Athanasius the Apostolic (patriarch for nearly half a century from *c*.328) commissioned the first bishop for the far away and lonely Empire of Abyssinia (*c*.356). The Copts preserve the heritage of Apostolic Christianity, but it is only in Ethiopia that this has remained the focus of national life in unbroken continuity up to the present day. At the time of the Council of Chalcedon in 451, the Ethiopians adhered to the Coptic profession.

John Cassian (*c*.360–435) studied in Egyptian monasteries for many years and transplanted some Coptic culture to Southern France. It has been suggested that Coptic monks, or Europeans who had lived in their monasteries, were missionaries in Britanny and the British Isles. The missionary enterprise of Copts, or their associates, may possibly be indi-cated by a litany preserved in the Royal Irish Academy in Dublin, which invokes "Seven Egyptian monks in Disert Ullaigh", though Coptologists do not agree about the historical reliability of a prayer which may be patient of many interpretations. Nearer home, the ancient Nubian king-dom certainly received Bishop Longinus "the apostle of Nubia", in the sixth century. Some records suggest Coptic Orthodox involvement in the Yemen (Arabia Felix), amongst the existing Orthodox churches of South India and even in Sri Lanka. Outreach seems to have ended at the time of the Arab Conquest in the seventh century.

For centuries the Coptic vocation in Egypt was mere survival, but the missionary and evangelistic traditions of the Copts were revived in the twentieth century, especially in Africa. This began modestly enough with work amongst Coptic migrants in South Africa. In 1950 Abouna Ishaq al-Bishoi went to minister in Johannesburg. By 1964 it was reported that 400 families had joined the Coptic congregations in the Republic of South Africa.

In 1962, Pope Kyrillos the Sixth declared a new age in evangelism with the opening of a Department of African Studies in the Coptic Institute, Cairo. The post-colonial period in Africa would offer special opportunities for an indigenous African Church, which had survived in

Egypt since Apostolic times. The Pope reported that President Nasser –
"the carrier of the flag of political liberty in the African continent" – had
confidence that the Copts were capable of strengthening such liberty.
Kyrillos sent Fr. Yusuf Abdou Yusuf to represent the Copts at the first
meeting of the African Christian Peace Conference in Freetown, Sierra
Leone and when the priest went on to speak at a Conference in Dar-Es-
Salaam, Tanzania, the Middle East News Agency reported that the
Africans considered the Copts to be "the Church of Africa". A Church
hidden from the world for centuries was slowly taking a central place
on the stage of Christian Africa, thanks largely to the political revolution brought by Gamal Abd El Nasser and others like him. The Copts
seemed destined to take the place of white missionaries in Black Africa.

After the accession of Pope Shenouda, Bishop Antonious Marcos was
to become the leading exponent of the neo-Coptic missionary movement. He was born in Cairo in 1936 where he also trained as a doctor of
medicine. He specialized first in paediatrics, and later worked in
orthopaedic and general surgery. In the 1960s, as a layman, he served
as a doctor and self-supporting servant of the Ethiopian Church in
Addis Ababa, travelling extensively in the surrounding countryside. He
returned to Egypt in July 1975 and became a monk in the exquisite
Monastery of the Romans in the Western Desert. In January 1976, as
Abouna Antonios El Baramousi, he began to work in Nairobi, but
returned to Cairo on 13 June 1976 to be consecrated Bishop of African
Affairs. Commenting on his change of work from medicine to monk he
once remarked: "There are so many doctors in the world, but so few
Christians to spread the Gospel of the love of Christ."

Bishop Antonious Marcos has the pastoral care of churches in Zaire,
Kenya and West Africa. He lives in a monastery in Nairobi, but is
forever on the move. His appointment was, like so many things, foreseen by Pope Kyrillos when he sent his Chaplain to Kenya and Uganda
in 1961 because he had heard of Africans who wished to join the Coptic
Orthodox Church. There are several thousand independent churches in
Africa, and Bishop Antonious Marcos has visited many of them. He has
emphasized traditional Coptic spirituality and theology on his visits so
that these people can see that there is an authentic African Christian
tradition. In 1978 the bishop invited the leaders of independent
churches to meet in Cairo. They formed the Organization of African
Independent Churches, delighted to discover that Christianity had
early African roots and was not simply a European import. This
discovery has been extremely important in discussions and disputes
with Islam. It was customary for Islamic apologists to attack Christianity
as the "white man's" religion, especially bearing in mind the theological attitudes of the Dutch Reformed Church in South Africa. The Copts

showed that Christianity was not only much older than Islam, but also an African religion. Christianity may be seen as mystical and eastern rather than institutional and western. This has been a primary pronouncement in the Coptic missionary endeavour.

The Coptic mission in Africa is admired in ecumenical circles and has many successes to its credit. Antonious Marcos has encouraged social, educational and medical missions. Thousands have been baptized. On 11 January 1981 three Kenyan priests were ordained. By January 1989 the Liturgy was being celebrated for the four major tribal groupings in their own languages: Kikuyu, Luo, Akamba and Abaluya. Some independent churches, which had used the adjective "Coptic" in their title, were absorbed into the ancient Church of Alexandria. One young Akamba woman trained for five years in Egypt and returned to Kenya in 1985 as Deaconess Naomi, ministering to women in several communities.

Pope Shenouda spent ten days in Zaire in 1979 as guest of *L'Eglise de Jesus-Christ sur la Terre par le Prophete Simon Kimbangu*. The Kimbanguist Church is an African Church founded by an African prophet, but is sufficiently orthodox to be admitted to the World Council of Churches. Shenouda hoped to attract the three million Kimbanguists with the obvious antiquity of the Coptic Orthodox Church. Coptic monks have taught in the Kimbanguist Theological School, but ecumenical progress has been very slow in Zaire. The Coptic Church in Zambia, on the other hand, has been a state-registered church since 1984 and Egyptian residents with their priest have successfully evangelized amongst the native population. Similar work is underway in Zimbabwe.

Antonious Marcos has attempted to develop an Orthodox presence which is truly African whilst retaining all that is necessary in the Tradition. Converts to Orthodoxy have not found it easy to distinguish between what is sacred in the Tradition and what is purely ethnic. The triumphs and deficiencies of this missionary venture are demonstrated in the life of Father Mark of Scetis who was an African. The title given to him here is an English form of his Arabic name in the Coptic Orthodox Church: Abouna Marcos el-Askiti. The English usage celebrates his first language. He was born in the borderlands of the modern states of Kenya and Uganda on 27 February 1942. He was murdered in the United States of America on, or about, 17 April 1982.

Father Mark of Scetis was known in the world as Raphael Bernard Wanyama. The meaning, which Raphael attached to the name Mark and to the title "of Scetis", is clear. Upon entering the Coptic Orthodox Church, first as a monk and later as a priest, Raphael Bernard Wanyama chose to be associated with the Apostle of Africa and with one of the most famous monastic foundations of late antiquity. He was consciously rejecting a western mode of being a Christian, which he felt he had witnessed in the missionary churches of East Africa. He was intentionally embracing the Coptic way because he believed that it was an ancient African–Christian way.

Raphael Bernard Wanyama was born in Busia on the Kenya–Uganda border. He may have been either Kenyan or Ugandan at the time of his birth. The borders were changed in the Colonial period. The name Wanyama is common amongst the Luhya people of the Western Province of Kenya and occurs often in the Ugandan communities close to the modern border. These people share a close tribal, cultural and linguistic background. In the 1990s Busia is a district within the Western Province of Kenya. Busia is also the name of a town on the Kenyan side of the border. Raphael carried a Kenyan passport in 1967 when he visited Egypt.

Raphael was baptized a Christian in the Roman Catholic Church in the year of his birth. He was baptized with his twin brother. They came from a very large family, which had sixteen children by the time of Raphael's departure in the 1960s. Later in his adult life, Raphael remembered his family as happy and protective. His parents were both strict and devout Catholics. His mother had a special devotion for the Blessed Virgin Mary and taught the boy to pray as soon as he could speak.

At the age of only five years, Raphael was separated from his twin brother and from the big and contented family. He was sent to a very rigid, authoritarian Catholic boarding school. The plan was to give him the best available education. At the school Raphael was totally controlled by the European priests who taught and brought up their African charges. The education was excellent, but Raphael believed that he suffered for much of his life from the feelings of inferiority imposed upon him by the discipline in the boarding house. He also came to believe that he suffered psychologically because of the separation from his parents. He was not even allowed parental visits for several terms until the priests were sure that he had settled down.

On his rare visits home he became especially fond of one younger sister. She shared her inner life with him and in her teenage years, when she became eligible for marriage, expressed her anxiety about the practice of arranged marriage. It was the custom for fathers to select husbands for their daughters. Raphael was not entirely surprised when his favourite sister disappeared early in the morning of her wedding day. She left a message saying that she did not love the man chosen for her. She had run away. After a search of three years, conducted in holidays and at free periods, Raphael found her as a novice in a remote Catholic Convent in the rain forest. The convent was enclosed. She remains a member of the congregation to this day. Raphael later remarked upon the impression of peacefulness which the religious life conveyed to him through this important moment in his family life.

Raphael did a number of jobs after leaving school. His twin brother excelled in mathematics and science and went to College where he qualified as an engineer. Their father thought that Raphael should do something similar. It was important to make something of yourself, to acquire material advantage in the emerging countries of the developing world. There was a great future in Kenya.

Despite his rejection of the western priests at the boarding school, Raphael was attracted by religion, not in its outward appearance but in its inward reality. He liked to pray and to think of God. He spoke often in later life of the need to Remember God. He had latched onto a central concept in the contemplative life.

Raphael wanted an African Church. African congregations were springing up all over the place. These independent churches survived the malign attacks of Europeans and the contempt of nationalists. They gained in numerical strength. By the 1960s there were several thousand independent African churches. Their problem, from Raphael's point of view, was that they were rootless, without sufficient African–Christian roots and without a mature and considered theological system. Raphael wanted an independent church as long as it had secure African and doctrinal foundations.

In response to the missionary commission from Pope Kyrillos the Sixth a well-educated Coptic monk was sent to East Africa. He was Abouna Makari Es-Souriani and as Bishop Samuel he will have an important role in our narrative. The Egyptian priest, who became generally known as Father Makarios amongst English speakers, at first visited Kenya and Uganda in 1961. He undertook a careful study of the current religious situation in those countries. He was also commissioned to see if the Copts could help the newly emerging independent churches of Africa. That first visit was followed by many regular visits to various parts of Africa by the enthusiastic Coptic priest. He even began to learn Swahili. Raphael Bernard Wanyama and the future Bishop Samuel met in Nairobi, Kenya in 1966. It was an important meeting for both of them. Raphael was immediately attracted to the man and to his message. Father Makarios was thrilled to became the spiritual father of the young African. He invited Raphael to Egypt. Wanyama accepted the invitation and already spoke about becoming a Coptic monk.

The family were distressed. They had already lost a beautiful and lively daughter and sister to the convent. Raphael's mother said little about her son's plans but his father was against the possibility of his son joining an alien church. Becoming a monk was wrong. It was important to avoid poverty, not embrace it. Monasticism was opposed to the

African family tradition of marriage and children. Raphael should continue his education. He should become a man of means. If Raphael wished to follow any religion it ought to be the family religion. Raphael believed that the Copts offered him the possibility of an authentic African–Christian Faith. Saint Mark was a spiritual father from Africa. The Coptic Church was a spiritual mother within the African continent. Her theology was historically famous and distinctive. The pressure in the family was stormy.

After his departure in the 1960s, Raphael returned to Kenya only once. In 1976 some American friends in New Jersey paid for the trip. It was for a few weeks at the end of his final semester at Drew University. It was an important visit, which brought him peace of mind. In the intervening decade he had found his spiritual family, but he knew that he wanted to put himself right with the fifth commandment in the Decalogue: to honour his parents. The homecoming was happy. Friends and family met him at the airport. His father was among them. They were reconciled and that night, when everyone else had retired, Father Mark took his mattress and placed it on the floor between his parents' beds and slept there as a son in his father's house. He visited his sister in her enclosure, a meeting made easier by the innovations of the Second Vatican Council. His twin brother was now a successful engineer and owned his own aircraft to engage in his hobby as a bush pilot. The twins flew together around the beautiful East African countryside. One night they flew to Entebbe airport in Uganda under the cover of darkness. His brother was a frequent visitor there. It was a routine trip. They sat on a darkened runway. In the silence, they witnessed the far-from-routine Israeli rescue of their people forced down there in 1976. It was a dramatic moment in an otherwise peaceful return to his family. On his second departure from Nairobi the Kenyan Orthodox priest was at peace with his family and with himself.

The new Coptic convert, Raphael Bernard Wanyama, arrived in Egypt in 1967. He was met at the airport by Bishop Samuel and taken first to rest at the beautiful monastery of the Syrians in the Wadi Natroun. His first year as a Cairene theological student in the capital of Egypt coincided with the apparitions of the Blessed Virgin Mary at Zeitoun.

In April 1968, Raphael went to the Church in Zeitoun where the Virgin had appeared. He stood there in the warm evening air and waited. Thousands witnessed the appearance that night. Raphael entered the courtyard and he heard crying and shouting. He looked to the top of the church over the Northeast dome: "I saw the Virgin Mary in a very bright light. She raised her hands in front of her. It was a waving motion. Palms up. From the tips of her fingers lights was flowing down to the ground where I was standing. She remained like that for some time. Then she vanished."

His description of this event was always quiet, contemplative. It was impossible to mistake the awe and wonder he felt as a consequence of this event. It was an incident which confirmed the childhood faith learnt at his mother's knee, and validated the integrity of his commitment to the Copts. He was able to refer back, in the difficult times lying ahead, to this support received from Mary the *Theotokos*, the Mother of God. Mark was certain that he had seen Mary.

For five years Raphael studied Theology in Cairo. He was regarded as an earnest and assiduous scholar. In 1971 he obtained a Bachelor's degree in Theology. At one stage he was required to teach in English as a member of the faculty. In later years it was said that his difficulties in the Coptic Diaspora were caused by his lack of adequate Arabic. This is untrue. Some arabophone colleagues in the USA have said that Father Mark was fluent, responding very quickly in Arabic during discussions. He did not learn the arts of deceit, which are the same in any language and any culture.

Raphael was originally baptized by a Roman Catholic priest, but the Copts do not recognize the validity of western baptisms. The Catholic Church is, of course, the largest Christian body in the world and grave offence is caused by the continual rebaptism of converts to Coptic Orthodoxy. Western women of Catholic families who marry Copts in England or the USA are ordinarily required to submit to rebaptism. It is a common occurrence. The question of rebaptism was something of a crisis for Raphael and for many years after the event he remained anxious about the teaching of the Roman Catholic Church. The dispute about Saint Peter's place in the Church continued to worry him through his long theological education, but he slowly accepted traditional Orthodoxy polemics against Rome. In Egypt, he was baptized "as a Copt" and took the name of Marcos: Mark. As a convert he was a special case. He absorbed Coptic culture, thought in Arabic and developed a deep compatibility with Coptic liturgical language. This is rare. A Dutch clergyman, Dr Jacob Blom von Assendelft and a French colleague, Bernard Canepa, have both devoted a quarter of a century of faithful work to the Coptic congregations in Europe as Metropolitan Markos of Toulon and Bishop Athanasios, general bishop for France. They work from a Coptic *Ermitage Saint Marc*, near Toulon and at a Coptic Centre in Venice. Abba Markos and Abba Athanasios are articulate, well-educated and sensitive exponents of Coptic Tradition. Both are polyglots. They have done admirable ecumenical work throughout Europe, but it would be true to say that, though consecrated by Pope Shenouda himself, they have experienced grave difficulties in the

Church. The new convert Mark was more fortunate. He spent a long period in Egypt. He was eventually able effectively to celebrate the liturgy in Arabic and Coptic. This is essential. No existing translation of the Liturgy in any European language is convincing as literature, liturgical drama or cultural expression. The indispensable Coptic music rests entirely upon the Arabic and Coptic languages. No Coptic Liturgy can be taken seriously as liturgy without the age-old Egyptian music that is its backbone. The spirituality of the Coptic Mass is rooted deeply and uniquely in the Dar al-Qibt. Any Church which requires its Patriarch to have been born in the national homeland as a qualification for office cannot seriously claim universality. It is the great strength of the Coptic Orthodox Church that it is solely the Church of Egypt. In an important sense, the convert to Coptic Orthodoxy must somehow become an Egyptian to become a Copt. To a surprising degree Mark achieved this.

Mark-Raphael was ordained as a monk in the Wadi Natroun at the Monastery of Holy Virgin and St. John Kame, also called the Monastery of the Syrians. Following the example of many Coptic monks before him, Mark the monk was allowed to live for a brief period in the total isolation of a desert cave as a hermit. He was there in the desert on 9 March 1971 when the aged patriarch Kyrillos fell asleep in the Lord.

The election of Pope Shenouda the Third was unexpected. It was to prove momentous for the Kenyan monk. His friend and mentor Bishop Samuel was the most popular candidate, but the lot fell to another. Pope Shenouda ordained the Kenyan monk Mark of Scetis a priest on 12 July 1972. For a brief period he was attached to the patriarchal staff as a secretary to the new Pope. Shenouda enjoys the company of foreigners. He is also convinced that the Coptic Church is not an Egyptian sect. He has ordained a number of foreigners, including a white American and two black priests from the Caribbean. This has not taken place without much criticism in Egypt and in the Coptic Diaspora.

Father Mark was something of an embarrassment after his priestly ordination. They were not quite sure what to do with him. Could an African be a Coptic bishop for the Africans? Mark knew what to do. He was sure that he ought to engage in as much post-graduate theological study as possible. He had an insatiable thirst for knowledge of Orthodoxy and he wanted to know how to apply it in the modern world. He was uninterested in preferment. It was decided that he would go first to an Orthodox country and then to the West to further his theological education. Father Mark of Scetis became a wandering scholar–monk, not unlike those known in the European Middle Ages.

For most of 1973 he studied Patristics in an Orthodox monastery in Greece. The differences between the two families of Orthodoxy are a major issue. For the rest of his life Mark attempted to build bridges between the Copts and the Greeks. He always wanted to learn more about the Orthodox faith. Had he lived, he would have seen some fruits in this dialogue, though the two families have yet to enter into Communion. Many significant and unprejudiced Greek and Russian theologians are opposed to any adjustment of their historic position with regard to the Copts.

In 1974 the World Council of Churches awarded Father Mark a scholarship. With the active support of the Overseas Division of the Methodist Church, he became a student at Kingsmead College, Selly Oak, at Birmingham in England. He spent most of 1974 in Selly Oak.

Kingsmead, like several of the other Selly Oak Colleges, was originally a college preparing missionaries for service overseas. When Mark was there half of the student body was drawn from Africa and Asia. They were engaged in specialist courses and attached to Birmingham University. Mark studied Biblical Theology and Mission. He contributed a great deal to the spiritual and social life of the college community. The Methodists liked him. He was kind and gentle, a person with a delightful sense of humour. The college community, informed by a rather strong Protestant tradition, which did not follow any special liturgical or ascetic custom, was particularly impressed with his self-discipline and devotional life. They were amazed and affected by his fasting. They admired his enthusiastic singing of their hymns. The Methodist hymns, which hold a central place in Wesleyan spirituality, were particularly helpful to Mark. He was particularly fond of those by Charles Wesley, which supported his spiritual life.

The Copts reject the usual western interpretation of their Christology, which suggests that they believe in one divine nature in Christ. The Copts claim that they confess the full humanity and full divinity of Jesus Christ united beyond separation in the one Nature of God Incarnate. Father Mark found his understanding faithfully confirmed in a Methodist hymn:

> He deigns in flesh to appear
> Widest extremes to join;
> To bring our vileness near,
> And make us all divine:
> And we the life of God shall know,
> For God is manifest below.

The Methodist hymn also supported his highest aspirations as an Orthodox on the path to holiness. It is a clear statement of the central orthodox concept of *theosis* or deification.

At Kingsmead, his Methodist friends often raised the question of the value of Tradition, and this always occupied an important place in

Mark's mind. Theology must answer questions for the sake of his own peace of mind, and to support his ministry as a Copt. Mark now travelled across the Atlantic to the United States of America where he enrolled at Drew University in New Jersey in 1975. At this time, the question of appointing a Coptic bishop in East African was raised again in Cairo. It was thought that the preferment must be preserved for an Egyptian who had the Coptic tradition in his blood. The thinking was conditioned by centuries of Egyptian control in Ethiopia.

At this time Mark wrote his 23-page paper on *The Ecumenical Council and the Ministry of Peter*. It was his personal answer to the crisis that he had felt at the time of his conversion to Orthodoxy. The long essay is notable for its careful citations in French; each of these are studiously marked in pencil with the correct accents. It is likely that Father Mark, a skilled linguist by now, originally created this essay in French. His secondary sources are all eminent French Catholic theologians.

The general effect of the paper is of a typical, rather tedious Orthodox polemic against the Roman Catholic position, "a case which lacks any religious, spiritual and theological foundation to support it". Although the arguments presented by Mark are entirely derivative, this paper has since reminded many Catholics how far they are from Orthodoxy, despite external appearances to the contrary. Catholics often fail to understand Orthodox hostility or indifference to western-style Papacy. Father Mark understood it at the time of his Orthodox baptism and he gave his thoughts structure and academic form at Drew University. The paper affirms the Orthodox tradition "that the authority of the Councils is above their (the Apostles) authority as individuals", and says of Saint Peter that "he was just one of the Council of bishops". The paper may have had some appeal to Protestant professors at the university for it treats the Bible, and especially those chapters in the Epistle to the Galatians and the Acts of the Apostles which deal with the Council of Jerusalem, with extreme literalism. It completely disregards the problematic circumcision of Timothy in Acts 16. The dissertation is a tidy piece of self-justification. When Father Mark attended Drew Theological Seminary in Madison, New Jersey he was still deeply concerned with the understanding of classical Orthodoxy and its application in the world today. Because he wanted to show that Orthodoxy had practical uses, he decided at first to work in a hospital to study holistic medicine and its relation to Orthodox spirituality.

Drew University offered a Master of Ministry degree and as a part of this course Mark decided to move on from the study of holistic medicine to attend a more traditional clergy course at Overlook Hospital, Summit, New Jersey. He graduated in Clinical Pastoral Education after following the Programme from 23 September 1975 to 14 May 1976.

Within the CPE group he was alone in being a foreigner, a black, a celibate and an Orthodox. Mark was at first shy but in a short time became completely integrated in the group. He felt that he more than anyone on the course learnt most from his contact with well-educated western Christians, but for all members of the gathering there was a strong feeling of reciprocity in the dynamics of the group. Father Mark impressed the Director of the Department of Pastoral Care as "a truly holy man".

Whilst in the United States, Mark heard that Bishop Antonious Marcos had been appointed the Coptic Orthodox bishop in East Africa. The African priest was pleased to know that people in his motherland were to have their own Orthodox bishop to stand beside the Anglican and Catholic episcopate. Perhaps one day there would be an African bishop for the Africans?

Mark's relationship with God was unchanged by his contact with western modes of religious thought. From the beginning to the end of his course at Drew he impressed everyone as being a dedicated man. The difference was not so much in his obvious sanctity, or in the depth of his spiritual life as in his availability as a person. He was open to the group and to the individuals. He was described as a man who was both humble and proud. Everyone who met him during his decade in the West commented upon his intelligence and personal charm. He was physically attractive, a fact which was often called against him by his critics. He was spiritually enchanting to those who sought that kind of authenticity. The overwhelming characteristic of religious professionals in the traditional ecclesiastical structures is of their mediocrity, people like Mark are rare. His supervisor at Drew recalls him as a man of fine sensibility, patience, dedication, strong faith, sincerity, love and affection. "He is a man whom one is blessed to have had as a friend."

He was an omnivorous reader. With English as his first language, he could not have been in a better place than the USA to learn about Orthodoxy. Father Mark could pour over the publications of St. Vladimir's Seminary in New York, Holy Cross at Boston and the numerous publications of the Russian Orthodox Church Outside Russia. He loved them all. He impressed many as a man with a profound knowledge of Orthodoxy. His piety and knowledge were carried with simplicity and quietness. Yet a few simple questions were enough to get him to expound an aspect of Theology with style and depth. One day at a gathering of Christian friends a discussion took place about the worship of the Orthodox Church. To illustrate a point, Mark suddenly burst into a chant from the Divine Liturgy of St. Basil the Great. Everybody stopped what he or she was doing. The kitchen and the parlour fell silent. The voice of the black priest sounded quietly, persistently, at length, throughout the house. He was at home and his listeners felt at home with the sacred words.

Many Coptic priests and monks who come to serve the churches in the West live in considerable affluence, with lavish accommodation that would be considered to be inappropriate for the average western minister of religion. Mark lived simply. He was a monk in his inner being. He was a poor man. He had embraced poverty in response to an evangelical injunction. Mark carried no money. He was often without food. He worked at washing dishes in the university cafeteria so that he could earn enough to buy food. Whilst he was cleaning crockery to earn his living, some Copts said that he had left the church, others that he had become a Protestant minister because he failed to wear the robes of a monk. The faithful had no faith in him. Father Mark, the little, poor dishwasher of New Jersey found his Coptic critics a great burden.

To the young, the Copts of the second generation of immigrants, he was a friend and adviser. They loved him and he loved them in return. He was happy in his holiness. He could laugh and play. He loved to watch the late night television movies with his young American–Coptic friends. It is said that he abandoned traditional standards to be American, others say that he lived his faith within the new and different culture, sanctifying the modern world instead of creating yet another ghetto. Mark's years as a travelling theologian confirmed his place as an outsider. He had embraced Coptic culture but his opponents thought this incompatible with embracing American culture at the same time. When it came to questions about his knowledge and practice of the mystical Theology of the Eastern Fathers, taken as a standard for Orthodoxy, Mark was emphatically an insider.

By December 1979 Father Mark was settled as the pastor of Saint Mark's Coptic Orthodox Church, at 424 Mulberry, Bellaire, Texas. Bellaire is a small, incorporated city within the boundaries of the greater City of Houston. Mark wrote to some of his old friends back in New Jersey: "I have seen Jesus more through my ministry here." He organized classes in the Orthodox catechism for over one hundred young people. People who had been very occasional "attendees" at church back in Egypt were drawn to Mark and the Church. Others were not sure about him. He had difficulties with traditionalists: "The majority seem to embrace the idea of teaching the Sunday School classes in English but those who have moved down here from the East coast think that God cannot understand any language except Arabic."

The remark is innocent enough and may even be thought to be playful, but there is an underlying sadness. When challenged by an Egyptian national at his church in Bellaire with the question, "What kind of a priest are you anyway?" Father Mark replied, "I am a Coptic

His Holiness Pope Shenouda the Third
Born Nazir Gayed on 3 August 1923
Consecrated 117th Coptic Pope and patriarch 14 November 1971

Modern monastic cells and water tower in the Wadi Natroun: frequently used by guests of the Pope. The fourteen crosses in this photograph illustrate the ubiquity of the Coptic cross on church-owned buildings throughout Egypt

The monastery of St. Antony the Great (c.251–356) is hidden away in the barren cliffs of the Qalalah mountains on the edge of the Wadi Arabah. It is about 300 hundred kilometres – a six-hour drive – from Cairo and some thirty kilometres from the Red Sea coast

Traditional Coptic marquetry cross – polished wood and ivory – on the Iconostasis in a Coptic monastery

A group of Coptic boys with the
Guest Master
at the monastic fishing farm in
the Wadi Natroun

Saturday 18 July 1992: Pope
Shenouda (centre) with monks
and bishops celebrating the
thirty-eighth anniversary of his
monastic ordination

Main Gate of the Monastery of the Blessed Virgin Mary, Al-Muharraq, Assyut Province
On 11 March 1994 two monks and two laymen were martyred here

A Tower in Deir Anba Bishoi, the Monastery of Saint Bishoi in the Wadi Natroun, the Western Desert of Egypt

His Holiness Pope Shenouda the Third
From September 1981 to January 1985
he was under house arrest. This
autographed photograph was taken
during that period. Shenouda is wearing
the traditional *qolunsha/qalansuwa*,
originally a Syrian Orthodox monastic
head-dress. It is a tight fitting cap
covering the head and neck,
embroidered with thirteen yellow or
white crosses representing Christ and
the Apostles.
In his hand he holds the cross of
blessing.

Raphael Bernard Wanyama
Born 27 February 1942 died
circa. 17 April 1982
Abouna Marcos al-Askiti (Father
Mark of Scetis)

His Holiness Pope Shenouda, a photograph taken in the Monastery of Saint Bishoi during his house arrest 1981–5. The patriarchal throne is symbolically covered, whilst he is deprived of his authority. The monastic Tau-stick of Saint Antony rests on the patriarchal seat

His Holiness Pope Shenouda with his Arabic biographer Fr. Mikhail Salib and the author. January 1990

ΠΑΠΑ ΑΒΒΑ   ΚΥΡΙΛΛΟC

An unofficial icon of Pope Kyrillos the Sixth (1902-1971) by Professor Isaac Fanous Yussef. In the collection of the author; Kyrillos is not yet canonised, but many, including Dr. Fanous, think he ought to be.

President Gamal Abd el Nasser laid the foundation stone of St. Mark's cathedral on 24 July 1965. At the inauguration of the cathedral on 25 June 1968 Nasser was again present and the United Arab Republic issued a special stamp for the 1,900[th] anniversary of the martyrdom of Saint Mark, on the following day a relic of the Evangelist was placed in the crypt of the new building

His Holiness Pope Kyrillos the Sixth
Born 2 August 1902 Died 9 March 1971

His Holiness Pope Shenouda the Third with Metropolitan Marcos of France and Bishop Athanasius of Toulon

Dr Stephane Rene examines the gilding on his 1995 icon of the Flight into Egypt

Small modern Coptic icons of Saint Antony the Great, the Resurrection of Christ and Saint Athanasius used for private devotion in the home. Dr. Stephane Rene wrote these icons, which are in the private collection of the author

Popular mass-produced icon of Saint Demyana and the forty virgins:
Martyrs under the Persecution of the Emperor Diocletian (245-313)
The icon is the work of Isaac Fanous Yussef

An icon of Bishop Samuel, who died alongside Sadat on 6 October 1981. The bishop's robes, with the bullet holes clearly outlined, are kept in a Martyrs' room, with this icon, at Abbasiya in Cairo

Ashraf Fayek Ishak, associate professor of Iconography in Cairo, produced this icon for the Coptic Orthodox Church in France

رئيس التحرير: صاحب القداسة البابا شنوده الثالث

السنة الثانية والعشرون | الجمعة ٨ أبريل ١٩٩٤ - ٣٠ برمهات ١٧١٠ش | الثمن أربعون قرشا | العددان ١٣، ١٤

اجتماع المجمع المقدّس

عقد المجمع المقدس جلسة فى صباح يوم الخميس ٣/٣١ برئاسة قداسة البابا ، وسكرتارية نيافة الأنبا بيشوى ، وبحضور ٥٣ من الآباء المطارنة والأساقفة .

وقد تغيب بعض الآباء الذين يعملون فى الخارج ، فى القدس والسودان وأفريقيا وأمريكا وفرنسا. كما تغيب ولكن أرسل تأييداً

لقرارات المجمع كل من أصحاب النيافة : الأنبا غريغوريوس، والأنبا أنطونيوس مرقس، والأنبا يوسف (أسقف عام جنوبى USA) .

وقد تم توزيع تقرير عن العلاقة مع الكنيسة فى أثيوبيا. ثم تلى عليهم مشروع البروتوكول للعلاقة معها بمواده الـ١٦ .

◄ وبعد المناقشة قرر المجمع الموافقة على البروتوكول بالإجماع .

وكان المجمع المقدس فى أثيوبيا قد وافق عليه من قبل .

وينتظر أن يوقع عليه قداسة البابا، ويرسل مع نيافة الأنبا سرابيون إلى أثيوبيا لتوقيعه أيضاً من هناك .

Al Kiraza, the Coptic Church weekly edited by the Pope. *Al Kiraza* is one of the leading publications for Copts, even those of a secular mind

His Holiness Pope Shenouda the Third and the author

Orthodox priest." His inquisitor commented, "You may, for all I know, be an Orthodox priest, but a Copt you will never be. You have to be born a Copt to be a Copt. I was born in Egypt. I am a Copt." It was typical of a certain Coptic mentality, but it was hurtful and damaging and it did not augur well for the future.

Father Mark transformed the Board meetings in the church at Bellaire. The meetings started with prayer. Bible Study and discussion would take up most of the time. Mark always wanted to find out how the local community could serve God. At the end of the Board meeting a little time was left to discuss "material items". This was the character of every meeting. It was only after some time that members of the group noticed that the priest never used a Bible. He knew all the passages off by heart. In some Coptic circles it has become acceptable to refer to congregations like that at Bellaire as "churches of the migration". It is suggested that the individuals have left Egypt for purely professional reasons. The term "Diaspora" is disliked because of its historical associations with the scattering of Jews for political and social reasons. Mark thought the preference for the phrase "churches of the migration" a fraud, covering-up the endless discrimination against Copts in Egypt throughout the centuries. Most Copts who have left Egypt have done so for reasons relating to fundamental human rights. Some Copts become well assimilated in their countries of adoption, but many are always looking back over their shoulders.

When the Christians of Egypt feel cold the Coptic Orthodox Diaspora in the United States of America sneezes. The crisis of the Egyptian Church, when Pope Shenouda was placed under house arrest from 1981 to 1985, is analyzed in the next chapter. It suffices at this point to state that Father Mark remained always and only "the Pope's priest", believing this to be the necessary fulfilment of his ordination vows. It is sometimes said that Goodness is boring. Father Mark of Bellaire, Texas was a good man. His goodness was extremely dangerous. Late in September 1981, Father Mark led a demonstration outside the Egyptian Consulate in Houston. He protested the exile of the patriarch in a desert retreat, the establishment of a government committee of bishops to rule the Church in place of the patriarch and the imprisonment of some bishops and priests. Mark's former mentor Bishop Samuel headed the Government Committee. The church in Houston like the mother Church in Egypt was now deeply divided.

On 7 October 1981, the day following the assassinations of President Sadat and Bishop Samuel, who had also been Mark's confessor and spiritual director, the Bellaire priest telephoned some old friends in New Jersey. He was deeply distressed and full of sorrow but with a sense of deep conviction and a determination about what he must do now.

Father Mark had given the impression that he was holding back from any criticism of the Government Committee of Bishops, which was usurping the functions of the Pope, because of his personal association with Bishop Samuel. When challenged about this just after the assassination, Mark said "I know that God stands for the Truth. I must stand for the Truth". By this time the Copts outside Egypt had generally decided to keep quiet about the situation in the Coptic heartland. Only three Egyptian-born priests in the entire Coptic Diaspora spoke out. Abouna Ibrahim Aziz and Abouna Antonious Henein in California were to defend the Pope and the Coptic Church until the amnesty of January 1985. Abouna Antonious Farag in London cooperated with the priests in California. Most priests decided to keep quiet. They entertained the enemies of the Pope when they came to the West, but all the Coptic clergy of the Diaspora dramatically became Pope Shenouda's admirers and supporters in 1985 when he reappeared at the Cairo cathedral.

Father Mark became the ally of Father Aziz and Father Henein. Some of his congregation believed that this was unwise. Some said that Mark was not an Egyptian, not a real Copt. His work and study in the West had made him "political". He was unworthy to be a Coptic priest. It was regretted that Pope Shenouda had a reputation for ordaining foreigners who could never really be Copts. One friend of the black priest tried to defend him and raised the question "Do you suppose that it is because he is not Egyptian, that he is black and that he is in the south, where race has been a great factor, all this rejection and criticism takes place?" The reply was an emphatic, "No."

The Egyptian Government's Committee of bishops became angry at the statements of the priest in Texas. On 10 March 1982 they published a document excommunicating Father Mark. Bishop Gregorios signed it. The warrant was stamped by the legal department of the Foreign Ministry in Cairo, and the assistant to the under Secretary of State for Foreign Affairs. It carried the Egyptian State Seal. The document refers to "Mr. Marcos Askaty" and concludes with the words, "He is no longer recognized as a priest". The document is reproduced on pp. 151–2.

There being no possibility of appeal to the Pope, Mark and his local Church Council appealed to an American Court. The case of the Committee against Father Mark was first heard on 17 May 1982 before sixty-year old Judge Robert L. Smith. It was adjourned.

At the height of the Church Struggle, Mark wrote to one of his congregation. The correspondent wanted to leave the church. He was deeply distressed by the committee of bishops. Above all, he was disgusted by the behaviour of US Copts in Texas who acted against Mark. The priest's letter is justifiably a part of Fr. Mark's martyrology. The letter is dated 23 June 1982:

I know that it is hard for me to express myself and my deep feelings. Yesterday we met the two lawyers with the four members of the Board. I learnt from them that I was the cause of dividing the whole Community. They said that I should sacrifice myself for the sake and benefit of the community by leaving the Church.

I do not want you to have some doubts about your Church. Do not be spiritually disturbed at all. God is always standing beside the innocent in such downs and trials. I do pray for those who engineered all these things against me.

It is impossible to understand the stress he must have experienced when faced with these authorities. Mark was a man who had lived with authoritarian structures all his life, from the boarding school in Kenya to the monastic tradition in Egypt. He knew himself and expressed himself almost entirely in the role of a priest. The rigid, arbitrary modes of control left their mark upon him. The Committee was powerful. Pope Shenouda was politically weak and banished. Priests from London, Canada and Australia phoned Mark to tell him to support the five bishops against Shenouda. He should leave the church and the priesthood quietly. The black priest rejected their advice. Father Mark's importance is moral and religious: it lies in his decision to support a patriarch chosen by altar lot, a device perceived at this moment in Coptic history as the means of expressing God's will for his people. At great personal cost, he fought for the Coptic Tradition.

It tells much about the man that his response to the crisis was essentially spiritual and theological. At this time, Father Mark deliberately made available his twenty-one hand-written pages on the understanding of Tradition in the Coptic Orthodox Church. It went back to the questions raised by theologians when he had studied in England and New Jersey. It related directly to the struggle faced in Houston. For Mark the contest was on the highest spiritual level:

When we speak of the Church we do not mean a social or a secular organism, or even a humanitarian society concerned with the moral betterment of human life. By Church we mean the life-giving Body of our Saviour and God, Jesus Christ. We mean Jesus Christ Himself transmitted and extended to the ages. We mean the transmission of Life.

The attempt to undermine the position of the Coptic Pope was a heresy and a blasphemy: "The denial of Tradition's importance is essentially the denial of the work of the Holy Spirit in History and the doubting of His charisma."

Father Mark saw that the canons of the Church, which were being undermined by the Committee in Cairo as a sop to the Egyptian government, were the only means of asserting the independence of the Church: "The canons are the expression of the Church's independence, of her external limits and inner structure. They render her a visible and concrete body."

Theology was the ground under his feet. In this sense the African became the teacher. Everyone else in the ugly tale was operating on a different basis, and even the patriarch was forced to appeal to secular courts for his reinstatement. Fr. Mark taught that the theological and spiritual issues had their priority. Spirituality armed only with its own integrity won.

The bishops decided to test the resolve of the Copts in Texas by appointing the Hegoumenos Maximos Sadek Ibrahim as parish priest in Houston. Some Copts refused to accept him. Mark appealed to Bishop Antonious Marcos in Nairobi who said that the matter must be left to the Pope.

The case came before Judge Robert L. Smith again on 12 July 1982 and was again adjourned while a Notary Public went to Cairo. He received a handwritten letter from Bishop Gregorios, confirming the legality of the earlier excommunication and the appointment of a new priest. The Cairo Committee had already claimed (15 May 1982) that they had taken over "the spiritual status" of the Pope. For the first time in Coptic history there were bishops supporting the notion that a Coptic Patriarch is someone who may be hired and fired by the civil power. Mark was rejected by five of the most senior bishops of the Coptic Church, two of them monks from his own monastery.

In his residence attached to the monastery of St. Bishoi, hidden far away in the easternmost point of the Sahara desert, another Coptic monk was imprisoned. He heard the news from Texas and he decided to act. The letter from His Holiness Pope Shenouda to the Houston Judge is dated 5 June 1982 and is stamped with the Papal seal. The text, in full, is hand-written in English:

> Father Marcos Al Askeety [*sic*] is one of the monks and priests of the Coptic Orthodox Church. He is the pastor of our church in Houston and the head of its congregation. I ordained him and sent him to USA.
>
> He is working under my direct jurisdiction and hierarchy, as we have not ordained yet a bishop or more for our Coptic churches in [the] USA and didn't authorize any bishop to preside our church [*sic*] in Houston or in any other place in America.
>
> As for the deposal [*sic*] or excommunication of priests, the canons of our church states [sic] that the priest many not be deposed or excommu- nicated or dismissed unless after being tried by a legal ecclesiastical council [court] and found guilty. In such case, he should have chance [*sic*] to defend himself against any accusation. If the priest is found worthy of

any penalty, this should be approved by his bishop.

As the direct and supreme chief of the Coptic Orthodox churches in America, I state that Father Mark al Askeety is still the pastor and priest or our congregation in Houston and the head of its congregation.

The letter was smuggled out of the monastery and some weeks later taken out of Egypt in the private baggage of a courier. It reached Texas and was offered in evidence at the third hearing of the case on 29 July 1982. Whilst the Copts continued to fight among themselves, Judge Robert L. Smith, a combat-veteran of the United States Marine Corps and a traditionalist Protestant of South Main Baptist Church, signed an order in favour of Pope Shenouda and Mark, thus upholding the ancient canons of Orthodoxy. It might have ended there, but many Copts look back upon this historic court case and see in it the beginning of the Passion and Martyrdom of Father Mark of Scetis.

For ten years a study was made of the relevant documentation and a mass of verbal evidence concerning the life and death of Father Mark. Letters from people who knew the priest, both friends and opponents in the Coptic Orthodox Church, have been the subject of careful scrutiny. It has not been proven that agents of the Egyptian Secret Service, or any other State agency, were responsible for the death of Father Mark. There is no conclusive evidence that the murderer or murderers of Father Mark were paid by members of the Coptic community in America or by any officials of the Coptic Church. Some Copts, like the late Mansour Sidhom of Illinois, a good and serious person, held with the intensity of an act of faith, that Father Mark was murdered by the enemies of Shenouda in the Church, if not directly then by hiring an assassin. It is possible to understand the passion lying behind such convictions, but there appears to be no evidence to support them. If blame is to be apportioned for the bitterness and divisiveness occasioned by this tragedy then a great weight must lie upon the hearts of the committee.

Some of the documents relating to the trial found their way into the public domain, thanks to the work of Human Rights activists and the helpful public information legislation in the USA. Copies of these manuscripts can be found, as a permanent historical record, in the Appendix to this volume (pp. 152–3).

Father Mark of Scetis was murdered less than a year after the trial.

The black priest of Saint Mark the Evangelist Coptic Orthodox Church at Bellaire, Texas was last seen on Friday, 15 April 1983. His disappearance was not reported until he failed to appear for the public church services on Sunday, 17 April. The police report noted that his car, a 1981 Oldsmobile, was also missing. The priest's absence from church on Saturday, 16 April was highly irregular, and the police were surprised and annoyed that it had remained unreported for twenty-four hours. Detective D. L. Oglesby was reported as observing: "It's been real hard, working with these people. The church is divided. One group wants the pastor out. The other wants him in, and the people just aren't saying anything to help the investigation."

United Press International regularly carried the story in the following years. The UPI affirmed that some people in the Coptic community in Houston believed that the priest was killed because of his outspoken opposition to the banishment of the Coptic Pope. Others were reporting that he was the subject of racial controversy. It was said that he had not been able to communicate with the Egyptians in his congregation. The UPI coverage divided the Coptic community even more and some people left the Church. Some have not returned. It was reported that the police were called out several times to break up quarrels between disputing factions in the missing priest's church. One Copt who had left the church because of the court ruling in favour of Shenouda said that Mark had just taken off. Nothing harmful had happened to him. "Whatever the factions are in the Egyptian community, they would not go that far, to murder him."

Father Mark had an Exxon credit card to get petrol. When the card was used after his disappearance, a suspect called Michael Gray was identified and eventually arrested at Syracuse, New York on 6 April 1984. Gray was arrested as the result of a complaint from a known homosexual. Gray also claimed to be a homosexual. Some Copts, who were known supporters of the episcopal committee, began to claim that Mark too was a homosexual. No evidence has even been given to support these claims and they have died down, though some individuals continue to raise the issue of the connections Mark might have had in the Gay community. The accusation was a means of indirect attack upon the patriarch's discernment. Gray was released after his return to Texas. There was no proof at the time of Gray's release that the priest was dead.

On 15 October 1984 Father Mark's car was found in Nacogdoches, Texas. Human bloodstains were found in the car. The FBI took samples but, because of the condition of the specimens, no adequate grouping could be made. A Texas Ranger called Max Womack investigated the possibility that Gray had dumped the priest's body somewhere. Before the beginning of the deer-hunting season, in the middle of November 1984, an appeal was made that hunters be on the lookout for skeletal remains in the area outside Jefferson Texas. On 27 December 1984 human remains were found in the woods of Marion County, Texas. A human skull with maxilla, but no mandible, was found. There were very few other bones. The pelvis was discovered. A windbreaker jacket was also recovered near the skeletal remnants. Two dentists who had both seen Mark as a patient compared the dental records belonging to the priest with the maxillary dentition of the skull. They identified the remains as those of the Coptic Orthodox priest.

Michael Gray was indicted with the murder of Father Mark. It has never been established that Gray was part of a wider conspiracy, and it has not been verified that he was not. The exact details of the murder remain a mystery at the beginning of the new millennium. Many Copts would share the emotions of one Coptic Orthodox Christian from New Jersey when she wrote:

> I was not present in Houston, Texas when captors took Father Mark away, but I see them taking him in the dark. His black body blended with the darkness, writhing in horror and fear. But I see his white eyes shining so pure. I see all the final moments of his life; with his last breath he pleads with God to forgive those in such ignorance. Those who murdered him. Those who had him murdered.

About five hundred people, a tiny number considering the enormous number of Copts in America, attended his funeral in St. Mary's Church, Los Angeles. Father Ibrahim Aziz and Father Antonios Henein were the officiating ministers. The Coptic Diaspora, in general, ignored the occurrence. In the Western Desert of Egypt, Pope Shenouda wept and began a fast. He felt the horror.

The earthly remains of Abouna Marcos el-Askiti were not buried. They are kept in a reliquary as the relics of a martyr. People pray before these relics and there have been reports of healing of mind and body. His act of witness awaits the judgement of the Church but many believe that his glorification as a Coptic saint will take place in the not too distant future.

As a convert to Orthodoxy and as an Orthodox priest, Mark of Scetis embodies an invitation and a warning. His life was an invitation to all those who search for the authentic originals of Christian life and thought. He devoted much time and great passion to the study of the sources of Christian Theology and Mysticism, and this aspect of his life portrays the inclusive dimension of Orthodoxy. As a priest within an inevitably narrow national church he warns us that Orthodoxy is exclusive. It was given to a black African of non-Orthodox origins to uphold the genuine practices of the Oriental Orthodox even when senior bishops were denying them. If not a martyr, he is at least a confessor of the Faith. He defended Orthodoxy against it detractors. Some words of Isaac of Nineveh have been considered to be an appropriate gloss upon the direct lessons learnt from this child of Coptic missionary enterprise:

Love is sweeter than life.
Sweeter still, sweeter than honey and the honeycomb
is the awareness of God whence love is born.
Love is not loath to accept the hardest of deaths
for those it loves.
Love is the child of knowledge . . .
Lord, fill my heart with eternal life.

Chapter Seven

The Egyptian Church Struggle

We reject the false doctrine, as though the State, over and beyond its special commission, should and could become the single and totalitarian order of human life, thus fulfilling the Church's vocation as well. We reject the false doctrine, as though the Church, over and beyond its special commission, should and could appropriate the characteristics, the tasks and the dignity of the State, thus itself becoming an organ of the State. The Barmen Declaration, Germany, May 1934

Early in the morning of Thursday 3 September 1981 "the visitors of the dawn" (armed state security police) visited thousands of homes in Egypt. They arrested a mixed assortment of politicians, lawyers, teachers and journalists, with a hotchpotch of prominent intellectuals in many professions. A special category of prisoner was that of "religious leader", both Muslim and Copt. By Presidential decree No. 493 of 1981, President Sadat detained 1,536 named people without charges or trials. On Saturday 5 September, Pope Shenouda III was placed under house arrest. In a Presidential telecast lasting nearly five hours on 15 September, Sadat explained that the September revolution had been made under article 74 of the Constitution which gave him power to abolish constitutional guarantees in a time of national emergency. He had suspended publication of opposition newspapers, including Coptic Church publications.

The political situation in Egypt in September 1981 was anxious but not hopeless, certainly not desperate enough to justify the arrest of so many. Sadat's foreign policy of reconciliation with Israel, which seemed admirable to some western observers, was disliked by many at home and did nothing for the crumbling economy. In July 1979 at Alexandria

– on the 27th Anniversary of the Republican Revolution – Sadat had said: " With the signing of the peace treaty with Israel there is no longer any excuse for not solving the acute problems under which the majority of Egyptians live." It might well have been the epitaph for his tomb two years later. The economic policies of the National Democratic Party, like the *infitah* (opening), abandoning a planned economy in favour of a free market, were ineffectual. The poor did not understand the workings of the International Monetary Fund, and did not know that Egypt was entirely dependent upon American wheat supplies. Sadat claimed seventeen thousand Egyptian millionaires in 1981, in a country where seventeen million families live on about £15.00 a month. Some attacked the president's own lifestyle. Graffiti during the riots of the early eighties read: "Nasser built a dam for Egypt, Sadat builds palaces for his wife." Mrs. Sadat was unpopular and informed commentators spoke of the "Evita syndrome" in Egypt. Several parliamentarians opposed Sadat's acceptance of the credentials of Eliahu ben Elissar, Israel's first ambassador to Egypt, and his offer of asylum to the ex-Shah of Iran. The government liked to give the appearance of democracy, but governed increasingly by referendum, achieving numerically overwhelming but quite incredible support. Sadat's famous visit to Jerusalem on 8 November 1977 and the signing of the Camp David accords in 1979 were criticized by many Egyptian leaders, including some imprisoned in 1981. The critics believed that the visit to Israel and the signing of the agreements were signs of Egypt's weakness. Sadat always claimed that he had only been able to open up the possibility of serious dialogue because he was vindicated by his early victories over Israel in the early moments of the Yom Kippur War.

The *New York Times* of 10 September 1981 carried a report of an interview with the Egyptian President who charged all those arrested in the previous week with having fostered sectarian–communal strife. In Egypt this is a very serious charge. The inevitable struggle between Copt and Muslim, whilst usually kept under control, is always bubbling beneath the surface of national life. Commentators generally regarded Sadat's attempt to raise the spectre of communal strife at this distressing moment as an attempt to distract his people from wider economic and foreign policy issues, though some political analysts in the National Democratic Party really believed that a full-scale civil war was a possibility.

The entire religious scene in Egypt has always been and remains extremely complex. Any attempt to explain it is bound to appear partial and must be subject to the vicious polemics that generally characterize the sectarian debate in Egypt, but an attempt must be made.

The Egyptian Constitution proclaimed by President Nasser on 23

March 1964 provides for an exceptionally strong presidential form of government, and affirms that the religion of the State is Islam. To the visitor, Egypt looks like a secular society. The presence of Islam is clear from the constant call of the muezzin from the thousand minarets of Cairo and there are churches everywhere, but the overwhelming perception is that the majority of the population are what may be most conveniently described as secular Copts and Muslims. The instinct of most Egyptians would almost certainly be to affirm the political slogan once adopted by Copts and Muslims alike: "Religion is for God alone and the Homeland for all its people" (*Al-Din l-Allah w-al-Watan l-il-Jami*).

Although eight bishops and twenty-three Coptic priests were amongst those detained by presidential decree No. 493, the majority of those arrested were Muslim activists. In the West the latter might be called Fundamentalists, a problematic term in itself. Sadat had conducted a long campaign against these groups, but he had sown the seeds of distrust in the Christian minority by his earlier ill-judged endorsement of the idea that a larger Islamic identity would be possible in the Egyptian state and society. He enjoyed being known as "the pious president" and sponsored a number of programmes suggesting the *Islamization* of the most secular state in the Arab world. He encouraged some very obtrusive events like the interruption of all radio and television programmes for the call to prayer five times every day. The Copts had no comparable public presence in the media, and no broadcasts consistent with their government estimated numbers in the population. In his discussion before the National Assembly on 14 May 1980, the President affirmed: "Throughout its history, Egypt has never been a country with sectarian discrimination", and of his personal attitude, "I am not a fanatic and am well known for not being a fanatic. If the ruler were a fanatic, reaction might be possible. But I am not a fanatic." Egypt was secular. It had room for the Copts. It was also Islamic, though only up to a point.

Everyone was aggrieved in 1981. The Muslim activists claimed that modern Egypt was unIslamic, living in a pagan plight similar to the "time of ignorance" (*jahilliyah*) in Arabia before Muhammad. It seemed that influential media personalities, like the blind demagogue Sheikh Kishk, had denied the Islamic legitimacy of the modern Egyptian State. Others supported the view of the martyred writer Sayyid Qutb (hanged in 1966) that this *jahilliyah* was a sufficient cause to use force to overthrow the irreligious government. Such revolutionary religious theories were insulting to the Muslim establishment in prominent places of theological learning, like Al-Azhar, which had been reformed and brought under government control in 1961. Theologians of Al-Azhar were amongst those who had been obliged to affirm that President Sadat's visit to Jerusalem and his rapprochement with Israel were consistent with orthodox Islam. The Copts were under siege from Islamic activists. They were not adequately defended by the State. Above the hurly-burly of political debate, representatives of the elite in Official Islam and the Orthodox Hierarchy wished to avoid confrontation. There were many Coptic critics of Shenouda whenever he asked the government for protection for the Copts. These well-placed members of the Coptic community were not unhappy to see the patriarch under house arrest. One well-placed Copt was heard to describe the September crisis as a "blip" in two thousand years of church history.

In the aftermath of the September arrests, powerful elements within the Egyptian State began their long campaign against Pope Shenouda. The semi-official Egyptian newspaper *Mayo* (7 September 1981) claimed that the Pope had "turned into a leader who declared war on the government in order to regain Coptic rights by force." Sadat deemed Shenouda responsible for written attacks and demonstrations against Sadat by émigré Copts during the Egyptian President's visits to the United States. The newspaper listed a number of incidents in which the patriarch seemed to have encouraged communal strife. What the Copts regarded as legitimate defence of Coptic property and lives was regarded by Sadat's journalists as the rising militancy of the Copts in their response to the abhorrent militant Muslims. The government had shown that it too was opposed to Islamic militancy, but Shenouda should be warned that the Coptic riposte was out of all proportion to the Muslim threat. All Egyptians knew that outsiders were only too willing to give the Muslim activists financial and military assistance. P. J. Vatikiotis was later to report that President Sadat was shocked by intelligence reports of the possession of sophisticated small arms by both communities. The Coptic Patriarch had caused deep anger amongst the Presidential party when he had "banned" Easter in 1980. Shenouda had summoned the Holy Synod in March 1980 to discuss the increasing incidence of physical attacks upon Copts. Churches had been burnt. Some Copts had been killed. The Synod decided to cancel all official Easter festivities and ordered the hierarchy to retire to their desert monasteries during Holy Week as an expression of the desperate plight of the Copts in Egypt. The "banning" of Easter attracted international attention and concern. This enraged Sadat. The government press also accused the Pope of making donations to the political opposition. A general criticism was that the Coptic Patriarch supported the establishment of a Coptic State in Upper Egypt: the BBC repeated this accusation more than once in both 1982 and 1983.

Shenouda accepted attacks from outsiders as a routine part of patriarchal life. Hewais a polemicist and natural debater. He had his enemies, but the withdrawal of support by some of the finest spiritual and intellectual guides in his own Church was deeply wounding. *Time* magazine (28 September 1981) reported the comments of Father Matta El Meskeen, the abbot of Egypt's greatest monastery:

> Shenouda's appointment was the beginning of the trouble. The mind replaced inspiration, and planning replaced prayer. I see the Church going from bad to worse because of his behaviour.

Although the patriarch was shocked by this criticism, it was possible to dismiss it as sour grapes. Shenouda and Matta had been rival candidates in the Papal election of 1971. It was certainly true that Abba Shenouda had boosted the communal pride of the Copts, affirming them as separate from and older than the Muslim majority. His duty was to speak up for his people, after endless harassment and persecution. Matta preferred to follow the Government line concerning the September arrests. In the same *Time* interview he said: "I can't say I'm happy, but I am at peace now. Every morning I was expecting news of more bloody collisions. Sadat's actions protect the Church and the Copts. They are from God."

From the moment of Pope Shenouda's arrest and detention it was apparent that questions above and beyond the realm of secular politics would engage the Copts as they attempted to interpret this new phase in their long and tortured history. Sadat realized, before 5 September, that he could not leave a vacuum where a charismatic leader had been. The president was fortunate in finding a small group of bishops who agreed to accept "the Executive Capacity of managing the Church affairs" as a "Papal Committee". Shenouda heard the news that he had been suspended, and that his functions were transferred to a council of five senior bishops, from his chaplain who had caught it on the television. In the same week that *Time* magazine published Fr. Matta's interview, the new Patriarchal Committee reported to the Egyptian media that the Coptic Orthodox Church was "in complete obedience to the regulations of the Egyptian State". For many Copts, it seemed that the State had taken control of the Church. In Coptic tradition, the Pope is chosen as spiritual leader for life. The election process is designed to involve all the faithful and to reflect the practice of the ancient Church. The Egyptian President had no right to replace a leader whose election was viewed as the work of Divine Providence. The President was a Muslim who had no place in the counsels of the Church. The bishops who agreed to work with Sadat knew this as well as anyone.

The five bishops must have recalled the violent incidents in Alexandria and Upper Egypt, which had earlier led the patriarch to refuse to take part in the Easter rites. Fear is a very potent force in a beleaguered minority, and the bishops would remember with horror the murder of a Coptic priest in daylight in Cairo on 6 June 1981. A series of disturbances in the same month left 20 Copts dead and 100 injured in the *Zawiya al Hamra* district of the city. The spark which caused the violence on that occasion was a proposal to build a mosque on church property. In August 1981 a bomb exploded in Shoubra killing over a dozen Copts and injuring nearly fifty other people. The bishops were witnesses to these aspects of resurgent Islamic activism. They perhaps became preoccupied with one question: Is Egypt's Muslim majority intent upon the annihilation of Coptic Christianity through the government, or is it merely a matter of a personal vendetta against Pope Shenouda? They certainly agreed with Sadat and Matta that the Pope was known for his rather aggressive, activist views regarding the promotion and defence of the rights of the Coptic community.

Shenouda read the list of bishops appointed by the government to act in his place. Most names did not surprise him, but he was badly shaken when he saw that Bishop Johannes of Gharbia and Tanta had given his name to the process. Bishop Johannes (d. 1987) was Secretary of the Holy Synod, the body governing the Church in conjunction with the Patriarch. He was widely admired as a man of profound spirituality and deep humility, and the author of a popular work of Spirituality. Johannes was also respected outside Egypt, being a friend and colleague of the notable English Egyptologist, the Reverend Professor Jack Plumley of Selwyn College, Cambridge. Shenouda had consecrated Johannes at the beginning of his patriarchal reign. Before his episcopal ordination the bishop had carried the patriarchal name as a monk. When the two served together in the Monastery of the Syrians the Pope was called Fr. Antonious as-Suriani (1954) and the Bishop was Fr. Shenouda as-Suriani (1955). They were very close. If Johannes was opposing him, Shenouda thought, then the patriarch must seriously re-examine the position, but it was now far too late for such reflection. The battle lines in the Church Struggle were already drawn.

When the Church in Germany confronted the policies of Adolf Hitler, there were people of sincerity and integrity on both sides. History now appears to be on the side of Dietrich Bonhoeffer, who opposed the Nazis and was executed for his part in the plot to kill Hitler. But the much-loved Bishop Marahrens of Hanover, whose own clergy were devoted to him, had at first praised Hitler and later kept silence in the face of Nazi horrors. Marahrens was attacked as a Nazi, which he was not, and eventually forced from office. The universal Church has a record of resistance to tyranny and of martyrdom for that stand, but it has always failed to heal the wounds of internal conflict. The Church in Germany has not completely recovered from the disagreements of the thirties and forties. There is a resonance in the 1981–5 Egyptian Church Struggle.

Anwar Sadat was not a dictator. The checks and balances of the Egyptian Constitution, though not as refined as those in western democracies, do prevent any ultimate presidential *folie de grandeur*. Critics of Sadat were quick to seize upon the information given by Saul Bellow in his 1976 book *To Jerusalem and Back*, where the novelist wrote about Sadat's admiration for Hitler and identified the Egyptian President as the author of a 1953 eulogy of Hitler. In fact, Sadat was merely echoing the views of many Arabs who at that time shared a common enemy in Israel. If Sadat thought that the Coptic Orthodox Church could be easily cowed after some imagined German model, it was because he believed that the Church had no political clout in Egypt. Anwar Sadat did not understand the fact that a central religious principle was at stake in removing the Pope from office. He was relieved when he realized that his action had divided the Copts, though it is extremely doubtful that he had plotted to this end. The Church in Egypt was now split in two just as the German Church had been. Outside Egypt, the Coptic Diaspora and the ecumenical community were similarly broken into opposing factions. Church opposition to Shenouda was formidable.

Alongside Bishop Johannes of Tanta, three of the most respected, mature and experienced Coptic bishops were serving on Sadat's Committee. They were bishops Athanasius, Gregorios and Samuel. The detached fifth bishop was an old schema-monk known for his piety. Only Athansius was a diocesan bishop. He had been consecrated Bishop of Beni Suef by Pope Kyrillos on 9 September 1962. A man of penetrating intelligence with a fine command of English, Athanasius was tough and prepared to stand his ground. He worked in a busy Egyptian province where he had witnessed what he believed to be the ill-effects of Shenouda's political interference. Bishop Athanasius had served on the Central Committee of the World Council of Churches, understood the operations of international ecclesiastical politics, and remained unapologetic for his stand throughout the Church Struggle. On visits to the West he successfully curbed some Coptic dissenters with the threat of an Egyptian Qaddafi or Khomeini.

Bishop Gregorios was born Waheeb Attalla on 13 October 1919 at Aswan. He is a scholar. In the 1940s he obtained a BA at Cairo University, later a BD and a Diploma in Egyptian Archaeology. He moved on to the prestigious Department of Biblical Studies at Manchester, England, where he was awarded a doctorate in 1955. He established an international reputation as a lecturer in Britain and Europe. He studied with the great Orientalist Walter Till and was appointed a lay observer for the Copts at the Second Vatican Council in Rome. Gregorios was ordained a priest in June 1963. For two decades, he pursued a scholarly life at the Institute of Higher Studies in Abassiya. In 1981 he was co-opted onto the Papal Committee to give some academic authority to their presentation and their deliberations. Collectively, the council looked very impressive, but the most important individual representative of the Papal Committee was the Bishop of Social and Ecumenical Services at the Coptic Orthodox Patriarchate in Cairo.

Bishop Samuel was born Sa'ad Aziz on 8 December 1920. He graduated in the Faculty of Law in Cairo University in 1942, obtained a post-graduate Diploma in Theology in 1944 and a BA at the American University in Cairo later in the same year. In 1944, soon after the liberation of Ethiopia from the Italians, he was invited to teach at the School of Theology in Addis Ababa. In 1946 he returned to teach in the Nile Delta but, increasingly aware of a vocation to the monastic life, he became a monk in the Western Desert in March 1948 with the name Makari as-Suriani. Shenouda, Johannes and Athanasius all joined the same monastery. There has been much speculation about the strange chemistry at work amongst these monks of the Wadi El Natroun. It is generally agreed that Fr. Makari was a natural leader. The Church respected his maturity of judgement and he was sent to head the Coptic delegation to the World Council of Churches in 1954. He went on to Princeton University where he received an MA in 1955; his dissertation was on Education. According to his American supervisor, it was only the lack of a Masters degree in Egypt that prevented Princeton from awarding a Ph.D., such was the quality of his work.

In the late 1950s, the saintly Pope Kyrillos appointed Abouna Makari as-Suriani as his Secretary and Chaplain. Those who met Makari were impressed with his seriousness and competence even though they occasionally suspected some signs of patriarchal ambitions. He gave the impression of being a good tactician when dealing with issues of the moment, though it is often said that he lacked deep analysis. His foreign travels helped him to communicate with visitors. Father Makari was well received in East Africa, where he became extremely popular. He had an excellent manner when dealing with the ecumenists who began to pour into Cairo during the era of Kyrillos. Even before his consecration as a bishop with ecumenical responsibilities, Father Makari was in effect the Coptic Orthodox Minister of Foreign Affairs.

In September 1962 Makari, "a small bustling man with a big heart", became Bishop Samuel and embarked upon a course which was to make him the most famous Copt inside and outside Egypt. He was passionately concerned for the poor, and established the *Kanisat al-Zabbalin* so that the garbage collectors (*zabaleen*), who were mostly Copts, could be granted some dignity and their children some opportunities. In conjunction with the projects of his colleague Abouna Bulus Bulus, Samuel established the Diaconate of the *Rif* (countryside) through which he penetrated the distant and isolated villages of Egypt where a Copt was often only a Copt by name. Politicians in Egypt admired his social work and his name was often heard in government circles.

Bishop Samuel became a permanent member of the Central Committee of the World Council of Churches. He was a founding member and vice-president of the All Africa Conference of Churches. In eastern Europe he joined the Continuation Committee of the Christian Peace Conference where he became close to Hungarians of the Reformed Church and hierarchs of the Russian Orthodox Church. Samuel was almost a career diplomat, being well known in all the foreign embassies in Cairo and in the corridors of power in Washington and Moscow. These contacts were to be of immense value when the Church Struggle came to crisis point in 1981. Samuel's contacts in England prevented Shenouda's supporters from gaining access to the BBC World Service from 1981 to 1985, and, with the notable exception of the Catholic international weekly *The Tablet*, Christian publications in the West supported Samuel and his successors against Shenouda.

In the 1960s and early 1970s, Bishop Samuel was increasingly prominent in national affairs and was at the centre of a building programme in Cairo. His efforts for the urban and rural poor attracted wider attention and his institute for the blind received state support. He became the first head of department for the Coptic Social Studies Department in the Coptic Institute.

Bishop Samuel was not too proud to learn from younger churches. He felt that the Coptic Orthodox Church should be seen to be up-to-date. His programmes were progressive. His actions were revolutionary in Coptic Orthodox terms, but he did not believe that his innovations were in any sense incompatible with Tradition. He emphasized, more strongly than any hierarch did in modern times, that lay participation in Church administration and decision making was essential and followed the traditions of the Apostolic Church. He wanted the secular clergy in Egypt to wear plain clothes outside the sanctuary. He had seen this practice as an advantage in Russia and he thought that it would help in Egypt. The Copts had to be at the heart of Egyptian life, but they did not have to flaunt themselves. Shenouda was of the opposite mind. He introduced rigorous dress codes for all clergy, imposing Syrian monastic headdress unknown for centuries.

Samuel was a champion of women. He welcomed their participation in worship, especially as readers. He saw that intercommunion worked, and at ecumenical celebrations of the Liturgy he was delighted to give Holy Communion to Christians who were not Copts. He was a reformer at every level. He regarded a Coptic Ecclesiology denying the reality of Catholic and Protestant Baptism as a shallow blasphemy, though there was a sharp division in the Coptic episcopate between those who recognize other baptisms and those who deny the sacramental integrity of other churches. Bishop Samuel was firmly on the side of those who recognize the baptismal fellowship of all Christians. His views were advanced with skill and with great personal charm.

Although he obtained the maximum number of votes in the patriarchal election of 1971 his name was not drawn from the chalice at the final lottery. He continued to fill his national and international roles under Shenouda. The patriarch's outspokenness and apparently aggressive style dismayed him. Egypt's communal violence increased throughout the first decade of Shenouda's pontificate. Samuel attributed some responsibility for these developments to the Pope's personal style. He was especially alarmed by Shenouda's growing tendency to promote young hot-heads as bishops, while many experienced men on the Episcopal bench, who had a life time of experience to draw on, seemed to be totally ignored. When Sadat proposed that Bishop Samuel should lead the Committee of 5 September 1981 the bishop accepted immediately and said that he was acting "for the Orthodox Church and the Egyptian Nation". The phrase was not wasted on some listeners. Shenouda had been accused of employing the construction "the Coptic Nation". After 5 September, Samuel became the principal representative of the Copts on public occasions in Egypt.

Although the Papal Committee became the official agent of Government policy concerning the Copts, it may be true that President Sadat always preferred to apply to the monastery of St. Macarius for advice. Samuel would hardly have objected, for as a young man he had been a member of the Giza parish educational department with Matta El Meskeen. It might have been natural for the two to exchange views about anything effecting the Church at this difficult time, though there is no concrete evidence of Father Matta's active involvement with the Papal Committee itself.

Mohamed Heikal, one of the most important and best-informed journalists in the Arab World, has been closely associated with presidents and generals; his close friendship with Nasser was continued with Sadat until disagreements over policy in the aftermath of the 1973 War. Heikal was among those who found themselves in prison following Sadat's mass arrests in September 1981, but was released two months later by Mubarak. He has written a major study of the period under review. According to Heikal, Matta represented an acceptable Coptic alternative to the Papal Committee. Matta represented a school of Coptic thought in which religion was essentially a matter for the individual conscience, having nothing to do with party politics. Since Shenouda seemed to teach that the Church was an all-embracing institution they were bound to disagree. Heikal portrays Matta as Sadat's fifth column in the church, "in close touch with the President", with a power base at St. Macarius. Matta had been the recipient of a gift of presidential land for his "huge agricultural enterprise". To the extent that Matta had a political viewpoint it is represented as one in which everything political could be left to President Anwar Sadat, the Father of the Nation.

If Father Matta is the Egyptian *éminence grise* portrayed by Heikal he has disguised the fact with a Machiavellian skill which most politicians would envy. He is idolized by many educated Copts. He has written works of outstanding importance. As far as one can see, he stands above the storm of internal ecclesiastical politics and in the margins of society. He was approached by *Time* magazine for the notorious interview quoted above because he has an international reputation as an ascetic and theologian. Occupying approximately the same ground as Matta in the Church Struggle were a number of bishops appointed by previous patriarchs. Amongst these can be found the towering figure of Metropolitan Mikhail of Assyut, presiding over the Copts in the most populace Christian Province in Egypt. Bishop Mikhail had been a bishop for nearly forty years when the storm of 1981 broke over the Church. He had been ordained a priest, Abouna Mitjas El Makari, in the monastery of St. Macarius in 1939 and consecrated as Bishop of Assyut on 25 August 1946. Assyut is a dangerous place where sectarian violence is a regular feature of life. Amba Mikhail retained a powerful hold on the Coptic community and resisted all the attacks of Islamic activists. He remained distant from the Coptic Pope. In Assyut, Mikhail is his own patriarch. He is also the bishop responsible for his old Monastery of St. Macarius, and so the Episcopal authority for Fr. Matta and his monks. In the Church Struggle, which now ensued, Fr. Matta and Bishop Mikhail represented those vast numbers of Copts who stood firmly on the touchline. In Assyut, Amba Mikhail deals with crisis after crisis. He remains "solid as granite in the face of adversity". He is a patrician but pastorally sensitive.

Support for Shenouda was muted in Egypt. Militant monks were either in prison or in their desert monasteries. In any case, their reputation was such that they could only have done the patriarch more harm. A name frequently heard as a possible force for conciliation within the Church was that of Amba Bimen of Malawi. Unlike some of the Pope's supporters, he was a mature and reflective person. He was recognized as a man of outstanding intellectual gifts whose analytical approach had often worked to the advantage of the Church in his region. He had entered the ministry much later than most of the Coptic clergy. Bishop

Bimen was born Kamal Habib in Cairo in June 1935. He held degrees in Theology and Psychology and gained prominence working amongst young people in Cairo. He was ordained in the Western Desert not long after his thirty-eighth birthday. He was content as Abouna Antonious El Anba Bishoi in the monastery, but was sent abroad to read a Masters degree at Princeton in the USA. Upon his return to Egypt, on 22 June 1975, Father Antonious was consecrated a bishop with the name Bimen. Although a specialist in Education and an individual whose wisdom and tact were badly needed at the centres of Coptic power, he was sent to guide the Diocese of Malawi in Upper Egypt. Bishop Bimen built new churches, ordained many priests and improved the social, educational and moral position of Copts throughout the diocese. His work inevitably came to the attention of the secular authorities and, at the moment when his wise counsel was most urgently needed, in September 1981, he was imprisoned. President Mubarak released Bimen on health grounds in 1982. Although very sick, and obliged to seek medical attention abroad, he continued his ministry of reconciliation, persuading some Copts to support their patriarch whilst telling others to be less voluble. He was quite simply a saint. He died on 19 May 1986. Shenouda's tragedy during the Church Struggle is that he had no cautious and considered Coptic voice to speak on his behalf. The Papal Committee was absolutely authoritative. Coptic militants were shrill. Most Copts had decided to fall in line. The most effective moderate was at first jailed and then sick.

Christian institutions outside Egypt waited. The most influential were disposed to accept any explanation given to them by Bishop Samuel. An exception was the American Coptic Association (ACA). This group of Coptic migrants had been formed in 1974 to monitor human rights abuses in Egypt, and especially to report on the plight of Copts. On 11 April 1980, when Sadat was in the United States of America to discuss the peace process with Israel, the Association placed full-page advertisements in the major American newspapers denouncing "the persecution suffered by Christians in Egypt". The advertisements also described the Egyptian President as a prisoner of Muslim Fundamentalism. Sadat was embarrassed and angry. When he returned home, Sadat attacked the Coptic hierarchy, and especially Shenouda, but worse was to come. In the following summer, Sadat was in the United States again. This time the ACA took an advertisement in the *Washington Post*, published in the form of a open letter to Sadat, which claimed that "Coptic men have been burned alive. The Christian religion has been attacked and ridiculed by the state-controlled media." "Mr. President", the advertisement concluded, "you have often condemned state-sponsored fundamentalism as exemplified by Qadaffi and Khomeini. Why do you not put an end to this same madness in Egypt?"

Sadat was angrier than ever. One week after his return from America the detentions began. For the American Coptic Association it was a confirmation that Egypt was not a democratic state and that its President was a dictator. The migrant Copts had learnt that American expectations with regard to Human Rights are much higher than those in Egypt. Armed with American citizenship and from the relative safety of the United States they had decided to work for the Copts in their own way. After the confinement of the Pope in the Western Desert, the ACA mounted an international campaign, conducted virtually on a day-to-day basis, for his release.

The ACA is a combative organization. Many of its members were born in Egypt and have first-hand experience of religious persecution. Their interpretation of events is quite clear: "the objective of the Egyptian government is to crush the structure of the Coptic church and to apply Islamic principles on Egypt's Christians by making these principles the basis of civic laws which will either enslave them or convert them by force to Islam." Shenouda was also concerned with the legal threat to the Copts. His reactions to Islamic law were known from the time of his enthronement. There are continuous cries from all parts of Muslim society for the introduction in Egypt of the Shari'a (the Law of Islam derived from the Qur'an and the Sunna). Islamic courts have existed in Egypt alongside other communal courts. The Shari'a courts were abolished in 1956 but in general Egyptian civil law has its roots in classical Islamic law, more than it does in any European interpolations. In the 1970s the National Assembly began its re-examination of Muslim demands for the strengthening of constitutional affirmation of Shari'a. The politicians looked first at all the modifications of established Islamic law, which were already in place in Egypt. It was claimed that the Shari'a had been affirmed by a series of statutory enactments which aimed to make Islamic law more congruous with the conditions of modern Egyptian life, but which nevertheless derived directly from the Shari'a. The threat of "more Shari'a" is a constant issue for the Copts. This is especially true in relation to personal and family law, where the Egyptian Constitution had gone some way to attempt to protect Christian marriage, but where Copts remain dissatisfied. Shenouda certainly raised the Shari'a issue throughout the next few years, but the ACA "house style" was to present the worst possible scenario in Egypt and propose it as the norm. Patriarchs negotiate behind closed doors, human rights organizations with tabloid headlines.

The President of the American Coptic Association, Dr Shawky Karas was born on 6 October 1928 in Akhmim, Sohag province. He is a mathematician and graduated from Cairo University in 1949. He gained a fellowship to the United States in 1959 and earned his doctorate at Columbia. Karas stayed in the USA and gained a further advanced degree in Mathematical Statistics from Rutgers. Since 1967, he has been the director of the Research programme in Behavioural Sciences at Connecticut State University. Karas is a faithful Copt who found religious freedom in the United States, which he had never known at home. Every report of harassment, persecution and sectarian violence in Egypt angered and frustrated him. When the Church Struggle came he worked to mobilize the Coptic Diaspora. Dr Karas inspired Coptic organizations to arrange demonstrations in Canberra, Montreal, Washington and New York. In September 1981, Shawky Karas instituted a media war for the Copts at home, but in Egypt itself the situation was about to get much worse.

On Tuesday, 6 October 1981 Anwar Sadat greeted Bishop Samuel and the Muslim Sheikh of Al-Azhar in the reviewing stand at a military parade. They were celebrating the eighth anniversary of the October 1973 war against Israel when the Egyptian army, in a memorable and heroic action, crossed the Suez Canal and broke through the Bar-Lev Line in Sinai. In full view of the television cameras, Islamic activists from the army assassinated the President. Bishop Samuel was killed on the stand. The Sheikh of Al-Azhar escaped. An uprising in Assyut was suppressed with considerable loss of life. At the time of his death, Sadat was only 62 years of age. In Syria there was dancing in the streets and Radio Damascus reported: "The traitor is dead. It is a victory. Our comrades of the Egyptian Army have avenged us." In Libya there were car accidents as enthusiastic drivers waved their hands in the air. In Beirut formidable arsenals sounded "fires of joy". *Time* magazine called these three demonstrations "dancing upon the assassinated corpse of one of the world's last great men". Jackie Kennedy Onassis wrote: "Sadat was one of the most visionary statesmen who has ever lived. His legend will grow through the ages."

Sadat's funeral was a predominantly western affair. When Nasser had died his body was carried through the heart of Cairo in scenes that could never be duplicated in the West: spontaneous and unforgettable cries of lamentation followed the dead man and Egypt was wrapped in immense grief. Now it was quite different. Gerald Butt reported: "There was an eerie calm over the city. No mourning, no celebration. Just a hint of anxiety." Sadat's gun carriage was followed by Prince Charles and Lord Carrington, representing the United Kingdom, with three American presidents: Nixon, Ford and Carter. Schmidt came from Germany and Giscard d'Estaing from France. Menachem Begin, with whom Sadat had negotiated the Camp David Accords, was there for

Israel. The security was tight. Thousands of police stood with their backs to the procession. The people of Egypt were not there. One national leader, Numeri of Sudan, represented the twenty-four members of the Arab League. Claude Cheysson said that Sadat was buried without the Egyptian people and without the army.

There was an ambivalent internal response to the slaying in Egypt, but the international response was tense and offensive. The United States Sixth Fleet sailed in Egyptian waters, the American Airforce provided B52s as a warning to anyone contemplating action against Egypt and the US 82 Airborne Division made parachute drops in the Western Desert. The Soviet Union complained about "gross pressures on a sovereign state", but in fact Hosni Mubarak had been established as president within minutes of Sadat's death, confirmed by a presidential referendum three days after the funeral. He was sworn in on 14 October 1981. President Mubarak was 53, a former Commander of the Egyptian Airforce and hero of the 1973 War, who had held the office of Vice-President since 1975. His straightforward, plain-speaking and practical style of leadership appealed to many Egyptians. He inherited a system where the roles of Chief Executive, Head of State and Leader of a political party are inextricably bound together. It is a dangerous and exposed position. Mubarak is unlike Nasser or Sadat; he is quieter, much more reticent and with little charisma. Publicly, he is a secularist. The majority of fair-minded commentators agree that President Mubarak's period of rule has seen an improvement in the internal and international circumstances of the Egyptian Republic. The function of the Papal Committee and the position of Shenouda could not have been high on his list of priorities in October 1981. In any case, Mubarak, like Sadat, had at least one Coptic Minister to advise him. For the next three years Mubarak was accused of vacillation with the Shenouda case, but the Egyptian President is a master of circumspection.

At the time of the Coptic Christmas (7 January 1982) the BBC Outlook programme interviewed Bishop Athanasius. He said that it was the government's role to decide what to do about the pope, and that "most Copts want peace". In the same programme it was suggested that the patriarch had taken inappropriate political initiatives, and destroyed what was described as "the classical friendship" of Copts with Muslims. It was said that the Coptic Church under Shenouda had sounded like a great giant waking up, trying to compete with Islam and even to manipulate it.

The programme angered the ACA but they were soon to face a much more serious confrontation in the American judicial system. On Monday, 1 March 1982 the Cairo Committee of bishops appointed Fr. Maximos Sadek Ibrahim as parish priest of St. Mark's Coptic Church in

Houston, Texas. They informed Fr. Maximos that they had excommunicated and defrocked Fr. Marcos, the resident parish priest. News of the appointment was followed on 14 March with a letter to Kamal Hassan Ali, the Deputy Prime Minister and Foreign Minister. This explained that three priests – Fr. Antonios Henein, Fr. Ibrahim Aziz and Fr. Marcos of Houston – had led "a movement of rebellion and disobedience, which is harmful to the Copts" and that Henein and Aziz, who were Egyptian citizens, had been suspended. Bishop Gregorios asked the minister to advise the Egyptian Embassy that the priests must be tried in Egypt and "to do what is necessary". This was the first time, in a thoroughly documented exchange, when the Egyptian Church Struggle drew the Pope, the Committee and other parties into open conflict.

We have seen in the previous chapter how the Papal Committee failed to convince the American courts that it had the authority to remove Father Marcos. The most important moment in the trial had been when Pope Shenouda's letter, smuggled out of Egypt, had been accepted by the court. The Pope had affirmed his international control over the Copts and rejected the excommunication of Marcos. The Judge in Houston agreed. Some in the ACA believed that the issue of catholicity, or "universality", was to be important in their argument with the Egyptian government.

Shenouda had spoken to the world through his letter to the Houston court. He had exposed the canonical impotence of the committee and rejected the notion that he could be made redundant by the government. The ACA now drew attention to the concept of the Coptic Church as an international body, transcending barriers, which are national, social, political and racial. G. R. Scharoubim, an ACA writer, pointed out that there is nothing theoretical about the assertion of the essential catholicity of the Egyptian Church. There are Europeans, Americans and Africans who are ordained Coptic deacons and priests. Scharoubim drew a comparison with the Roman Catholic Church: "In Rome we have a Polish Pope with an international See. He has no obligation to the Italian Government except as an individual." Then Scharoubim asked: "What would the world say if the Italian Government imprisoned Pope John Paul II in Monte Cassino?" Boutros Boutros-Ghali and other Coptic intellectuals easily demolished this argument. Egypt has no Vatican State. It is true that there is a minute number of unusual, eccentric foreign clergy in the Church. Shenouda's extraordinary enthusiasm for outlandish aliens is well known, but it is odd that there should be any foreign clergy because the Coptic Law does not permit any foreigner to be Patriarch. Whilst it is true that a theological and spiritual definition of Orthodoxy permits Copts to recognize other national branches of

Oriental Orthodoxy as the true Church of Christ in Ethiopia, Syria, Armenia and India, the Church in Egypt is resolutely and finally Coptic, that is to say Egyptian.

It is certainly true that the Coptic Orthodox Church is most clearly defined by national identity, probably much more than it is theologically determined, but Scharoubim should not be dismissed too lightly. Copts like Bishop Samuel have responded to international ecumenism in the last fifty years. Coptic consciousness of their continental obligations as one of the ancient churches of Africa has weight. At the very least, the Copts have a right to expect some response from the wider church when their chief pastor is placed under arrest.

The World Service of the BBC interviewed Bishop Athanasius again for their Report on Religion programme in September 1982. He was asked if he hoped for the Pope's release and replied that he could not accept the word "release" because the Pope was "not in any way under arrest". Athanasius reminded listeners that the whole Middle East was in a state of unrest. This was no longer a purely Egyptian affair. Speaking of the Copts, the bishop concluded, "We don't like to be a political Church." The Bishop of Beni Suef was speaking for most Copts, for they were afraid.

The World Council of Churches (WCC), the Vatican and Lambeth Palace kept a watching brief on the Egyptian situation. The WCC had good contacts with the Committee. The Vatican acted through its established diplomatic channels, always conscious of the overwhelming needs of the Coptic Catholic community. Vatican approaches were professional and confidential, but persistent. The Vatican was aware that the Copts have a long history of anti-Catholic sentiment. The Anglicans decided early on that no protest would be of help to the Copts. Anglican experts were opposed to the American Coptic Association, and came to believe that Egyptian government statements to the effect that the ACA was financed by Israeli sources were accurate. Archbishop Runcie of Canterbury was convinced that Sadat's murder and Mubarak's rise to power would lead quickly to normalization in the relations between Copts and Government. Early in 1982, Lambeth Palace was conferring with Athanasius of Beni Suef. The Anglicans had long and valued contacts with Matta El Meskeen and appreciated the input of his confidants in the Anglican Establishment.

The Anglicans, Catholics and the WCC always questioned Shenouda's judgement. It was constantly said that he was no judge of men. He had given preferment to unstable characters at home. His friendships, even with those who had been very close to him at the Monastery of the Syrians, were vacillating. Rome constantly questioned his involvement with fringe episcopal sects in Europe. The Anglican bureaucrats were less curious about ecclesiastical oddballs who converted to Coptic Orthodoxy, but both Rome and Canterbury contrasted the older bishops like Amba Mikhail in Assyut or Amba Athanasius in Beni Suef with the combative, political bishops chosen by Shenouda. Rome was especially impressed with the moral and spiritual authority of Bishop Johannes of Tanta who endorsed their assessments of Shenouda's naïvety and misjudgement.

Cardinal Franz König, formerly Archbishop of Vienna and President of the Vatican Secretariat for non-Believers, is by general consent one of the most astute intelligences at the disposal of the Catholic Church. He knows the Middle East well and first met Shenouda over thirty years ago at the meetings of *Pro Oriente*, a theological "think-tank" working for the reunion of Eastern and Western Christians. He was the obvious choice to act for the Vatican as a go-between with the Egyptian Government and one who could reassure Shenouda. His presence would make it clear that Rome cared about the Copts. On Saturday, 23 October 1982 the Cardinal arrived in Egypt on the first stage of what he described as "an ecumenical pilgrimage". The Egyptian press reported Cardinal König's arrival and his reception by "a member of the Papal Committee". It was reported that the archbishop would attend the Coptic Liturgy, visit some museums and travel in Sinai. The paper did not mention his carefully prepared meetings at the Al Azhar University. On 27 October the Muslim newspaper *Al Akhbar* reported that the Cardinal had been to the Foreign Ministry to engage in discussions with the Copt Dr Boutros Boutros-Ghali, at that time the Minister of State for Foreign Affairs. On Thursday, 28 October the State media reported the departure of Franz König for Jerusalem and added that the Vatican Nuncio in Egypt had said that the Cardinal's visit had not had the object of "pleading the cause" of Pope Shenouda.

On 10 November, *Al Ahram* revealed that Cardinal König had been to the Wadi El Natroun during his time in Egypt and had engaged in dialogue with the Coptic Pope. It seems that König had made an application for the entire Pro Oriente delegation to go to the Monastery of St. Bishoi to meet Shenouda. This application had been made six months before the visit. In the event, the government issued only one permit, for the Cardinal himself. When he arrived at the pope's house he was obliged to sit through a meeting between the Pope and two members of the government committee. König and Shenouda then spoke alone for a long time. The concession of König's permit was an attempt to open up relations between the Pope and the Government, through Professor Boutros Boutros-Ghali. The weekly newspaper *Al Ahali* reported that it was obvious "to infer that the government is now studying the probability of Shenouda's return to his guardianship of the Copts in Egypt".

Cardinal König made no public statements about his meeting with Shenouda, but in his private reports the cardinal stated his belief that the Coptic Patriarch could only be released if the internal security situation improved.

Encouraged by the information supplied by the Vatican, Geneva decided to send its own mission to Cairo. The Director of the WCC's Commission on International affairs was in Egypt from 27 December to 31 December 1982. Ninan Koshy, a member of the Church of South India, had served on the International Commission for many years. His authority in this field may be judged from his appointment as a Law Fellow in the Human Rights Programme of the prestigious Harvard Law School, where he was an admired advocate of religious liberty as an inalienable and non-negotiable human right. Shenouda had now been in enforced exile for one year and three months. Koshy was qualified to test the temperature of the Nile.

The WCC intermediary discovered that negotiations between the Copts and the ruling National Democratic Party were underway. There was a possibility of movement. Boutros Boutros-Ghali received Ninan Koshy, but "because of the lack of adequate time" the WCC representative did not meet any supporters of Shenouda in Cairo. Dr Ghali said that the ecclesial and spiritual position of the Pope was untouched by events, and emphasized that the real friction was no longer between the State and the Church but with many highly placed Copts who felt that life in Egypt was quieter without the pronouncements of Shenouda. Mubarak intended to release the Pope, but while Islamic militants were on trial in Egypt it was not the right time. Impartiality was everything.

When they met, Shenouda told Koshy that Mubarak was generally pursuing realistic domestic policies, but that the desire to be even-handed, so that any action taken against Muslim militants had to be balanced by action against Copts, was nonsense since the Copts are not armed and have not engaged in assassinations. Koshy thought that the policy of relating Shenouda's release to the treatment of Islamic activists could leave the patriarch in exile for a matter of weeks, months, a year, two years or even a generation. It was all too vague. Shenouda wished the WCC to know that he would not accept conditions for his release, but that he would negotiate. He was confident that "our people do not accept the papal Committee because it is illegal, against our ecclesiastical tradition and against Canon Law." The Committee was creating confusion in the Church, and probably at the WCC too. This was certainly true.

Shenouda had discussed the possibility of a new advisory committee working with him. He would agree to the appointment of a committee if the composition was acceptable to him, and if its functions were clearly defined. He could not accept any members from the existing Committee. Shenouda was sensitive to the criticism often made against him that he was a demagogue, who loved nothing so much as the sound of his own voice. Many Copts disliked the way in which he pandered to crowds. His public Bible studies often seemed little more than political rallies. Shenouda told Ninan Koshy that when he became Pope he had to make a deliberate choice of his patriarchal style. Either he had to be quiet in the earlier manner of Pope Kyrillos or he could adopt a high public profile, principally through preaching and teaching. Pope Shenouda knew that he should take the latter course and now he had to bear the responsibility for it. He still thought that he had done the right thing.

With the patriarch's international responsibilities in mind, Ninan Koshy was happy to have the chance to hear from Shenouda on a number of external issues. The Coptic Pope expressed his concern about the migration of many Christians from the Middle East to Australia and the West. He lamented the consequent weakening of Christian communities in the lands of the ancient churches of Jerusalem, Antioch and Alexandria. Lebanon was a cause for constant anxiety, and the Copts were close to the Palestinians. Koshy left with a feeling of uncertainty, but he had to be hopeful. He was very impressed by Shenouda's high morale and hopefulness. Koshy went on to meet Athanasius and Boutros-Ghali for a carefully guarded debriefing and a cautious diplomatic assessment of his visit to Egypt. He saved his detailed and critical analysis for the General Secretary of the WCC in Geneva.

As a result of negotiations between the Government and the Pope there was a significant, possibly symbolic, exchange of messages in January 1983. On the 5 January, Shenouda sent a New Year message to Mubarak, expressing confidence in the president's work for national unity. On 7 January (Coptic Christmas) the President reciprocated with seasonal greetings, adding that he had faith in all Egyptians. This was the first time the Head of State had directly addressed the Patriarch since the events of September 1981. Some Copts pointed out that this was a *de facto* recognition of Shenouda as the lawful Pope.

Shenouda applied to the Courts to contest the legality of the committee and his detention. Medically qualified monks from St. Bishoi monastery constantly monitored his health. His personal security remained a primary concern for the Government, for he was believed to be a target for assassination, second only to the President. Incidents of sectarian violence continued. Shenouda was making it clear that he would not accept a Patriarchate controlled from outside his office.

Early in January 1983, Gabriel Habib, General Secretary of the Middle East Council of Churches (MECC), paid a visit to His Holiness at the

Monastery of Anba Bishoi. He reported that negotiations were going to lead to a positive outcome, but that there was no government timetable. When asked if there was anything MECC could do for him, Shenouda replied, "Pray for me at your gatherings".

At the beginning of 1982 the Anglicans had approached the Egyptian Ambassador in London with a request for an ecumenical visit to Shenouda. Permission was given in December 1982, and David Roycroft, a British Foreign Office official, prepared the trip for Bishop Graham Leonard of London. Dr Leonard was an unusual choice for this mission, being known as the leading Anglican proponent of union with Rome and as one who had intellectual and spiritual confidence in the fraternal primacy of the Bishop of Rome. Shenouda has frequently spoken of Anglican priests who convert to Roman Catholicism as those who left "one error to embrace another that is worse". But Archbishop Runcie chose Bishop Leonard, and the Anglican Church made extensive preparations in Cairo receiving careful briefings from the Papal Committee.

Dr Leonard was told that the situation was extremely optimistic. A negotiating committee was close to agreement. The Pope's lawyer, Hanna Nairuz, expected that the Pope would make concessions including the acceptance of a new Community Council. The Anglicans were immensely impressed with Bishop Athanasius, but slightly suspicious of Shenouda. Dr Runcie's advisers were also convinced that the enemies of Egypt financed the ACA and that their strident voices were an irritant for the patriarch. Bishop Leonard was less comfortable at the meeting with Dr Samuel Habib the President of the Protestant Church Council in Egypt who was well connected with the Ministry of the Interior. Dr Habib complained that the Pope always acted without consulting the Protestants. Dr Habib accompanied the Bishop of London to the Wadi Natroun. As a Protestant liaison officer with the Government, Habib also represented the Anglicans, a fact that could hardly have pleased Graham Leonard, the leading Anglo-Catholic of the Anglican Communion, who was soon to become a Roman Catholic priest.

Sir Michael Weir, the British Ambassador, entertained Dr Graham Leonard to dinner before the trip into the Western Desert. On Saturday 15 January 1983 bishop and pope had a pleasant meeting in the papal residence adjacent to a desert monastery. Shenouda first stated his opposition to the expansion of Shari'a in civil law. The discussion struck the Anglicans as purely theoretical. They could not envisage stoning in a liberal country like Egypt. Shenouda went on to say that Family Law was the place where the Copts stood most to loose. If a bad Copt wanted to divorce his wife and then marry a Muslim his children by his Coptic wife would become legally Muslims.

Shenouda was critical of Sadat but not of Mubarak, and said that delicate discussions were proceeding. He did not expect the government to apologize, all he desired was to resume his full responsibilities. He had to contest the Constitutional nature of his banning in the Egyptian Courts because there would be other patriarchs after him. He firmly told Bishop Leonard that he could not fulfil his responsibilities to the Church and the Copts whilst in exile. The Anglicans were firm in their denunciation of the ACA, and similar groups in the West working for the Pope's release, and elicited an appeal for concessions and restraint from Shenouda, which they eagerly promised to pass on when they returned home. In later years, Shenouda came to believe that procuring this petition had been the real purpose of the visit. The Anglicans favoured Matta and the Committee and needed ammunition from the Pope to attack the ACA and its friends.

Shenouda rejected the Anglican view that the Egyptian Government needed to be seen to be even-handed. If Christianity cannot flourish unmolested in the face of Islamic fanaticism in Egypt, what hope is there for the rest of the Middle East? Graham Leonard and his travelling companions left Egypt absolutely positive that Shenouda shared their own pacific and discriminating approach to his detention, which was also the conviction of the majority of Copts in England, and entirely in line with the information received through the friends of Abouna Matta El Meskeen. Negotiations were within an inch or two of success. This was two years before the Pope's release.

Pope Shenouda's appeal was adjourned on the 25 January 1983 after a fracas in court when Government lawyers introduced an ACA pamphlet claiming that some Copts had been killed by Muslims. This incident hardened many against the ACA. On 14 April 1983 the High Court ruled that Sadat's decree revoking recognition of Shenouda's election was legal in Egyptian law, but that the appointment of the Council of five bishops was unconstitutional. The legality of Sadat's decree was said to be safe because Shenouda had not adopted the exact procedures at the time of his election in 1971, and was reported to have said that Presidential agreement was only a question of a rubber stamp by an official: "I was appointed by God." With regard to the five bishops, the Court affirmed that the Government only had power to recognize the appointment of an individual duly elected by the agreed processes of Coptic Canon Law. It was clear to many that the Government would like to have a new election for a new Pope. With the assassination of Samuel, the only suitable candidate seemed to be Matta El Meskeen who had retired to a desert retreat near his monastery. The High Court appeared to leave the Church without a legal Administration.

Amnesty International adopted Shenouda as a prisoner of conscience in 1982, but the resolution was treated with contempt in Egypt. In the Arab world Amnesty is generally perceived as naïve and confused. As if to prove the point for its critics, Amnesty adopted the blind Sheikh Dr Abd Al-Rahman, whose primary role as ideologue of militant groups was to follow the teaching of the militant Said Qutb who espoused armed rebellion. He successfully obtained asylum in the USA, but was later found guilty in connection with terrorist activities at the New York Trade Centre. Being listed with the Sheikh did nothing for the Pope's reputation.

By New Year's Day 1984, professional ecumenical interest in Shenouda had virtually died out. Dr Boutros Boutros-Ghali was sound. Shenouda had dabbled in politics and burnt his fingers. It was obvious that the Egyptian Government had a case against him, and only his sacred office, with the threat of Coptic violence, kept him from trial. His self-importance, and his far too vociferous demands for the Coptic minority that were insensitive to the needs of the secular majority, had carried Shenouda-the-politician away. In President Mubarak's own good time, Shenouda might return to his post. If he had learnt his lesson, he would keep quiet.

President Mubarak made a State Visit to the Republic of Kenya on 2–3 February 1984. It was an opportunity for Amba Antonious Marcos, the Egyptian-born Coptic Bishop for African Affairs, to continue the Church Struggle by engaging in vigorous debate with General Mohamed Hafiz of Central Security, Dr Boutros Boutros-Ghali, the Minister of State for Foreign Affairs, and President Mubarak. Hafiz was the first to meet the bishop and, when challenged about the difficulties being experienced by the Copts, explained that "there is contact between the President and the Pope and that is an indirect recognition". At a later Press Conference the bishop disputed directly with President Mubarak. For the first time since the events of 1981, Mubarak addressed the Church issue instantly: "Pope Shenouda is a Spiritual Father of the Church in Egypt. I know very well that nobody can replace him, but if I told you when he will be back in Cairo I would be stupid." The President repeated the argument about the recurrence of sectarian violence: "Do you want me to free the Pope now, and next day for someone to put a bomb in a church or a mosque and turn the country upside down, which would be hell for all of us? Pope Shenouda will be back. Definitely. I cannot tell you when. The Pope understands this very well. He moves around and we turn a blind eye. It needs time, but there is a great understanding between Pope Shenouda and me."

Mubarak turned dramatically to his Coptic Minister Dr Boutros-Ghali and said, "This is Boutros, you ask him, he gives me a constant headache about Pope Shenouda!" In a dispute with a Muslim militant, Mubarak indicated that it was the introduction of the Shari'a in the Sudan which had led the country to civil war: "I am President of a State full of Muslims and Copts and everyone is working for his own community. The situation in Egypt is difficult. Ninety per cent of Egyptian legislation originated from the Shari'a, so what is the difference?"

When the confrontation ended, Boutros-Ghali approached the bishop and said that he hoped that he now felt reassured: "Everything takes time. The problem is nearing an end now. Everything will be back to normal. I can assure you that we have not been silent." The altercation continued for some time, with no ground given by either side. Bishop Antonious Marcos felt that the interchange had been useful to the Church and the Government. The encounter had taken place at a decisive moment when real efforts were obviously being made to resolve the discord.

The Church Struggle did not feature in the Egyptian elections of 1984. There were definite signs of liberalization. Women held 33 out of a total of 448 seats in the People's Assembly. The president later appointed two more women in 1984 so that in total women constituted nearly 9 per cent of the Assembly. The fear of Muslim activism remained the most important reason for keeping Shenouda in the desert retreat. The Government's first consideration was the Economy. In the first nine months of 1984 it was calculated that American Aid amounted to 3 billion US Dollars.

In December 1984 the ACA heard, apparently before most Copts in Egypt, that the Pope had been given the choice of either going to Cairo to celebrate the Coptic Christmas in January 1985, and then returning to the desert, or moving to Alexandria where he would reside, celebrate the Liturgy but not preach or write. Shenouda rejected both suggestions. Negotiations continued. Then Rifaat El Mahgoub, the speaker of the Egyptian parliament, presented the conditions for the Patriarch's release. These included a commitment to avoid political statements, a regular return to the desert residence, with a special condition that the Pope should never be in Cairo on Friday, the Muslim holy day. Patriarchal appearances in Alexandria would be limited. The threat of Shenouda's assassination was given as a primary consideration.

Suddenly, Pope Shenouda was free. His first public appearance was at the Midnight Liturgy for Christmas on 6/7 January 1985. He had been detained for over three years (1,213 days). He described the Liturgy as a "wonderful meeting of Love, arranged for you by our President Hosni Mubarak". After a detailed exposition of Christian Love, the Patriarch spoke of the situation at home and in the world in general terms, but in language which was entirely conciliatory:

Egypt has lived in love throughout her history. We have lived as a nation in friendship and peace for centuries. We hope that love will govern our country and that peace will reign here in this age. We extend this hope: May Love rule the world.

   We pray that fratricidal war will end . . .If one part of the body is in pain the whole suffers. In Egypt, we hope to be of one spirit and one mind for the sake of our beloved homeland. At this Christmas Festival, all Coptic Orthodox Christians open their hearts to all their Muslim brothers and sisters. We Copts know that our Muslim brothers and sister are our flesh, our blood, our bones and in one family with us in this beloved country. We Copts send to all Muslims greetings from the bottom of our hearts, and we ask for all Egyptians a time of comfort, progress and prosperity.

His words were fine, but His Holiness knew that the divisions of Egypt were as strong as ever and that he now presided over a deeply divided Church. There could be no expectation of easy or early reconciliation.

   Perhaps Shenouda has changed as a result of his detention. Maybe he is more moderate. Possibly he has become conciliatory. Little else has changed. Muslim militants are frequently active in Egypt, probably more busy than ever. Ecclesial positions are firmly fixed. Bishop Athanasius carries on his carefully considered pastoral work, unassailable and unrepentant in Beni Suef. Metropolitan Mikhail is the model of Coptic Orthodoxy under attack: faithful and seemingly irreplaceable in the strife torn Province of Assyut. Abouna Matta El Meskeen has a thoroughly secure reputation as spiritual master and Orthodox teacher. Bishop Gregorios pursues the life of a monastic academic, untouched by ecclesiastical politics. All these men have seen patriarchs come and go and, in any case, they have their own priorities. Bimen, Johannes and, of course, Samuel are dead.

   His Holiness Pope Shenouda the Third has clearly learnt some things from the Church Struggle. He is now a jet-setting President of the WCC and travels to its Central Committee meetings and Assemblies in different parts of the world. If another crisis arises in Egypt, the WCC will know this time who the Patriarch is, and their sources of information will be different from last time. He regularly visits Copts who have migrated to Europe, America and Australia. Shenouda has distanced himself from the Catholics and the Anglicans, but encourages the indeterminate dialogue with the much larger Orthodox family of Byzantine tradition. In Egypt he has drawn too often on the enormous personal popularity invested in him in 1971. He is most frequently criticized by Copts. Since 1985, the Patriarchate has certainly given the impression of being preoccupied with purely ecclesiastical matters. Shenouda has placed his imprint decisively on the Coptic Orthodox Church by filling the Holy Synod with educated executives who are more like personal disciples than products of the established monastic system. Many members of the Holy Synod betray a disturbing, emotional attachment to Shenouda the man. Amongst the most fervent of his entourage are those, identified as extremists in the past, who have received considerable advancement. The cult of personality is pervasive. As a consequence of the events of 5 September 1981 there are several communities in the Egyptian Church, and the struggle for its heart and mind will continue for more than one generation.

Fortunately, the conflict continues only amongst those who feel a need to expend their energy in the quest for ascendancy in the institutional church. Mubarak can at least be grateful to Sadat for ensuring that these men would keep out of national politics, after their experiences of restriction or imprisonment. They have lost on the national playing field, but there is a better chance of victory in the narrower boundaries of the Church. They operate as party politicians do in the western democracies. Orthodoxy will still be in Egypt when they have gone. The Copts of the radiant Egyptian countryside, the great river Nile and the sprawling cities, with their golden skin and warmer hearts, are generally optimistic. They are a people of smiles, of sunshine and of sympathy. Their first consideration is survival. Their instinctive religious faith is modest and true, its expression unselfish and tangible. It is a faith at once barely institutional and constantly communal, traditionally growing its upright priests at home, as the sorghum grows at the Nile's edge. In the claustrophobic, swarming Egypt of sixty million souls, it is possible to speak of Muslims and Copts in the same words: Egyptians have a seemingly unshakeable optimism and direct their hopes to a future when things are bound to improve. Another considerable compensation for current hardship is their ardent belief in Divine Providence.

Chapter Eight

Thinking with the Church

The mind that has discovered spiritual wisdom is like a person who has found, in the midst of the sea, a well-equipped boat: when he gets aboard it, it conveys him from the sea of this world and brings him to the isle of the world to come. **Saint Isaac the Syrian, flor. 661**

The philosopher Plato (428–348 BC) purchased land in the Grove of Academe near Athens (*circa*. 386 BC). A place of trees and statues, where Plato's disciples met to talk and to walk, it has been called the first university. The first Muslim university was founded in Cairo over a thousand years later: *Al-Azhar*, the great Islamic centre of learning, dates from AD 972. In the period between these two universities we find, among the Copts, what may reasonably be described as the first Christian University, probably founded by Pantaenus (d. *circa* AD 200), at Alexandria in Egypt. The Catechetical School of the great Mediterranean metropolis is known by its Greek title *The Didaskaleion*, which signifies not only people and property but a body of thought. The school has a key place in the history of Christian thought, and in Coptic studies.

The *Didaskaleion* was perhaps the first place where the Christian Gospel was related to the context of a religious, philosophical and cultural life that was not Jewish. It provides illustrations of the Christian community making the gospel understood and known in and through local beliefs and customs. For that reason it has become a model for later theological enterprise. The curriculum in Alexandria included all the known areas of human learning brought into a relationship with faith in Jesus Christ. The School gave the Church a language that enabled it to speak intelligently and persuasively about the Gospel in the world of Hellenic learning. In Alexandria, Clement – Titus Flavius Clemens (*c.*150–215) – effected reconciliation between the ideas of Greek

Philosophy and the Gospel. He introduced the Coptic world to the value of Plato's metaphysics, Aristotle's logic and the ethics of Zeno's Stoicism. Clement viewed much classical learning with pleasure, but through spectacles provided by the Gospel. He invariably spoke of Christ as the *Logos* (Word), in a development of the fourth gospel that was to influence all his successors as they too tried to clarify Christology. In Alexandria, Athanasius, a native Copt (*c*.296–373), is called the Apostolic (*ar-Rasuli*). He gave assured elucidation of the Doctrine of the Incarnation in which God, the *Logos*, by His Union with manhood, restored to fallen man the image of God and who, by His death and resurrection, overcame evil and death. In Alexandria, Cyril the Copt (d. 444) was a major systematic theologian, teaching the doctrines of the Trinity, and of the Person of Christ with technical precision and skill. He constantly affirmed the divinity of the Logos and consequently spoke always of Mary as *Theotokos*, the God-bearer.

It is not merely prudent for a Coptic theologian today to claim association with these thinkers. If he is to be perceived as Orthodox he must enlist in the Alexandrine ranks. In the late nineteenth century Copts like Mikhail Sarubin (d. 1918) and Qummus Manasseh (d. 1930) created an image of the Coptic Patriarchate in Alexandria, the *Didaskaleion* and Alexandrine Dogmatic Tradition as the most ancient form of Christianity outside Palestine, predating the mutilations of Constantinople and Rome. It was a major contribution to Coptic self-understanding. Coptic historians of the twentieth century have been proud to industriously, though uncritically, affirm this Coptic primacy. Doubtful sources are frequently accepted word for word without discretion. One important expression of this approach is available to English readers in *The Story of the Copts* by Professor Iris Habib El Masri (1918–94). For the beginner this is a charming work, easy to read and emphasising the continuity and doctrinal purity of the Copts, but it is far too self-indulgent and ignores the voids in the Coptic chronicles. Iris was an important figure in the Coptic Revival. The last three Coptic Popes each appointed her as a Coptic delegate to the World Council of Churches General Assembly, the Middle East Council of Churches or the All-Africa Christian Conference. She is justly regarded as an important ambassador of the Copts and especially of Coptic women, who are invariably neglected by the hierarchy. It is also interesting to note, in the same general area, the valued contribution to Coptic self-awareness made by an outsider, Otto Meinardus, a genuine but not uncritical Coptophile. He is the author of many works, including *Christian Egypt, Faith and Life* (Cairo, 1970) *Christian Egypt, Ancient and Modern* (Cairo, 1977), *Monks and Monasteries of the Egyptian Deserts* (Cairo, 1961. 2nd edition 1989) and *Two Thousand Years of Coptic*

Christianity, (American University Press, Cairo 1999). The religious and communal pressures effecting the Coptic scholar have not restrained Meinardus, who is a Protestant, and his writings balance Coptic claims with a wider picture of the universal Church.

Meinardus is not a solitary external source of inspiration for the Copts. The Coptic revival of the twentieth century was deeply indebted to western scholarship. An Orthodox Christian consciousness, devalued for so long in Egypt, was significantly rejuvenated by study of the *Library of the Fathers* begun by E. B. Pusey (1800–82), the leader of the Oxford Movement most influenced by the Greek Fathers and the Christian mystical tradition. The first modern translations into Arabic were from these Anglican sources and not from the Greek or Coptic texts. Texts of the New Testament published in Cairo have relied upon the critical editions of the Coptic New Testament by G. Horner, published by Oxford University Press in the Bohairic dialect (4 volumes, Oxford, 1898–1903) and the Sahidic dialect (7 volumes, Oxford, 1911–24). In the search to reaffirm Orthodoxy, Matta El Meskeen has worked assiduously with English language editions of the Church Fathers and English translations of the Russian Orthodox theologians Vladimir Lossky (1903–58), Sergei Bulgakov (1871–1944) Paul Evdokimov (1901–70) and others. The impact of Russian theology on Coptic thought through the monastery of St. Macarius has been significant and helpful. One important Anglican scholar has been identified by some Copts as a seminal figure in the Coptic recovery of their own tradition. W. H. Temple Gairdner (1873–1928), a gifted priest, musician, playwright and author, has been called the apostle of Arabic Christian scholarship. Whilst working in Cairo he founded the distinguished journal *Orient and Occident*. Temple Gairdner's devotional, exegetical, doctrinal and linguistic output is still highly valued and remains a point of reference in Arabic Christian studies.

Western scholarship has played its part in reintroducing some celebrated Coptic thinkers to Egypt because the entire theological world owes so much to the old Church of Alexandria. Most theologians acknowledge an ancestry in Coptic thought, since one Copt has been characterized as "the father of all orthodoxy and heresy". This theologian, perhaps the greatest of all Copts, was Origen (c.185–254) aptly surnamed *Adamatius*, a man of steel or of diamond. His importance can hardly be exaggerated. In the School of Alexandria, Origen was the father of Biblical exegetes, the master of moral and ascetic theologians and the pioneer in the history of Christian speculative thought. There is no consensus among Copts concerning the place of Origen in their thought. In a private census of one hundred teachers in 1989, a number of Copts, including Pope Shenouda, agreed that Origen was "one of the greatest thinkers of our Church", but the theologically educated will always argue that the Egyptian Church is resistant to all speculative theology. The patriarch has said that there is one Origen, the author of *On Prayer*, whom we ought all to accept and another, the writer of *On First Principles*, who must be rejected. Henry Chadwick has said that Origen desired "with all his heart to be a man of the Church", defending Christian doctrine against Jewish, heretical and pagan adversaries. Certainly. He was a great apologist, but Origen was also a man of audacious conjectures. Areas of his teaching, like that concerning *apocatastasis* – when all creatures, even the devil, will be saved – are deeply disturbing to the Coptic mind. On occasions, even at the end of the twentieth century, Origen is publicly criticized by Copts. This suggests that his dangerous thoughts are influential enough to deserve condemnation. On the other hand, when it comes to safer teachers like Cyril, the Coptic tendency is adulation of an almost hysterical kind. When a western scholar in the 1980s questioned the murder of the Platonist philosopher Hypatia (d. 415) by Coptic Orthodox disciples of St. Cyril, he was actually subjected to physical assault, such is the intimacy of Coptic historical consciousness. Some Copts will claim, with pride, that Coptic thought ended in the fifth century. The rest is commentary. Devotion to the obviously orthodox Coptic fathers is only natural, but neglect of Origen could be a calamitous mistake, for as G. L. Prestige said, "the whole educated world is in his debt for the preservation of the old Hellenic culture, which he transformed by his genius into the beginnings of a *philosophia perennis* for Christendom". The model Coptic mind informed by Origen, but with his thought held in creative tension with the favoured giants of Coptic Patristics, can be enjoyed and does find expression among the Copts. It is rich and profound. It is not found in the mainstream of church life where Patristic Monastic texts are the most valued, and reflective philosophical texts are less commonly accepted.

There is a romantic image of contemporary Coptic Theology as a mirror of the *Didaskaleion*, but a visitor in Egypt looking for a modern seat of Coptic theological learning combining the evangelical and philosophical characteristics of the School of Alexandria will be disappointed. The kind of Theology which seeks to answer the questions of the temporal situation by addressing problems directly in the language and culture of the present, but in the light of the Gospel, is discouraged among the Copts. So is that kind of theology that offers a sustained scientific and critical examination of the Faith in the Swiss–German tradition. Every theological discipline in the Coptic Church is geared to Apologetics. Patristic Studies is directed against perceived errors in other churches. Church History, as we have seen a central component of Coptic Theology, affirms the historical prestige and superiority of the Coptic Church. Biblical Theology owes more to Protestantism than any other aspect of Coptic life, but operates in contrast to Quranic study. In this Theological environment, which requires the exercise of endurance on the part of a scholar who has not had the good fortune to be born a Copt, there is one area of current Coptic thought of enormous appeal, and one that has universal application and relevance. This can be called Ascetic Theology, and in Egypt is often designated Spiritual Theology. Pope Shenouda's two most important theological works are in this sector: "The Life of Solitude in Saint Isaac the Syrian" (Arabic; Cairo, 1963) and his masterpiece "The Release of the Spirit" (Arabic; Cairo, 1957 – there are at least four English translations, each one worse than the last). Matta El Meskeen's "The Communion of Love" (New York, 1984), a highly readable synthesis of mystical and psychological analysis rooted in Scripture, is the finest work of Coptic Spirituality available in English. Matta's greatest work "The Orthodox Life of Prayer" (*Hayat as-Salat al-Orthodoksia*, Monastery of St. Macarius Press, 1952) is arguably the most impressive Coptic publication in Arabic. It has not been translated into English possibly because of its acknowledged debt to the work of an Eastern Orthodox monk in the West. Weighty articles on Orthodox prayer appeared in English in Matta's monthly review from 1988 to 1991.

Historical Theology in modern Egypt usually involves uncomplicated exposition without any critical exegesis. For many Copts it is the preferred method of scholarship. Matta El Meskeen has produced a massive work on St. Athanasius of Alexandria, which faithfully follows all the classical texts, and unusually gives some attention to international scholarship in the field (Arabic: *Al-Qiddis Athanasius ar-Rasuli*, St. Macarius Monastery, 1981, p. 767). A more typically Coptic approach can be found in English in the work of the scholar–priest Matthias Wahba. His way of making St. Athanasius better known to us is by conscientiously pursuing the entire argument of the saint, finally resorting to the simple expedient of reproducing the material in summary form and simpler language. Father Wahba's "Doctrine of Sanctification" (Rhode Island, 1988) certainly illustrates how God calls man to sanctification, divinization or *theosis* and must be invaluable for the reader who only has English, but the logical end of this method is merely to produce a modern dynamic equivalent of the original text. Copts are apprehensive about critical exegesis, but Philotheus Ibrahim (d. 1904) was ready to propose a married Coptic episcopate on the basis of his patristic studies, and Butrus Miftah (d. 1875) was prepared to use his academic research to call into question the excessive fasting of the Copts in his time. Miftah compared contemporary excesses unfavourably with Early Church customs. In current Coptic practice, theological study is generally used to uphold the *status quo*. Matta El Meskeen's major studies of St. John's Gospel again demonstrate his awareness of Western scholarship (*Al-Madkhal el Sharh Injil al-Qiddis Yuhanna & Sharh Injjil al-Qiddis Yuhanna*, St. Macarius Monastery Press, 1990), the introduction and commentary alone running to nearly 900 pages, but Catholic and Anglican scholars are usually put up to be knocked down. Some of the secondary sources, like Bishop B. F. Westcott (1825–1901) are perhaps more than a little passé. The purpose seems to be to show that the Fathers were right after all; a foregone conclusion. Satisfaction from merely writing footnotes to the Fathers may appear droll in the West. In Egypt it is an ideal. The Coptic mind must be subservient to the past not critically engaged with it.

The theological methodology described here has increased in the context of the recent process of *clericalising* theology in the Coptic Church. Contemporary Coptic circulars state that the clergy, especially the bishops, have the right to teach, whilst laymen do not. This is in lamentable defiance of a noble tradition in which great Coptic theologians have been laymen. Critics of the clerical control of Theology notice that Dr Maurad Kamel (1907–75), a linguist and professor of Semitic Studies at Cairo University, Professor Aziz Atiya (1898–1988), Dr Mounir Shoucri (1908–90), Professor Iris Habib El Masri (1919–94) and Dr Yassa Abdel Messih (1898–1959), the Director of the Coptic Museum, were among the guardians of Coptic tradition. Their dates indicate their generation. Freeing the expert laity to elaborate the Coptic experience cannot come easily to a church where an attempt at greater hierarchical control is underway. This is a disappointing and depressing situation for those who do not experience ecclesiastical tradition as a living reality, but find in the Fathers a way towards a future in Faith.

Distinguished lay theologians are shy of criticising the *clericalization* of their discipline, but theological study among the laity is not entirely inhibited and some of it is most impressive. The Cairo Centre of Patristic Studies is retaining the tradition of lay theological study. It is independent of the hierarchy, and was the brainchild of a group of Coptic intellectuals. They were responding to accusations of a *trahison des clercs*, in a system that seemed to be marginalising the laity and reorganising their discipline as a clique. The project started in Cairo in 1982 under its Director Dr Nosshi A. Botros. Students from the Centre have studied in Greece and other Patristic Study centres. The Centre's principal work is the translation of Patristic texts into Arabic, with the encouragement of the study of the Fathers so that there is a basis for comparing the life of the modern church with that of the early church. The Centre has recently established its own quarterly periodical. If such studies continue to highlight the relatively late appearance of concepts like the monarchical episcopate and the institution of ministerial-priesthood the Centre may find it difficult to survive in an environment depending upon Apologetics. Fortunately, hierarchies tend to regard the study of patristic texts as obscurantism.

The Cairo Centre of Patristic Studies is not the only Coptic Orthodox academic foundation controlled by the laity. Dr Hany Takla a layman of the Coptic Diaspora has done dazzling work at the *St. Shenouda the Archimandrite Coptic Society for the promotion of Coptic Studies and Patristics* which he founded in Los Angeles, California in 1979. (St. Shenouda was an Abbot, fiery preacher and exponent of strict Christian ethics in Upper Egypt, d. *circa* 466). In Philadelphia Dr Rodolph Yanney, by profession a doctor of medicine, has produced the esteemed *Coptic Church Review* every quarter for two decades. Rodolph Yanney, a lecturer on several occasions at international Patristic Conferences in Oxford and North America, has been responsible for the first publication of several important Coptic patristic texts in English Translation, on several occasions the work of the Anglican scholar Tim Vivian. When the *Coptic Church Review* was launched in the Spring of 1980, Dr Yanney defined the journal's aim:

> To help the restless souls of the twentieth century along the ancient path of the Church Fathers. In this century, we have the biblical movement, the ecumenical movement, and the charismatic movement. Everybody is moving to nowhere, while what one really needs is a true encounter with God. But how can we find Him, unless we "follow in the track of the flock"?

Rodolph Yanney's devotion to the Church Fathers and his vision in which that Patristic past becomes the enriching experience of the Coptic Orthodox future is an inspiration for many. More. It is perceived as an inspiration of the Holy Spirit. At the turn of the millennium, Coptic publications in the USA also tend to be purely expository. This is their strength. It is also their weakness. Genuine insights from these sources are simply not yet adequately brought to bear on the structures of the contemporary church.

The ecumenical impact of the best modern Coptic Patristic studies should not be underestimated. Scholars cooperating with these remarkable Copts, employing the well-honed tools of modern Patristic Studies, are seriously committed to expressing the very being of the apostolic church. Western Patristic scholars are steadfastly aware of the need to reconnect modern man with his lost roots. Though not much interested in the Orthodox churches as they find them, these scholars frequently affirm that the apparently inexplicable can be explained by reference to established patristic doctrine. Byzantine and Western Christians outside the closed Coptic circle need the finest expositions of Hany Takla, Rodolph Yanney, the Centre of Patristic Studies and their kind. The Coptic mind needs to rediscover the critical intelligence and adventurous speculation of an Origen.

The influence of arcane models of interpretation from Late Antiquity is still so powerful in Coptic Egypt that it is not difficult for certain western visitors to have some sympathy with Sir Richard Burton when he expressed the outlandish opinion that Islam was closer to the original teachings of Jesus than Christianity. Burton was troubled by what he saw as Pauline and Athanasian "transmogrifications". In fact, anyone entering the Coptic world must be prepared to find the real context of Coptic thought, which is not secular pluralism, which besets the western theologian, and is not a sphere, time-locked in fourth-century Alexandria. The context of Coptic theology has been an anti-intellectual autocracy and has become renewed Islam. The Copts have enjoyed seeking out and embellishing their own *pharaohs*, like Saint Cyril, and they have apotheosized their *book*, the Holy Bible uncritically received. This process has its virtue, but it can become a terrible vice where "oldest is best because it is oldest" and where self-criticism is taboo. The Western Christian who seeks to learn from the Copts, and attends to them in the land of Egypt, waits to hear them answer the question so neatly formulated by Professor Hodgson when he asked; "What must the truth be, and have been, if it appeared like that to men who thought and wrote as they did?" In Europe, the biblical or patristic scholar who fails to answer this question fails completely. In the Coptic world the question barely has a place.

Of all the themes of Patristic thought, Christology has absolute priority in Coptic reflection. The Copts have been accused of being heretics by affirming that Christ in the Incarnation had one nature, and that a divine nature, into which his human nature was absorbed. In a pejorative sense this has been called *Monophysism* from monos (one) and physis (nature) and *monophysites* indicates those who admit to the one nature of Christ. In modern times it has become politically incorrect to call the Copts monophysites and, in any case, the term itself has often been redefined in recent years. Those who call themselves "Orthodox" in the 1990s are divided into a majority who accept the Christological definition of the Council of Chalcedon in AD 451 and acknowledge seven ecumenical councils (Orthodox churches of the Greek/Slavonic families) and the Oriental Orthodox minority (Armenian, Copts, Ethiopian, Indian and Syrian) who accept the definitions of only the first three Ecumenical Councils (Nicaea 325, Constantinople 381, Ephesus 431). The original division came about, at least in part, because the Oriental

Orthodox rejected the Chalcedonian Orthodox formula of "one person in two natures".

Pope Shenouda and most Copts, though not all, are anxious for a rapprochement between the two groups of Orthodox. They have used the term "family" for each group: the Copts belong to the Oriental Orthodox family, the Greeks to the Eastern Orthodox family. This attempt at compromise is not welcomed by all because some Chalcedonian Orthodox still regard the Copts as "Monophysite" heretics while some Oriental Orthodox continue to reject any language which implies a separation in the Person of Christ. Bishop Gregorios has written extensively on the subject and, though not obviously antagonistic to dialogue, remains concerned that any talk of two natures "implies duality". Pope Shenouda, whilst constantly accusing the Chalcedonian churches of a tendency to divide Christ, prefers the Coptic position to be defined by the term *miaphysite* rather than *monophysite*. "Mia" means one as a unity, one out of two natures, whilst "mono" implies one only, simply one, a single one. The Copts do not want to say that Christ is God and Man together for this implies separation. He is rather God Incarnate: Godhead and Manhood are united in a complete union: in being and nature. There is neither separation nor division between Godhead and Manhood in Christ. The most debated Christological slogan in Coptic Christology is that of Cyril of Alexandria: "The one nature of God Incarnate". In its Greek form it is patient of more than one interpretation. Cyril's formula is a banner under which the Copts wish to fight. Words which seem opaque to an otherwise theologically literate Western Christian are a matter of life and death for a Copt. There have been Coptic martyrs for some form of the *Monophysite* doctrine. In his devotions, the Copt most often addresses God Incarnate: One Being. One Nature. One Person. The Copts may say that Christ is One Nature out of two natures. Copts may speak of two natures before the union took place. But after the union there is but One Nature: One Nature having the properties of the two natures. If there is, as many believe, only a terminological difference between this and Chalcedon then some union of *Orthodox* may be possible. The Copts will not and should not abandon their terminology, or their interpretation of it. Christology is an area of theological combat, involving nothing less than the question of Coptic self-identity.

The language of Christological discourse is Greek, though some major works of the early Christian period appeared in Coptic. By the tenth century Arabic was becoming the language of theological dialogue in the Coptic Orthodox Church. There are many gifted linguists amongst the Copts and scholars with all the languages of Theology: Hebrew, Greek, Latin, and other languages. But, in general,

Arabic dominates the Coptic scene. This is complicated by a congruity of usage, if not meaning, in Islamic and Christian religious vocabulary. *Allah* – God. *Injil* – Gospel. *Rasul* – Apostle. *Iman* – Faith. *Kitab* – Book. Muslim activists would like to see this vocabulary reserved for Islam. Christians can choke on words. A shared sacred terminology creates tensions. A western scholar once asked Pope Shenouda if *Allah* – the God and Father of Jesus Christ, in the Arabic Bible – and *Allah* – the God of Muhammad, in the Qur'an – were the same *Allah*? Before Shenouda could reply, a bishop cried out with anguished voice: "No. No. The God of Islam is Satan!" The westerner was shocked. Shenouda was angry. He turned on the bishop: "You must not say this, not to an Englishman or to an Egyptian. We have to cooperate with moderate Muslims who are sincere in their belief in Allah. The word Allah remains the same word." It was a diplomatic but equivocal response. As if to carry the argument forward, the bishop continued aggressively in English "I am not a Muslim". Smiles of irony flitted across the face of Shenouda and of the westerner. One simply cannot say this sentence in Arabic, for *Lastu bi-muslimin* would mean that I do not submit to God and that would be blasphemous. It was a moment of disclosure.

Islam is always on the agenda, but it is written in invisible ink. Best to say it is the paper upon which Coptic apologetics must be written. If the Muslims have the infallible, unchangeable *Um al-Kitab*, the Mother of the Book, at *Allah's* side, then the Bible must be equally without error. This is to ignore the nature of a library of 66 books imparted in two or three ancient languages, compared with the great monoglot spiritual ejaculations of Mecca and the legislative spirituality of Medina, enclosed in only 114 memorable, poetic, rhythmical *surahs*. It is enough that infallibility is claimed for the Qur'an. The Copts must *quranise* the Bible.

Coptic Moral Theology also expresses itself in polarity to Islamic ethics. Fasting in Christian Egypt is much greater than that during Ramadan. Copts are sensitive to Muslim criticism of alcoholic drinks and frequently condemn other Christians who drink wine. The Copts are extremely confident of their moral superiority. The startling and widely distributed video of the meeting of the official dialogue between Copts and Anglicans at St. Bishoi monastery on 13 March 1990 is representative of the Coptic insight into its ethical supremacy. Anglican accommodation of women priests, homosexuals, biblical criticism and African polygamy are roundly condemned. In a typical summary the "shame" of homosexuality, God's "warning" of AIDS and "the sin of Sodom" are harshly exposed. Alexandria is not San Francisco and the context of this theology is not a liberal society but renascent Quranic traditionalism. Any notion of Development is heresy.

The modern Coptic Revival owes much to Protestantism and to American Presbyterian study of the Bible. Anglican missionaries of the Church Missionary Society were influential in the education of at least once patriarch, Kyrillos the Fourth (consecrated 1854, ruled for 6 years and 8 months). The canonical text of the Bible published under the authority of Kyrillos the Fifth (consecrated 1874, ruled for 53 years and 9 months) and published in Cairo in 1911, includes only the sixty-six books of the standard Protestant versions. In Cairo in 1992 it was impossible to find an Apocrypha, though the Coptic bishop responsible for literature said that he might be able to obtain one from the Catholics in Lebanon. This is of more than marginal significance. The Apocrypha, with the pre-Christian Book of Enoch (*c*.160 BC) and the later Shepherd of Hermas (*c*.1150 AD), were repeatedly accepted as divinely inspired and spiritually authoritative by Clement of Alexandria. The sister Church in Ethiopia has, for centuries, had a canon of eighty-one books, including the *Didascalia* from the second-century AD.

Arabic Bibles – usually the Protestant version of the nineteenth century, but occasionally a Catholic version – can be found everywhere in Coptic Egypt. Copts speak warmly of the work of the American Arabists Eli Smith (1801–57) and Cornelius Van Dyck (1818–95) in Biblical translation. But judged solely by copies seen on bookshelves in Egyptian Christian homes, the most popular of the twentieth-century recensions of the New Testament appears to be *Today's Arabic Version* (1979). In the Church, rivalry between Copts who believe they are advancing a patristic tradition and those who are Biblical Fundamentalists is never far from the surface of argument. The Copts are all proud of being biblically rooted. Shenouda taught the Old Testament at the Seminary before his elevation to the papal throne. Samuel was a life member of the American Bible Society. It is assumed that a Coptic mind, though effected by many changing influences, is in essentials shaped by Bible study.

The tools for Coptic Biblical studies are of special interest and confirm the Protestant bias in Coptic Theology. It is an extraordinary fact that the standard Bible Commentary used by the Copts is that of Matthew Henry (1662–1714). His many volumes are available in Arabic. Henry was a Puritan of extreme Protestant views. A number of Coptic scholars use concordances and commentaries from other Protestants and even the "Scofield Bible", a work generally biased towards the discovery of possible references to the end-time. Concentration upon the *Parousia*, the Second Coming of the Messiah, has some popularity amongst modern Copts and in 1994 Amba Dioscorus, a general bishop in charge of publications, wrote an eschatological study focused upon the Temple Mount in Jerusalem. A further surprising influence, as much in preaching as in Biblical exegesis, is that of the Baptist preacher Charles Haddon Spurgeon (1834–92) whose multi-volume sermon collection have been admired by the present Coptic patriarch. Scholars who have received part of their education in the West often prefer the solid approach of German scholarship. "Kittel", the massive multi-volume *Theological Dictionary of the New Testament* is not available in Arabic, but visitors have seen several editions in use in Egypt. "Kittel" is a model for some scholars. A well-worn copy of the lexicon is in the library of the monastery of St. Macarius where Germanic rigour is admired. Bishop Gregorios often uses the wordbook method to make his point, pursuing the shades of meaning of a word through the Bible and Patristic literature. In a Church which dislikes speculative thought it is an appropriately cautious method, though privately Gregorios is much more interesting, exhibiting an enthusiasm for abstract thought.

It is almost impossible to find a Coptic theologian who understands that the historical critical method, which is standard practice in other communities, is not necessarily negative, but urgently involves a judgement on the nature and context of the literature concerned. Professor Maurad Kamel, mentioned above as the professor of Semitic Studies at Cairo University, briefly espoused the German documentary theories of the origins of the Pentateuch advanced by K. H. Graf (1815–69) and Julius Wellhausen (1844–1918). Conservative commentators felt that the Graf–Wellhausen hypothesis led towards a general scepticism regarding the historicity of Genesis. Although Kamel was an independent academic and superb Hebraist, the church hierarchy silenced him.

In an Islamic environment, the hierarchy understood the Bible as a Christian Qur'an, an infallible Arabic *Kitab*, offering security in the continual struggle with Muslim thought. Most Egyptian Christians state their preference for the nineteenth-century Van Dyck Arabic Bible on the grounds that any new translation appears to undermine the reliability of the text compared with a changeless, ultimately untranslatable Arabic Qur'an. There have been long periods of silence in Coptic Theology, when the Bible was reserved for devotion, and when the Copts rested quietly upon ethnicity and tradition. Some of these periods have lasted for centuries. In periods of productivity Coptic theologians have been aggressively polemical and biblically conservative. When Arabic had become the language of Theology, Coptic theologians like Al-Wadi ibn Raga (tenth century) were vigorously engaged in polemics against Islam. In the same period Abd al-Masih El-Israeli was engaged in debates with Jewish thinkers. The latter represents a continuing trend because Judaism is, in Arabic consciousness, bound up with the emergence of the State of Israel. The Copts, as the principal Christians of the Arab world, have an immediate problem with the title "Israel". The

Arabic word *Isra'iliyun* refers not only to the Old Testament Jews but also to the people of the Zionist State. An attempt was made to expunge the word from liturgical texts, which proved to be difficult in view of the Jewish provenance of the Gospel. In the years following the disastrous Six-Day War of 1967, Pope Kyrillos, Bishop Samuel and Pope Shenouda have all been ready to make pronouncements against the *Isra'iliyun*. In 1965 the Second Vatican Council promulgated a declaration (*Nostra Aetate*) absolving the Jewish people of deicide and condemning anti-Semitism. Pope Kyrillos condemned the declaration as an imperialist–Zionist plot against the Arab nations and Arab Christians. Bishop Samuel used every occasion to attack the *Isra'iliyun*, and at the Fifth Assembly of the World Council of Churches in Nairobi (1975) led a motion to declare Zionism as racism. Pope Shenouda affirms his anti-Israel policy from time to time; most notably by ordering the excommunication of Copts who go on pilgrimage to Jerusalem while the Zionist State occupies the city. Many Copts have ignored him. It is reported that some 17,000 Copts have been excommunicated. Statements concerning Islam are studiously avoided or cautiously worded. It is politically expedient to attack the *Isra'iliyun*.

Coptic polemics are not limited to attacks upon non-Christians. Despite the sound of his name, the Coptic theologian and patriarch Christodoulos (1047–77) opposed the marriage of Copts to Greek Orthodox, and wrote against aspects of Byzantine Theology at the end of the eleventh century. In the later years of the twelfth Century, Boutros Sawirus al-Gamali launched a similar attack upon Eastern Orthodoxy with a parallel offensive on the heretical practice of Catholics. At the beginning of the thirteenth century one of the greatest Coptic theologians, a priest and physician called Abul El-Khair ibn at-Taiyib, was still engaged in the controversy with Islam and Judaism. El-Khair eschews philosophical discussion. His argument is entirely biblical, internal and circular: the internal witness of Scripture testifies to its truth. Islamic inroads into the Coptic Church were effective during the Ayyubid Dynasty (1169–1252) when El-Khair was working, and though a priest he was also a civil servant. At that time it was possible for Christian teachers to engage in vigorous disputes with Islam. Much later in the nineteenth century it seems that Roman Catholic proselytising was a major problem for the Copts: Ephraim Adad (d. 1897) and Philotheos Ibrahim (d. 1904) were both vitriolic in their condemnation of the unbiblical doctrines of the Immaculate Conception and Purgatory. For centuries, assaults upon Byzantine Orthodoxy, Judaism, Islam and Roman Catholicism were the stock-in-trade of the average Coptic religious teacher.

In the late twentieth century, when the Egyptian State is itself threatened by renascent Islam, it has become dangerous to write polemics against Muslim teaching. It is no longer politically correct to attack the Vatican, Orthodox Greece or Holy Russia. As we have seen, the *Isra'iliyun* are fair game, but today's debates are focused upon Scripture. The style of argument, turning round and round forever upon biblical texts, is immensely popular. Other weaker but vaguer objects for denunciation have been found, where implicit criticism of old rivals can be covered by explicit criticism of today's opponents. Coptic devotion to the Bible remains strong, and knowledge of the Arabic text is admirable. Shenouda has an encyclopaedic knowledge of the Bible, and has produced an enormous number of books. He often starts his work with a discussion of those many things shared with other Christians. Then he turns his guns upon them. His work is almost entirely polemical. The writer of the early spiritual masterpieces on Isaac the Syrian or spiritual freedom has been obliged to turn his mind to debating points in the service of Coptic Apologetics.

The patriarch's writings of the last three decades are an invaluable indication of the confrontational situation in Egypt. "Salvation: the Orthodox Concept" (New Jersey, 1977) explains how justification through faith also involves works and the sacraments. A deeper theological discussion of habitual, actual and prevenient Grace is notably absent from a work which is apparently designed to attack Coptic Evangelical teaching. "Return to God" (Cairo, 1989) is a popular analysis of Sin and Reconciliation, directed towards nominal Copts. "The Nature of Christ " (Ontario, 1988) is straight apologetics, claiming the superiority of Oriental Orthodoxy. "Comparative Theology" (Cairo, 1988) is a rugged assault upon Protestant Theology without the virtue of understanding it. Modern Coptic thought fails to distinguish between the distinct positions of John Calvin (1509–64) and Martin Luther (1483–1546). Instead Shenouda hammers home the point that teaching "was never the work of the laity". It is always important to look for the sub-text in Coptic Theology. Here, the patriarch employs most of his two hundred pages of text to engage in a sustained attack on Protestantism, but his real targets are those Copts who disagree with him. This volume is important for the Coptologist because it is a sure indicator of patriarchal insecurities in the face of internal debate. "The Divinity of Christ" (Melbourne, 1980) consists of over one hundred pages of polemic against the Jehovah's Witnesses. In the introduction Shenouda explains that the Witnesses have occupied his mind since the 1950s. This may be so. In Egypt the Copts are more likely recipients of *Watchtower* attention than Muslims, but the Witnesses provide Shenouda with an opportunity to attack the notion that Jesus is a created being. The reader is likely to draw the rather obvious conclusion that the argument is directed as much against Islam as the *Watchtower*, but with the virtue of appearing to shoot at the offstage target. The work itself is a largely circular discussion of biblical texts where one is used to prove another. In all the works produced since he became patriarch, Pope Shenouda is following a tradition in which the *odium theologicum* is normal. Coptic history and thought clearly show that there are no wars so sanguinary as religious wars, no persecutions so relentless as pious persecutions and no hatred so bitter as theological hatred. The Copts give us good as they get, and there can be a sharp, ugly edge to the Coptic mind.

Organized religious education has been a fundamental feature of the Coptic Revival. Kyrillos the Fourth (Patriarch from 1854 to 1861) was the forerunner of modern expansion, buying an Austrian printing press for religious publications, conducting a weekly seminar for clergy and founding high schools in Cairo. His work was modestly pursued by his student Father Philotheos Ibrahim who became the mentor of Habib Guirgis (1876–1951), the founder of the Sunday School Movement. Guirgis published a monthly periodical *Al-Karmah* (The Vine) and devised a curriculum for Christian education in the day schools, but his chief work was the establishment of the church-based Sunday Schools in 1900, with classes for every grade, youth meetings, teachers meetings and prayer groups. Biblical Studies and Church History were taught in four principal schools in Cairo and eventually in most Coptic churches. Although Abba Kyrillos the Sixth was not a product of this system, he recognized its value and in 1962 appointed the future Pope Shenouda to run the scheme. Shenouda, Athanasius, Johannes and Gregorios were all members of the Shoubra Sunday School in Cairo. Samuel and Matta El Meskeen belonged to the Sunday School at Giza, near Cairo University. It is sometimes suggested that the former were rooted in Biblical studies, with a Protestant orientation, whilst the latter were of Patristic orientation with emphasis on the Social Gospel. This is an over-simplification, but it is true that a consequence of the contrasting emphases at Shoubra and Giza has been the continuation of some antag- onism. The later progress of these educated and academically disciplined men into the monasteries confirms the general influence of the Sunday Schools. The German scholar Pfarrer Dr Wolfram Reiss of the Johannes Gemeinde in Frankfurt has presented the definitive study of the movement.

Because of the Sunday School Movement, the Coptic Orthodox Church has a theologically literate laity which would be the envy of many churches, though the focus of this system is extremely narrow. A direct offshoot of the movement has been the production of an enor- mous range of secondary-level religious publications in which the

Copts may be regarded as specialists. Shenouda is the leading exponent in this field, while Matta is the authority at tertiary level. But one Alexandrine priest working in the same area has gained a reputation outside Egypt. He is Father Tadros Yacoub Malaty (b. 1939). His many books have appeared in English editions in Australia, Canada, Egypt and the United States and include the following four important titles *Christology of the Non-Chalcedonian Churches* (Sporting, Alexandria, 1986), *The Coptic Church as a church of Erudition and Theology* (Ottawa, 1986), *Introduction to the Coptic Orthodox Church* (Ottawa, 1987), and *The Icons* (Alexandria 1970).

Malaty's work is especially useful for those who have no Arabic. Most of his books appear in parallel English–Arabic texts. They are arguably the best representatives of a prevalent Coptic approach. They clearly highlight the accomplishments and deficiencies of recent Coptic Theology. The following survey, touching briefly upon a wide range of topics, is offered in the conviction that Tadros Malaty has earned a place in any examination of modern Coptic theological reflection as one who wished to reach out from what had been an intellectual ghetto into the wider world.

A primary defect in this literature is the adoption of western terms, which have no real place in Coptic tradition. For example, Father Tadros repeatedly uses the term "transubstantiation" when he does not mean it. The Copts teach that the bread and wine of the Eucharist is mystically, though really, changed into the body and blood of Christ. A Copt gains nothing by the use of the term "transubstantiation", which was once serviceable in a philosophical treatise on the Eucharist where it was desirable to probe the conversion of the substance of bread and wine into the substance of the body and blood of Christ. The term does not appear in the Coptic Fathers. Bluntly. The Coptic Orthodox Church begins with plain bread and wine and it ends with the true Body and precious Blood of "Emmanuel Our God". Copts have Arabic and Coptic key terms, but there is no proper equivalent to "transubstantiation" in a Greek Patristic or Coptic Lexicon. Coptic Theology does not work when it employs Latin philosophical terms.

In dealing with western religious thought, writers like Malaty are at their weakest. Fr. Tadros has reviewed Black Theology, Christian Feminism, Liberation Theology, Marxism and Existentialism. The obvious lack of sympathy subverts any possible understanding, but even in the briefest survey we learn to empathize with Coptic isolation. Malaty says that the Coptic Church "has not intruded in politics". It may be prudent to say so but it is not true. He condemns Marxism. He may be right, but he should not expect us to believe that those who use Marxism in the Theology of Liberation have "lost their spiritual power".

The Latin American church has provided a new gloss on Theology. In a world where most people are poor and hungry, and too many are oppressed, it is unlikely that any church can afford to hide behind the *status quo* whether in Egypt or elsewhere. It might be thought that any theology offering more than liberation from sin and the hope of a distant heaven is especially relevant to oppressed Copts in Upper Egypt.

Tadros Malaty says that he was "astonished" in ecumenical exchange "to note that the black theologian of Africa had no idea of Coptic culture and concepts", and he elsewhere criticizes Black Theology because it creates "an exaggerated tendency against every order". He is unjust. The Church must offer itself as the means through which the human community is made to stand under the judgement of the values of the Gospel of Jesus. The Church is the witness *par excellence* to freedom, justice, peace, charity, compassion and reconciliation.

Philosophical Theology has not been a major part of Coptic thought for centuries. It is not surprising that Malaty misses the point in his blanket condemnation of Existentialism. Such a significant philosophical movement, emphasising the existence of the individual human being as a free agent who determines and interprets his or her own life, cannot be dismissed lightly simply because it seems to be so "remote from Alexandrine Christianity". Existentialism may not help us to express Church dogma, but it has played an invaluable part in western life, through its appeal for decision and commitment and its exhalation of authentic existence and genuineness. The western reader will find more philosophical theology in the novels of the Nobel Prize winning Cairene Naguib Mahfouz than in Tadros Malaty.

In his 1987 *Introduction* Fr. Tadros deals with the ordination of women and presents an admirable ideal of priesthood as a sacrifice of love and fatherhood. He says that priesthood is not an exercise of power and authority. In other writers we might suggest a degree of disingenuousness. Priesthood as it is commonly exercised among the Copts is authoritarian. We must agree with Fr. Tadros when he says, "ordination is not an administrative position for attaining honour but for suffering daily death", but such spirituality cuts no ice with women who are victims of male control and coercion. Tadros Malaty emphasizes Orthodox avowals about the role of women who are married to priests. He points out, quite correctly, that these women take the feminine forms of their husband's title: *khouria, presbytera* or *matushka*, in various Orthodox traditions. To be the wife of a priest may be a vocation as Fr. Tadros says, but that assertion does not advance the debate.

We are not surprised to find that Tadros Malaty is at his best when he is reporting Coptic tradition. He has been an official representative of the Copts in dialogues with other churches, and his evaluation of the

Byzantine–Oriental Orthodox dialogue in his essay on Christology is probably his most important work. The dialogue has affirmed the agreement of the representatives of both families concerning Christological dogma. They know who Christ is. Both affirm the perfect divinity and humanity of Christ. Both bodies recognize the difficulties involved in terminology. Malaty has confessed the Coptic position: faith in the one divine–human nature, will and energy of the One Christ. This affirmation is based upon the classical formula of Cyril: *Mia physis tou Theou Logou sesarkomene*. This he renders as "one Nature of God the *Logos* Incarnate" or as "One incarnate nature of God the *Logos*". This formula defends the church against any Christology that seems to divide the natures of Christ. Father Malaty is always saying that Jesus Christ is at once God and man, consubstantial with God the Father and consubstantial with us men. He is saying much more than that. He is not content with reaffirmation for its own sake. He wishes to find the new formula, which will express the Orthodox faith in an accurate, authentic and conciliatory way. Out of the most conservative, traditionalist background he is able to conceive a suitable term for a new time; perhaps something like "the one united nature of Christ". Like many Orthodox, Malaty impresses as he retains the continuity between faith theologically expressed in dogma and the worship of the Church. Thus he quotes with approval the liturgical expression of the Christology of the Copts:

> I believe and confess unto my last breath that this is the Life-giving Body which your Only-begotten Son, our Lord, God and Saviour Jesus Christ took of our Lady and Queen of us all, the Theotokos, the pure Saint Mary, and made it one with His divinity without mingling, nor confusion, nor alternation. His divinity never departed from His humanity even for a single instant nor the twinkling of an eye.

Christological debate has not diminished with the passing of the centuries. Divisions are still bitter in some quarters. Malaty is a representative Copt to the extent that he affirms the Tradition whilst tentatively reaching out for expressions which can survive the third millennium. Tadros Malaty is an occasionally hostile but finally hopeful theologian because he is attentive to other Christian ways of being beyond Egypt. That is rare in a Copt, but must be highly valued.

Coptic theological opinion came to public notice in the West at the 1988 Lambeth Conference. This gathering of the bishops of the Anglican Communion takes place once every ten years. The question of the ordination of women to the episcopate was recognized as the most important issue before the Conference. For some bishops it was too late to discuss the ordination of women priests. Women priests were normative in the USA and other provinces of the 70 million strong Communion.

Pope Shenouda sent an episcopal representative to the Conference with a written message entitled "The Viewpoint of the Coptic Orthodox Church regarding the Ordination of Women". It stated clearly some Orthodox objections to the ordination of women. Many familiar arguments were rehearsed. The bishops "must go back to the Scriptures". The "secondary source of reference is "Church Tradition" which knows nothing of female ordinations". The social conditions of the Apostolic age did not effect Christian teaching. Women did not participate in the ecumenical councils. Pauline teaching about *headship* must be taken seriously. The Blessed Virgin Mary made no claim to priesthood. The Copts regard the ordination of women as a novelty.

Shenouda's message also alludes to the effect of female episcopal and priestly ordinations upon issues of Fundamental Theology. This in turn effects liturgy and spirituality. The question of female ordination is often presented as a human rights issue. The real questions are obscured. The alleged inferiority of women is not the issue here. Such an allegation is unchristian and perhaps even unreal. If women are exercising their rights to freedom in secular society that is right. Women have no inferior status in the Church. If ecclesiastical power structures ever assert power over service they become unchristian. This all sounds fine. Not all Copts feel that ecclesiastical power is exercised in a humble and holy manner. In Egypt it is always possible to find a sufficient number of thoughtful Coptic women who believe that the ministerial structure of the Orthodox Church is not merely repressive but misogynist. These women were mature, well-educated graduates and some are technically "religious". Men do assert power over service.

According to the Coptic address to the Lambeth Conference, the most important question raised by female ordinations is "What will happen to God?" Shenouda believes that the doctrine of God is at stake. We are accustomed to seeing "the overzealous rushing towards innovations and tendencies, in which the female pronoun is to be introduced when referring to the deity whilst the term Heavenly Father is suppressed". The Patriarch concludes that this "will seriously endanger the doctrines of the Church. The doctrine of the Holy Trinity cannot remain unaffected; the relationship within the Godhead will become different if the gender used from apostolic times is changed."

Sacred Scripture has presented us with God's preferred way of speaking of Himself. Experience shows that this can only be unfavourably compared with a novel use of the female gender. Behind the movement for the ordination of women there appears to be the intention to revert to polytheistic modes of speech concerning a female deity, and this is seen in inclusivist versions of Scripture and Liturgy. The testimony of Holy Scripture requires a most rigorous re-examination in this debate. To take only one example: when St. John represents Jesus as calling upon God as his Father, the Evangelist is not importing "something alien into the mind and message of Jesus; he is bringing out something which was absolutely basic to it". Feminist Theology that seeks to supplant this image cannot pass unchallenged if a truly Biblical faith is to survive.

Father Matta El Meskeen has also seen the issue of changing Biblical language as vitally important in the debate:

> Issuing a Bible in which there is no reference to any masculine gender mainly to please the female sex is an antecedent to a general revolt. This would not be a revolt against the male sex or against the Holy Bible or the priesthood only; it would be a revolt against Divinity.

The Copts see the emasculation of Scripture as a constituent in the programme of the feminist reconstruction of the Christian religion, which asks also for women priests.

As far as the Copts are concerned, if the movement for the ordination of women in the West acts whilst knowing that doctrinal changes are necessary consequences of these ordinations, then it will automatically become an heretical movement. Language about the Fatherhood of God may be an analogy or a metaphor but it is not the language of mere analogy or bare metaphor. It is the analogy and metaphor preferred by God in Scripture. To change this language involves a loss of meaning. The holy icons are venerated, not worshipped, images. Their imagery is at once concrete and transparent. Icons are images. The mind too has its images. To disturb the image of Our Father disturbs faith. When the focus of prayer is changed so is the spiritual life of the believer. To destroy the icons of the mind is to destroy faith. This is an important argument. The Copts have not been answered.

Some Anglicans welcomed the Coptic intervention at Lambeth in 1988. Certainly, two traditions were laid open in their stark uncomprehending difference. Shenouda's representative, Metropolitan Bishoi of Damietta, was thrown into a group that included the radical American bishop Jack Spong and the Liberal Catholic Richard Harries of Oxford. Spong and the Copt were like two creatures from two distinct worlds meeting on an alien planet, but Harries could see that Christian honesty was at work in both bishops. Jack Spong is a man of integrity attempting to find a faithful way of redefining Christianity. He is ready to discard any traditions that stand in the way of the future. He sees faithlessness towards the future as the ultimate unbelief. The future is with women, with the oppressed and powerless, and with the homosexuals. Spong lives in an intensely moral world, but it is very far from the world of the Wadi Natroun whose representative was attempting to be scrupulous in his obedience to recent Coptic teaching: it is important to put it like that and not to pretend that he was rooted and grounded in the Fathers. He was thoroughly trained in the biblical models of the Coptic Revival. To the moderate bishops it was clear that Bishop Spong and Metropolitan Bishoi were both men of principle, but there was no relationship, only the dialogue of the deaf.

There is no doubt that the Western Churches will continue to move forward in their attempts to create an environment where there is a mutuality and reciprocity between the Church and Culture. The latter is likely to always have the same weight as the former in this dialectic. It is a very hard road to tread, but it is the only way open to Western Christians in societies where forms of materialism and hedonism dominate. There is a great gulf between Egypt and the West. The Copts are proud of their faithfulness to an ancient tradition, "We teach Christianity as it has always been taught" is the proud boast of many in Egypt, though there is some trepidation that they will be ill-prepared to respond to the clamouring questions of secular man when these arise in the future, as they are certain to do. Theology, like Technology, operates at many levels and develops at different speeds.

Since 1964 the Copts, with the other Oriental Orthodox from Syria, Ethiopia, Armenia and India, have been developing closer contacts with the great churches of Eastern Orthodoxy. After one of the most recent meetings, at St. Bishoi Monastery in 1989, the communiqué read: "We now pray and trust in God to restore communion on the basis of the apostolic faith of the undivided Church which we confess in our common creed." It is obvious that the appearance and historical experience of the Copts make them the most likely candidates for dialogue with the Chalcedonian Orthodox. Yet many aspects of Eastern Orthodoxy are entirely alien to Oriental Orthodoxy. The *apophatic* theology of the churches of the seven ecumenical councils, which is quite fundamental in Eastern Orthodoxy, certainly appears to have very few echoes among the Copts. Against an apophatic tradition which states that our concepts of God cannot properly be affirmed of Him, and where there is an assertion concerning the inadequacy of human understanding, the Coptic inclination is towards a *cataphatic*, affirmative and symbolic theology. It may be that the Protestant inroads into Coptic Orthodoxy in the nineteenth century were much greater than previously believed. If the terms Patristic Christian and Orthodox Christian are synonymous, and there is certainly an intellectual movement in Christian Orthodoxy today affirming this, then we may say that the Coptic Orthodox position is better described as a traditional Biblical

Christianity in the shadow of Islam. Their closest theological allies are certain Conservative Evangelicals in the USA. Many Copts recognize this. Some Copts long for Patristic models. The Coptic hierarchy has developed plans and programmes to express the debatable conviction that Christian Egypt is as Orthodox as Greece, perhaps, for those who think in an exclusive way, even more Orthodox than Greece.

For some Copts the programmes of the hierarchy and the monasteries remain a mystery. Throughout the twentieth century some of the finest Coptic minds were bent towards a redefinition of Coptic–Egyptian existence in which the Coptic tradition would be in fruitful discourse with the changing intellectual currents of the times. Salama Musa (1887–1958) represents a Coptic response to secularism. Although baptized and raised a Copt, Musa knew little enough about Coptic Theology to confuse the term *Monophysite* with *vegetarianism*, in a disconcerting but hilarious exchange with the British playwright George Bernard Shaw. GBS, on hearing that Musa came from Christian Egypt, inquired, "Are you a Monophysite?" To which the Copt replied, "No. We eat meat in Egypt." It would be good to imagine that Musa was a proto-Monty Python. He was serious.

Musa's political philosophy was more sharply defined. He believed that western civilization was the highest stage of man's spiritual and material development and that evolutionary science was an essential interpretative tool in the definition of a sociological image of the Copts freed from theological tradition. Politics, sociology and economics were to remain important for him all his life, but he also experienced a need for self-definition which only the Egyptian Church could meet: "I returned to the Coptic Orthodox Church with affection, finding in her our tormented and broken history." He was in some respects a precursor of Martin Bernal and the prophets of Black Athena, acknowledging Europe's debt to Egypt's wisdom. For Salama Musa, the perfect marriage would be that between Egyptian language and French literature. He could be fanciful: "I found the voice of the Pharaohs sounding loudly from the Coptic Orthodox pulpits". He dreamed of a de-classicized Arabic literature, which would provide a linguistic tool for a radically Europeanized "Egyptianism". He projected images of a socially active Coptic Orthodox Church and a politically liberated community. He expected a reformation of liturgy and tradition. The dreams of Salâma Musa point to a Coptic road not taken.

At the beginning of the twenty-first century, the type of Coptic mind represented by Salma Musa and his kind remains as insubstantial as a phantom, but irresistibly attractive.

On Saturday, 2 April 1994 the Easter edition of the American magazine *Newsweek* was on sale in Alexandria. More. At one of the city's largest Coptic churches young people were exchanging photocopies of a seven-page feature on *The Death of Jesus* by Kenneth L. Woodward. The piece surveyed opinions on the historicity of the New Testament ranging from those of the Catholic exegete Fr. Raymond Brown to those of Dominic Crossan and the Jesus Seminar. Brown and Crossan, in very different ways, are masters at deconstructing, decodifying and demythologising the Bible. In the West, it is possible to wonder how many people might read the article. Among the young Copts of Alexandria it was having a dramatic effect. A young Coptic man who said that he was reading Medicine at the city's university explained to bemused Anglicans from England: "Reading journalism like this is our only way of finding out what is happening on the frontiers of Christian thought. Most of our bishops are thought police. They are not interested in the questions, but have all the answers. Unlived answers, learnt in the Sunday School. For most Copts everything is literally true or not true at all. We are not answering the questions of today."

The exaggeration is pardonable, and the complaint should not be dismissed out of hand. Christians are universally anxious as a great civilization is breaking down everywhere. A response that involves a retreat from contemporary culture will be a mistake. Culture is something of too great a worth to be deprived of its value and meaning. The theologian in New York, Paris or Alexandria needs to know the culture. It is the environment where the Theology is done. The theologian also needs to know the ancient culture where the churches first spoke if he is to remain authentically Christian. The theologian has a privilege and responsibility to study today's problems, ideas and language – what words mean now – to communicate to the people of the present as the *Didaskaleion* once did long ago. The Coptic mind, as open to tomorrow as to yesterday, could inform the ecumenical discourse of the new millennium so that polarity is swallowed up by reciprocity.

Chapter Nine

Conclusion: Era of the Martyrs

The world cannot be served from a place of power, but it can be served from the cross. On the cross the world stabs its own heart, but the cross is a school and to run away from it is to run away from the future. Father Bishoi Kamel Ishak of Alexandria (1931–79)

The Copts have their own calendar. The Coptic year begins on 11 September and has 12 months of 30 days with a short month of five days at the end of the year – six days in a leap year. AD 284 was the year of the accession of the Roman Emperor Diocletian. Coptic time is reckoned from this "Era of the Martyrs" and its Calendar dates from August 29, AD 284. In Diocletian's Great Persecution (AD 303–305) many thousands of Egypt's churches were demolished, books were burnt and the land was baptized with Coptic blood. Eusebius (*c*.260–340), the father of church history, seems to have been an eyewitness of some Coptic martyrdoms. Though it has been observed that he avoids "a morbid avalanche of blood and gore in his narrative", Eusebius does speak of so many Copts being decapitated that the axe was dulled by executions and finally broken. The executioners were so exhausted that they had to take turns for several hours. The North African Church Father Tertullian commented: "If the martyrs of the whole world were put on one arm of the balance and the martyrs of Egypt on the other, the balance would tilt in favour of the Egyptians."

Three saints from the Diocletian period stand out in current Coptic devotion: Saint Demyana, Saint Mina and Saint George. Although demoted in western hagiography since the 1960s, St. George (Anba Guirguis) is a popular saint among the Copts. George was a Roman legionary who defied Diocletian's command to sacrifice to the emperor.

According to Coptic martyrology, George was sentenced to death and beheaded by his own legionaries in Asia. His body is said to have been brought to Egypt by the Coptic Patriarch Gabriel the Second (Pope from 1130 to 1144). On his annual feast day, the body of Saint George is taken from the shrine at the oasis of Al-Bahnassa and carried in procession round the town. A new veil is placed over the reliquary. The old veil is cut into pieces and sold as sacred relics, which may be placed upon the body of the sick in the ministry of healing. Devotion to the saints through their relics, or through material that has been in contact with the relics, has continued among the Copts throughout the ages. There are at least eighteen reliquaries of Saint George. They can be found in Cairo, Beni Suef and the Nile Delta.

St. Mina (Abu Mina) was an Egyptian officer in the Roman army at the time of Diocletian. He made a public profession of Christian faith at a time when it was proscribed. He was tortured but did not recant, and received the martyr's crown in Asia Minor. His body was returned to Egypt. The site of his shrine, in the Western Desert, near Lake Mareotis, is one of the most popular pilgrim sites in Egypt today. Mina was the patron of Pope Kyrillos the Sixth (d. 1971). Abba Shenouda transferred the bodily remains of Abba Kyrillos to the Mariout desert in 1972. They now lie in the crypt of the Basilica of Saint Mina. In the minds of many, including some Muslims, it is one of the most sacred spots on Earth.

The Shrine of Saint Demyana stands in the western part of the old church in the Monastery that bears her name (Deir Sitt Dimyana). It is near Bilqas in the Nile Delta, though many relics of the saint can also be found in Cairene churches. Icons of Demyana are widely used in popular devotion. Demyana was the only child of a Christian governor called Marcus. As a young woman she refused an arranged marriage and affirmed the virtue of virginity. Marcus built her a residence where she served Christ with the forty virgin daughters of other Christian noblemen who joined her. When Diocletian summoned all the Egyptian nobility and required them to burn incense to the imperial gods Demyana's father at first agreed. Marcus returned home and his daughter is reported to have told him that he would either confess his Christian faith again or she would refuse to be called his daughter. Marcus confronted the emperor. The Coptic nobleman was executed. Diocletian sent his imperial statue to Demyana and her companions instructing them to worship him. They refused and were killed. The icons of St. Demyana usually show her surrounded by the forty virgins. They are a constant reminder of Coptic faithfulness in the face of persecution.

The Coptic patriarch Peter the First was the last to lose his life in the Diocletian persecution and is known as *the seal of the martyrs* (d. 311).

From these events the Coptic calendar acquires the designation AM – *anno martyrii* – in the year of the martyrs. It is a designation for all times. The Copts live in the era of the martyrs. In the 1990s, in the forecourt of the patriarchal residence in Cairo, tattooists were doing good business, puncturing tattoos on the inside of the right wrist of their clients. For some it is a protective device, referring back to a Pharaonic practice, but for many it is the badge of a suffering tribe. From the reign of Diocletian to the modern world a Copt carries the martyr's cross.

The Copts have faced terror from other Christians. Byzantine imperialists, who accepted the definitions of the Council of Chalcedon (AD 451), regarded the Copts as schismatic. The *Melkites* (King's men: Christians of the empire and emperor) visited the Copts with humiliation, torture and death. The Arab Conquest of Egypt in the seventh century allowed the Copts to stand aside and watch the Byzantine enemy destroyed. If the Copts did not welcome the Arab invasion, they certainly had no reason to defend their Christian oppressors. The long centuries of Muslim rule began, in which the Copts were preoccupied with survival and very often with martyrdom.

Islamic dynasties came and went: while the Umayyads (661–750) controlled a single Caliphate from Central Asia to Spain, the Copts worked in the granary of the Empire; when the Abbasids of the ninth century ruled from Baghdad, the Copts suffered discrimination and destruction in equal measure; in ensuing centuries the Egyptian Christians hung on through the varying benevolent despotisms or vicious tyrannies of Tulunids (868–905), Ikhshidids (935–969) and Fatimids. Great Terror came in the time of the Fatimids (969–1170). The rule of Al-Hakim (996–1021) is a living memory for Copts. His bloodthirsty torture and killings of Egypt's Christians is thoroughly documented. Even those historians, including some Copts, who have tried to put the kindest pro-Islamic gloss on the martyrdom of the Copts, agree that this was a period of great horror. The Fatimid period ended with the rise of the Kurd *Salah al-Din Al-Ayyubi,* known in the West as Saladin. He built the great Citadel on the Mokkatam hills in Cairo, using two Coptic Christian architects, Abu Mansur and Abu Mashkur. The Ayyubid dynasty of Salah al-Din governed Egypt from 1170 to 1250. For centuries the Copts were to look back upon this as a relatively happy period. The Mamluks (1250–1517) were the next to rule Egypt, until the arrival of the Ottomans. Mamluk rule was decadent but from a Christian viewpoint varied from fierce oppression to accommodation, in the latter periods employing Coptic talent in government. Selim the Grim conquered Egypt and Syria for the Ottomans in 1517 while Sulayman the Magnificent extended the empire in Europe in 1526, but the Ottomans were absentee rulers leaving Egypt victim to local place-seekers. Fear was never far from the Coptic door. Muhammad Ali Pasha (*c.*1769–1849), the Albanian adventurer usually regarded as the founder of modern Egypt, was responsible for the taxation and persecution of the Copts. At the same time he had a policy dictating that the most qualified persons available should fill government posts. This led him to employ Copts in positions of responsibility. The number of Copts in the wealthy, educated class was out of all proportion to their overall numbers in Egypt, but Muhammad Ali still applied the hated Fatimid restrictions on Coptic movement and dress. Every year there were Coptic Orthodox converts to Islam. Discrimination does not always lead to martyrdom.

At the Arab Invasion, the Copts had become part of the *dhimmi* system. They were not faced with the brute choice of conversion to Islam or the sword. The *dhimmi* are protected, some would say *subjected*, peoples of monotheistic belief with a holy book. The system aimed at the protection and safeguarding of conquest by dispossession and colonization. In return for "protection" the *dhimmi* paid two forms of tax, the *kharaj*, a land tax at times amounting to a form of serfdom and the *jizya*, a poll tax that excluded the *dhimmi* classes from fighting for Islam. *Dhimmi* are unequal before the law. This may be experienced at a trivial but constantly irritating level. Ghazi al-Wasiti (fl. 1292) records an incident where a court did not accept a Christian's oath and there are many instances of Copts being required to wear "a differentiating garb" (Ibn Naqqash, d. 1362, is merely an example). The "persecution" was the niggling daily reduction of the Copts to the status of second-class citizens, and the real pressure was, and is, to convert to Islam. The Coptic Church was often in a state of acute decline, but the Copts were burgeoning. They were simply "passing to another nation", the House of Islam. The number of conversions has been enormous. Even in modern times, the American Edward Wakin estimated that 5,000 Copts per annum were converting to Islam, though in the sixties Bishop Samuel told a German researcher that 75 per cent of those accepting Islam eventually returned to the Church. In the 1990s it is not difficult to find Copts who have converted to Islam, but it is much easier to find those who are "nominally Copt" but prefer to be thought of as secular. To call an Egyptian an "atheist" can be harmful to them in their own community, whether they are secular–Muslim or secular–Copt.

If persecution has varied over the centuries, ranging from murder to minor forms of social exclusion, the modern phenomenon of attacks upon the Copts by Muslim extremists has been especially detestable. The Government of Egypt, in its struggle to be even handed, has failed the Copts. It is a desperate and complicated situation. Narrative confronts what analysis weakens. In following the experience of one "ordinary" martyr we may touch the lives of many. It is believed that an average of one hundred Copts per annum have been martyred in the last decade.

Raafat Fakher Khalil was born in the Province of Assyut on 9 August 1956. His parents were devout Copts and trained the boy in the Orthodox tradition. Whilst still young, Raafat was ordained into the minor order of Reader, and became an assistant in the sanctuary. He was noted for his singing in the Divine Liturgy of St. Basil the Great, which he knew off by heart before he was a teenager. He was a bouncy, obliging little boy.

The Copts work hard for the education of their children and it was a source of great pride when Raafat obtained good grades in high school. Pupils with these grades would usually attempt advancement in the secular field; there are many doctors of medicine in the average Coptic congregation. Raafat was more concerned with his incipient vocation to the priesthood: he had already decided to go to the Seminary at Al-Muharraq. He was attracted by the general and theological courses given there, and by the practice of incorporating seminarians in the liturgical life of the monastery.

About thirty miles from the village of Awlad-Elias, where Raafat's family lived, the great Monastery of Al-Muharraq was virtually a Coptic town on the edge of the desert, though within the fertile river valley of the Nile. In 1905 a Coptic Theological Seminary had been founded there. The buildings in the outer courtyard of the monastery were not completed until 1937, but by 1980, when Raafat joined the theology course, there were one hundred seminarians. The Diploma in Theology extends over a period of five years. It is a mixture of subjects with similarities to a general Humanities course in some western universities. Everyone was required to study Arabic, Coptic and English. Biblical and Systematic Theology were important aspects of the course. Raafat continued his ministry as a Reader in the monastic choir. Teachers, students and visitors commonly spoke of Raafat as a man of inner beauty, one of the pure in heart. At this time Raafat decided not to be a monk, with the prospect of becoming a bishop, but to be a parish priest. The parish clergy are married. He was soon to find a devout Coptic girl as his life-partner. Her name was Amgaad.

On 25 May 1980 Abouna Angelos El Amba Bishoi was consecrated as Bishop Andreos of Abu Tieg. He established a good relationship with the monastery–seminary. Amba Andreos got to know Raaaat and involved him in parish visits and in-service training. When Raafat graduated, Bishop Andreos sent him to work in the villages. He served in Sidfa, El-Berba, El-Nekheila and finally at Duena. Coptic tradition came to the fore when the people of Duena asked the bishop if Raafat could be their priest for life. Raafat was ordained on Sunday 15 March 1986 to serve in Duena in the church of St. John the Baptist. He was given the name Rueiss.

Saint Rueiss (d. 1404) became the patron of Father Rueiss of Duena. The great saint of the fifteenth century is one of the most remarkable figures of Coptic history. He is a sign of durability and continuity in a time of persecution. He wandered the length and breadth of Egypt, dressed in rags, barefoot and regarded as a "fool for Christ". He was famous for his teaching, sanctity, and miracles as much as for his eccentricity. Saint Rueiss lived through a period when churches were continually destroyed or turned into mosques. Christians were abducted in the streets and tortured to death if they refused to convert to Islam. Even on his deathbed, attempts were made to convert Rueiss, but he remained faithful unto death. Living conscientiously and heroically throughout a terrible period of Coptic history he became a symbol for the persecuted Church. Father Rueiss of Duena thought it providential that he had received this name.

When the "twentieth-century" Rueiss began his priestly ministry in Duena, the Coptic Liturgy could only be celebrated once a week on Sunday. This is a relatively common restriction on parishes in rural Egypt. Local mosques were permitted to broadcast the *adhan*, the call to prayer, five times each day and, as every visitor knows, this summons is more than adequately amplified. The inequality extends to many areas of Egyptian life. Friday, not Sunday, is the weekly day off in Egypt. Friday is the holy day of Islam. The Coptic Patriarch is not allowed to be in Cairo on Friday. Many Christians, not least school children, must take Friday off and work on Sunday. Fr. Rueiss was concerned for those who could not attend the Sunday Liturgy and he started an additional celebration on Friday. There was also a *Sunday School-of-Friday* to follow. It was the first time that Duena had a theologically educated priest and they wanted to hear him teach. The day ended with an *Agape* feast, a copy of monastic practice. The church building was also opened for lessons in Scripture and Doctrine during the week, then there were choir practices and the inevitable meetings of Coptic mothers.

Abouna Rueiss was a good pastor. He visited the twelve surrounding villages, which had no churches, and he established numerous social projects. The people were poor and there was much unemployment. He created some forms of "cottage industry" with sewing that he took to the villages on his visits. Village priests in Egypt have small salaries, which are usually supplemented by gifts from the richer members of the community. Rueiss now had a wife and a child, but he refused to live on more than his salary. He attempted, as much as possible, to live the simplicity of St. Rueiss. He was "too good for this world", and his wife relates how he prayed for his people with tears in his eyes, a side of him that his parishioners did not often see. A photograph taken at this time suggests a man of transparent kindness and self-respect.

Life in Duena and the surrounding villages changed as a result of the ministry of Fr. Rueiss. In two short years he lifted the morale of the Copts. They no longer felt that they were second-class citizens. They had an educated leader who exalted their ancient culture. Young people were flocking to study sessions. Nominal Copts were now reappearing in church. Prayer groups and social action groups proliferated throughout the parish. A building which had once opened only for a Sunday Liturgy was now open every day. Crowds of people attended every meeting.

In Assyut and throughout Upper Egypt members of *al-Gemaat el-Islamiya* (the Islamic Group) were active at this time. In the 1980s a major attempt to destabilize society had failed after the assassination of Sadat. Mubarak pursued moderate policies for seven years but *al-Gemaat el-Islamiya* had not given up their dream of an Egyptian Islamic Republic, perhaps similar to Iran. In Duena *al-Gemaat el-Islamiya* could not tolerate the Coptic Revival. In October 1988 a member of *al-Gemaat el-Islamiya* approached the priest and told him that he would have to return to the days when the church was used for a few hours on one day a week. Abouna Rueiss refused. Before retiring that night, he told his wife that his days might be numbered.

Thursday, 24 November 1988 was the feast day of the much-loved Coptic martyr Abu Mina of the Mariout Desert. Rueiss rose early and went immediately to pray in the church. The Divine Liturgy was celebrated, with a good crowd, despite it being a working day. The day passed in prayer and praise. There were some confessions and some pastoral counselling. Towards the end of the day, the priest offered the evening incense in the church. It had been a good day. Father Rueiss of Duena stepped out into the street, where local members of *al-Gemaat el-Islamiya* shot him dead in the front of the church. He was 32 years of age. His daughter Nardeen was approaching her first birthday. His wife Amgaad said, "I lost a father, a husband, a brother and a dear friend".

Rueiss was a martyr. One among many. In a church which thinks in centuries there is constant reference back to martyrdom under Diocletian, Al-Hakim and others, but according to statistics from the Centre for Egyptian Human Rights there have been 561 incidents of violence against the Copts since 1994. These following are simply representative: On 11 March 1994 two monks and three laymen were shot dead in the gateway to Al-Muhharraq monastery. *Al-Gemaat el-Islamiya* killed two Christians on 31 July 1996 for refusing to pay protection money. In February 1996 eight Christians were killed in a gun attack on the church at Ezbat al-Akbat. Twelve Copts were killed when *al-Gemaat el-Islamiya* stormed a church in Abu Quorqas on 12 February 1997. Later in the year, on Saturday, 6 and Sunday 7 September, forty Copts were killed in Minya province, some faces deliberately disfigured with the backs of spades. Five more were murdered on 17 November 1997: killed in Minya by having their throats cut.

There is great anxiety among the Copts. Their past has often been evil. Their present is unstable. Their future is unpredictable. No government in the history of Egypt has set out with a programme of Coptic genocide, had they done so they could surely have succeeded. The Copts are accepted as an element in Egyptian society, but the studied impartiality of the present regime is deeply disturbing. The more secular the government the safer the Copts, but the Islamic character of Egyptian society means that the secular Muslims themselves are not safe. One of the greatest difficulties in analysis and prognosis arises from the fact that all investigation is censored, sometimes self-censored out of fear for the Copts. We have come to such a pass that even the most secular Muslims deny the difference between popular western Islamophobia and honest criticism.

The Egyptian Government offers insufficient protection to Copts who are regularly exposed to attacks from Muslim extremists. Apostasy from Islam has dangerous consequences. The State Security organizations restrain Christian activity in keeping with Islamic law but in defiance of normal Human Rights. There is no freedom of choice, and there is compulsion in Religion. The Government hinders the repair and construction of Christian property. Copts experience general discrimination in education and employment. The pressure on the Copts is daily, unrelenting and pervasive. All this is so thoroughly and reliably documented and authenticated that no denial of it can stand. Ironically, the Copts must hope that this untrustworthy, unresponsive system of administration will remain. The alternative is too terrible to contemplate.

The future of the Coptic Orthodox Church is as uncertain as the future of everything, but Coptic culture is so vital, life-affirming and yea-saying that it is always being richly lived. The deepest Coptic being of Abouna Matta El-Meskeen, Isaac Fanous and Abba Justus al-Antouni is mystical, spiritual and inward – the essential Christian gnosis of the Church of Alexandria, which transcends the boundaries of Egypt. The Coptic vocation is still best conveyed by aphorism, on this occasion not from the desert but from a pious city priest, Fr. Bishoi Kamel Ishak (1931–79), who died in the grip of cancer. He left some eloquent words about suffering. They have an obvious personal reference. Coming from a Copt, there is an historical and communal connection. But these words rise above the particular, comprehending the universally Christian:

> Powerlessness has its own speech. Weakness has its own triumph.
> The world cannot be served from a place of power,
> but it can be served from the cross.
> On the cross the world stabs its own heart,
> but the cross is a school and to run away from it
> is to run away from the future.

Appendix

The facsimiles of two letters reproduced for this appendix are the key documents referred to in chapters six and seven. The documents came into the public domain because of the careful work of Human Rights activists and the invaluable public information legislation in the USA. The letters are presented here as a permanent historical record. They had a decisive role in the religious and legal debates of the time, convincing theologians and canon lawyers of the patriarch's authority, and turning the tide of Western public opinion in Pope Shenouda's favour.

The case of the Papal Committee against Fr. Marcos was heard in the 165th Judicial District Court, Houston, State of Texas on 17 May 1982 and 12 July 1982, and the order was signed on 29 July 1982. The Hon. Judge R. L. Smith presiding. The letter of the Papal Committee was presented at the first hearing. The court received the rebuttal from His Holiness Pope Shenouda the Third on 12 July 1982. Judge Smith signed his order in favour of Fr. Marcos and the Pope on 29 July 1982.

A full transcription of the letter reproduced overleaf, signed by Shenouda III, Pope of Alexandria and Patriarch of St. Mark See (sic), and dated 5 June 1982, is given on pp. 88–9.

The second letter, dated 10 March 1982, is the warrant excommunicating Father Mark. Bishop Gregorios signed it. The warrant was stamped by the legal department of the Foreign Ministry in Cairo, and the assistant to the under Secretary of State for Foreign Affairs. It carried the Egyptian State Seal.

This is to declare that Mr. Marcos Askaty(El-Iskity) of St Mark Coptic Orthodox Church, in Houston – Texas is excommunicated and defrocked. He is no longer recognized as priest. He is not permitted to officiate the Mass Liturgy, nor admitted to celebrate any other Coptic Church service, neither the liturgy of Baptism, Chrismation, nor the Liturgy of Matrimony, nor any other Church service whatsoever, not even to deliver any sermon or preaching in the Chuch. In a word he is no more authorised to act as a priest.

Coptic Orthodox Patriarchate
FROM H. H. POPE SHENOUDA III
Deir Anba Ruies, Ramses Avenue, ABBASSIA
CAIRO, EGYPT.
CABLE ELANBARUEISS, CAIRO.

Date | 5, 6, 1982

Father Marcos Al Askeety is one of the monks & priests of the Coptic Orthodox Church. He is the pastor of our church in Houston and the head of its congregation. I ordained him and sent him to U.S.A.

He is working under my direct jurisdiction & hierarchy, as we have not ordained yet a bishop or more for our Coptic churches in U.S.A. and I didn't authorize any bishop to preside our church in Houston or in any other place in America.

As for the deposal or excommunication of priests, the canons of our church states that the priest many not be deposed of or excommunicated or dismissed unless after being tried by a legal ecclesiastical council (court) and found guilty. In such case, he should have chance to defend himself against any accusation. If the priest is found worthy of any penalty, this shall be approved by his bishop.

As the direct and supreme chief of the Coptic Orthodox Churches in America, I state that Father Marcos Al Askeety is still the pastor & priest of our church in Houston and the head of its congregation.

5/6/1982

Shenouda III
Pope of Alexandria & Patriarch of St. Mark See.

COPTIC ORTHODOX PATRIARCHATE
CAIRO U. A. R.

March, 10, 1982

TO WHOM IT MAY CONCERN

This is to declare that Mr. MARCOS ASKATY(EL-ISKITY) of St. Mark Coptic Orthodox Church, in HOUSTON - TEXAS is excommunicated and defrocked. He is no longer recognized as priest. He is not permitted to officiate the Mass Liturgy, nor admitted to celebrate any other Coptic Church service, neither the liturgy of Baptism, Chrismation, nor the Liturgy of Matrimony, nor any other Church service whatsoever, not even to deliver any sermon or preaching in the Church. In a word he is no more authorised to act as a priest.

The Patriarchate

The Papal Committee

+ Gregorios

A Coptic Chronology

Dates of general importance are presented in light type.

Dates of particular significance for the Copts are given in bold type.

*c.*3200 BCE	First dynasty rules in Egypt.
*c.*2580	Great Pyramid of Egypt, still the largest stone building on Earth, built on a site which is now on the edge of modern Cairo.
47 BCE	Julius Caesar captures Alexandria and the Library is burnt.
***c.*150 CE**	**Clement born; teacher and author in Alexandria. Died *c.*215.**
***c.*190**	**Death of Pantaenus, the founder of the Catechetical School in Alexandria ("the first Christian University").**
***c.*251**	**Birth of St. Antony the Great, hermit and "father of Coptic monasticism".**
284–305	**The Diocletian Years. The Coptic Orthodox Church dates its calendar from the Era of the Martyrs (29 August 284).**
***c.*296**	**Birth of St. Athanasius the Apostolic. In 325 he attended the Council of Nicaea as Secretary. 328 consecrated Patriarch of Alexandria. Died 373. Author of the *Life of Antony* and many other works.**
357	**Athanasius writes the *Life of Antony*.**
***c.*375**	**Birth of Cyril of Alexandria. Coptic Patriarch, CE 444. Prolific theologian and "father" of a distinctive Coptic Christology.**
407	**First devastation of the monasteries of the Wadi Natroun by Barbarians.**
431	**Council of Ephesus.**

434	**Second devastation of the monasteries of the Wadi Natroun by Barbarians.**
451	**Council of Chalcedon.**
641	Conclusion of the Arab Invasion of Egypt with the capture of Alexandria, during the Caliphate of Umar ibn Abd al-Khattab (634–644).
909	The Fatimid Dynasty begins its reign in Egypt, which will last until 1171. The Fatimids claim descent from Fatima, daughter of the prophet and wife of the fourth caliph Ali.
996–1021	**Al-Hakim the Third Fatimid Caliph, a period of persecution for the Copts.**
1047–1077	**Patriarchate of Christodoulos, who moved the patriarchal seat from Alexandria to Cairo.**
1169	The Ayyubid Dynasty commences its rule of Egypt under Salah-ad-Din (Saladin). It will reign over the country until 1252.
1250	The Mamluks rule Egypt for two and a half centuries until 1517, having risen from the ranks in the army: Mamluks (literally "those possessed, slaves"). A period of economic prosperity, cultural flowering and superb architecture.
1717	**Fr. Claude Sicard SJ (1677–1726) drew the first scientific map of Egypt (1677–1726). He visited the Coptic monasteries and wrote their names in his maps in Greek, Coptic and Arabic.**
1798	French Occupation of Egypt by Napoleon Bonaparte.
1805–48	Mohammed Ali, Governor of Egypt, a Turkish soldier in the Ottoman army who became governor or *pasha*, and pioneered westernization in the Middle East.
1809–1852	**Patriarchate of Peter the Seventh, who established the Coptic bishopric in the Sudan.**
1822	Publication of Jean-François Champollion's letter to French authorities establising the correct reading of hieroglyphs.
1854–1861	**Patriarchate of Kyrillos the Fourth, "The Reformer". Iconoclastic controversy.**
1869	Opening of the Suez Canal.
1902	**2 August. Azer Yussef Atta (Pope Kyrillos the Sixth) born in Toukh El-Nassarah, Nile Delta.**
1910	**Naguib Shah-hat (Abba Justus al-Antoni) born in Assyut.**
1919	**September. Birth of Yussef Iskander (Fr. Matta El Meskeen).**

1922	26 November. Howard Carter and Lord Carnarvon open the antechamber of Tutankhamen's tomb in the Valley of the Kings.
1923	**3 August. Nazir Gayed (Pope Shenouda the Third) born in Assyut Province.**
1952	Sadat Announces the Free Officers' Revolution on Cairo Radio.
1953	17 April. Nasser appointed Prime Minister.
1956	23 June. Colonel Abd el Nasser elected President. July. Nationalization of the Suez Canal. October–December the Suez War, ending with Egyptian victory.
1959	**19 April. Election by lot of Pope Kyrillos the Sixth as Coptic Patriarch.** **10 May. Pope Kyrillos the Sixth enthroned as the 116th Successor of Saint Mark.** **27 November. Pope Kyrillos lays the foundation stone for a new monastery of St. Mina, close to the site of the ancient Coptic Basilica in the Mariout Desert.**
1964	23 March. Proclamation of Nasserite Egyptian Constitution.
1965	**24 July. President Abd el Nasser lays the foundation stone of a new Coptic Orthodox cathedral in Cairo.**
1967	June: Arab-Israeli Six-Day War.
1968	**2 April. Apparitions of the Blessed Virgin Mary at the Coptic Orthodox Church of St. Mary Zeitoun in Cairo.** **20–24 June. Coptic Orthodox bishops to Rome, collecting relics of St. Mark from Pope Paul VI.** **25 June. President Abd el Nasser, Emperor Haile Selassie and Pope Kyrillos inaugurate the new cathedral in Cairo.** **26 June. Relics of St. Mark placed in the crypt of the new cathedral commemorating the 1,900th Anniversary of the martyrdom of the Evangelist.**
1970	21 July. Completion of the Aswan High Dam project. 28 September. Death of President Nasser.
1971	**9 March (Coptic: 30 Meshir 1687). Death of Pope Kyrilllos VI.** **29 May. The final apparitions of the Blessed Virgin Mary at Zeitoun.** **31 October. Election by lot of Pope Shenouda the Third as Coptic Patriarch.** **14 November. Pope Shenouda the Third enthroned as**

	the 117th Successor of Saint Mark.
1973	October War: Victorious Egyptian crossing of Suez.
1976	**17 December. Death of Abba Justus.**
1977	8 November. President Anwar Sadat makes his historic journey to Jerusalem.
1979	March. Egyptian–Israel Peace Treaty.
1979	**UNESCO declares the St. Mina-Mariout site one of the world's districts of "universal value".**
1981	**5 September. Pope Shenouda placed under house arrest.**
1981	6 October. Assassination of President Sadat at the Military Parade commemorating the 8th Anniversary of the October 1973 War.
	Bishop Samuel was killed with the president.
1985	**January 5/6 Pope Shenouda was released in time to celebrate the Coptic Christmas Liturgy in Cairo.**
1986	**Abba Justus' uncorrupted body moved from a grave into sanctuary in St. Antony's monastery.**
1991	**The Seventh Assembly of the World Council of Churches, Canberra Australia. Pope Shenouda is elected a President of the Council.**
1996	**14 November. Silver Jubilee of Pope Shenouda's enthronement in the throne of Saint Mark.**
1999	26 September President Mubarak re-elected for a fourth term, making him the longest serving head of state since Mohammed Ali, the founder of modern Egypt, who ruled from 1805 to 1848.

Further Reading

Books

Two Thousand Years of Coptic Christianity by Otto F.A. Meinardus

Dr. Meinardus lived in Egypt for many years as the Professor of Philosophy at the American University in Cairo and as Pastor of the Maadi Community Church. This book, in English, can be recommended. It is a revision and summary of his major studies *Christian Egypt, Ancient and Modern* (American University in Cairo Press, 1965) and *Christian Egypt, Faith and Life* (AUCP 1970). This neat one-volume digest is packed with information. Meinardus avoids criticism and his analysis is always cautious but, though he occasionally reads like an encyclopaedia, he has mastered and presented masses of material unavailable elsewhere in the English-speaking world.

Monks and Monasteries of the Egyptian Desert by Otto F.A. Meinardus (AUCP 1989) and his *The Holy Family in Egypt* (AUCP 1986) are both fascinating works and are widely acclaimed.

These books can be obtained through http://aucpress.com or by surface mail at The American University in Cairo Press, 113 Sharia Kasr el Aini, Cairo, Arab Republic of Egypt.

Journals

The most important English-language publication in the Coptic Orthodox Church is the *Saint Mark Monthly Review*, published by the Monastery of St. Macarius the Great, Wadi El Natrun under the direction of Fr. Matta el Meskeen. Ten issues a year can be sent by AirMail for US$20.00 from St. Mark, PO Box 31, Shoubra, Cairo, Egypt. The prestigious *Coptic Church Review* (Subscription and business address: PO Box 714, East Brunswick, New Jersey 08816, USA) can be visited on their Internet Home page: http://home.ptd.net/~yanney/. The *Review* presents a wide range of material, with articles on Orthodox Spirituality, Patristics, History and contemporary issues. *St. Shenouda Coptic Newsletter* is a useful quarterly of Coptic Studies, mostly linguistics, and can be obtained from

St. Shenoudah the Archimandrite Centre for Coptic Studies, 1494 S. Robertson Blvd., Ste. 204, Los Angeles, CA, USA or at:

http://www.stshenouda.com/coptlang.htm. The Society also issues an outstanding CD for the study of Bohairic Coptic, the liturgical language of the Church.

Internet

The scholarly site of the International Association for Coptic Studies can be visited at http://rmcisadu.let.uniroma1.it/~iacs. The admirable Newsletter of the Association, in several European languages, is at: orlandi@rmcisadu.let.uniroma1.it/

The Catholic Encyclopaedia at: www.newadvent.org/cathen/ has several accomplished articles on Coptic Literature. For the widest imaginable range of photographs, icons and music there are several colourful sites through http://www.coptic.net/Menu.html. Authentic Coptic music can be heard at mailto:mike@salib.com. The Religious News Service of the Arab World offers superb reportage on contemporary Egypt with frequent attention to the Coptic Orthodox Church. Contact by e-mail: jourcoop@intouch.com.

Bibliography

Chapter 2 *Copt and Coptic*

Aziz S. Atiya, *A History of Eastern Christianity*, London: Methuen, 1968.

——, ed. *The Coptic Encyclopaedia*, 8 vols. New York: Macmillan, 1991.

——, *"Kibt"* in *Encyclopaedia of Islam*, 6 vols., Leiden: Brill, 1960.

Bishop Athanasius, *The Copts through the Ages*, Cairo: Ministry of Information, 1974.

Winifred S. Blackman, *The Fellahin of Upper Egypt*, London: George G. Harrap, 1927.

Henri Boulad, *All is Grace*, London: SCM, 1991.

B. L. Carter, *The Copts in Egyptian Politics, 1918–1952*, London: Croom Helm, 1986.

Judy Chicago, *The Dinner Party*, New York: Viking Penguin, 1996.

Maria Dzielska, *Hypatia of Alexandria*, Cambridge, MA: Harvard University Press, 1995.

Nelly van-Doorn-Harder and Kari Vogt (eds.) *Between Desert and City: the Coptic Orthodox Church Today*. Oslo: Novus forlag, 1997.

Adrian Fortescue, *The Lesser Eastern Churches*, London: Catholic Truth Society, 1913.

Boutros Boutros Ghali, *Egypt's Road to Jerusalem*, New York: Random House, 1997.

Theodore Hall Patrick, *Traditional Egyptian Christianity: A History of the Coptic Orthodox Church*, North Carolina: Fisher Park Press, 1996.

Fouad N. Ibrahim, *Social and Economic Geographical Analysis of the Egyptian Copts*, Geo Journal, vol. 6.1, Wiesbaden, 1982.

Jill Kamil, *Coptic Egypt*, Cairo: American University Press, 1987.

Thomas O. Lambdin, *Introduction to Sahidic Coptic*, Macon: Mercer University Press, 1982.

S. H. Leeder, *Modern Sons of the Pharaohs*, London: Hodder & Stoughton, 1918.

L. S. B. MacCoull: various papers, including in *Akten d. XVI Internationale Byzantinistenkkongress*, Vienna, 1982. *The Fate of Coptic*, Bulletin of SAC, Cairo, 1985, International Congress of Classical Studies, August 1984, *Coptic Orthodoxy Today*, Coptic Church Review 4, 1983, *The Strange Death of Coptic Culture*, Coptic Church Review 10, 1989.

Otto F. A. Meinardus, *Christian Egypt, Ancient and Modern*, Cairo: American University Press, 1977.

——, *Two Thousand Years of Coptic Christianity*, Cairo: American University Press, 1999.

Andrew Palmer, ed. *The Oriental Churches: A Brief Introduction*, London: School of Oriental and African Studies, 1995.

G. Scattolin, *G. Anawati*, Encounter 203, Rome : PISAI, 1995.

Chapter 3   *In the State of Angels*

Alain and Evelyne Chevillat, *Moines du Desert* d'Egypte, Lyon, 1990.

Derwas Chitty, *The Desert A City*, Oxford: Mowbrays, 1966.

Trans. Derwas Chitty, *The Letters of St. Antony the Great*, Oxford: SLG press, 1975.

Pieternella van Doorn-Harder, *Contemporary Coptic Nuns*, University of South Carolina Press, 1995.

Sister Emmanuelle, *Sister with the Ragpickers*, London: Triangle, 1982.

St. Mark Monthly Review published by the Monastery of St. Macarius the Great, Cairo, Egypt.

Paulo Freire, *Pedagogy of the Oppressed*, Penguin, 1972.

Robert C. Gregg, Trans. and Intro. *Athanasius: The Life of Antony*, Classics of Western Spirituality, London: SPCK, 1980.

Jean Leclercq et al., *Contemporary Monasticism*, Oxford: SLG Press, 1981.

Maximus al-Antuni, *The Life of the Anchorite Saint Yustus Al-Antuni* (Arabic), Cairo, 1989.

Otto F. A. Meinardus, *Monks and Monasteries of the Egyptian Deserts* (Revised Edition) Cairo: American University Press, 1989.

Farag Rofail, *Sociological and Moral Studies in the Field of Coptic Monasticism*, Leiden: University of Leeds & E.J. Brill, 1964.

Benedicta Ward, *Sayings of the Desert Fathers*, Mowbrays, 1979.

——, *The Lives of the Desert Fathers*, Mowbrays, 1980.

——, *Harlots of the Desert*, Mowbrays, 1987.

John Watson, *Abba Justus: A Modern Desert Father*, London: Medan Books, 1993.

Takao Yamagata, *Coptic Monasteries at Wadi Al Natrun in Egypt*, Tokyo: Institute for the Study of African Cultures, 1983.

Rodolph Yanney, *Father Justus of Saint Antony*, Coptic Church Review, vol. 6, Pennsylvania, 1985.

N. Youssef, *Mechanics and Dynamics of a Successful Holy Flight*, New York, 1991

Chapter 4   *In Liturgical Time*

Jacqueline A. Ascott, *Towards Contemporary Coptic Art*, unpublished PhD thesis, Higher Institute of Coptic Studies, Abbassiya, 1988.

British Library Catalogue, *The Christian Orient*, London, 1978.

The Coptic Liturgy of St. Basil, pubs. Mark's Robertson Blvd. Los Angeles (Arabic, Coptic and English in parallel columns).

Christine Chaillot, *Role des images et Veneration des Icones dans les Eglises Orthodoxes Orientales*, Geneva, 1993.

Paul Evdokimov, *The Art of the Icon*, Oakwood, CA, 1990.

M. Gerspach, *Coptic Textile Designs*, New York: Dover Publications, 1975.

H. Hondelink (ed.), *Coptic Art and Culture*, Cairo: Netherlands Institute, Shoundy, 1990.

Fayek M. Ishak, *The Horologion: An Arabic-English Version*, Toronto: Coptologia Publications, 1992.

Murad Kamel, *Coptic Liturgy and Music*, Cairo, 1968.

Nabil Naoum, *Impressions d'Afrique du Nord*, Paris: Institut du Monde Arabe, 1998.

John Julius Norwich, *Byzantium: The Early Centuries*, London: Viking, 1988.

Leonid Ouspensky, *Theology of the Icon*, New York: SVS Press, 1978.

The Philokalia, English translation G. E. H. Palmer, P. Sherrard and K. Ware (4 vols. 1979 ff.).

Stephane Rene, *Coptic Iconography*, Ph.D. thesis, Royal College of Art, London, 1990.

Marian Robertson on *Coptic Music BSAC* 26 & 27, Cairo, 1984, 1985.

His Holiness Pope Shenouda, *Release of the Spirit*, Melbourne, Australia (undated).

Gerard Viaud, *La Liturgie des Coptes d'Egypte*, Paris: Jean Maisonneuve, 1978.

John Watson, *Transfigured Matter: A Theology of Icons*, Philadelphia: CCR, 1992.

Chapter 5   *Patriarchs: Fathers of the Fathers*

Fr. Cyril OAR, *Coptic Christianity in Egypt and Nubia*, New Mexico, 1984.

F. Johnston, *When Millions saw Mary*, Devon: Augustine Publishing, 1982.

Edwar al-Kharrat, *City of Saffron (Turabuha Za'fara)*, London: Quartet, 1989.

Peter Mansfield, *Nasser's Egypt*, London: Penguin African Library, 1965.

Kyriakos Mikhail, *Copts and Moslems under British Control*, New York: Kennikat Press, 1911.

Peter Moore, ed., *Bishops, but what kind?* London: SPCK, 1982.

Karekin Sarkissian, *The Witness of the Oriental Orthodox Churches*, Beirut, 1968.

P. F. Vatikiotis, *The History of Modern Egypt* (4th Edition), London: Weidenfeld and Nicolson, 1991.

Edward Wakin, *A Lonely Minority: The Modern Story of Egypt's Copts*, New York: Wm. Morrow, 1963.

John Watson, *Abba Kyrillos: Patriarch and Solitary* double issue of Coptic Church Review, Pennsylvania, 1996.

John Watson, *Signposts to Biography – Pope Shenoudah III* in Nelly van-Doorn-Harder and Kari Vogt (eds.) *Between Desert and City: the Coptic Orthodox Church Today*, Oslo: Novus forlag, 1997.

Chapter 6   *Mission: For Africa and the World*

Norman Anderson, *An Adopted Son*, Leicester: IVP 1985.

D. Desanti, *Une religion Chretienne d'Afrique*, Kinshasa, 1971.

Historical Documents regarding the role of the Government Committee of Bishops, Copts (Christian of Egypt), London, 1982.

K. S. Latourette, *A History of the Expansion of Christianity*, 7 volumes, London, 1937–1945.

Bishop Antonious Marcos, *Developments in Coptic Missiology*, Geneva: Missiology 17, 1989.

Stephen Neill, *A History of Christian Missions*, Penguin, 1964.

Chapter 7   *The Egyptian Church Struggle*

Archives: Centre for the Study of Christianity in Islamic Lands, Walmer, UK (September 1981–September 1992).

Saul Bellow, *To Jerusalem and Back: A Personal Account*, New York: Viking 1976.

Robert Brenton Betts, *Christians in the Arab East*, London: SPCK, 1979.

Gerald Butt, *The Arab World*, BBC, London, 1987.

Jimmy Carter, *The Blood of Abraham*, London: Sidgwick and Jackson, 1985.

Kenneth Cragg, *The Pen and the Faith*, London: Allen and Unwin, 1985.

Fouad Guirguis, *The Difficult Years of Survival: A Short account of the History of the Coptic Church*, New York: Vantage Press, 1985.

Mohamed Heikal, *Autumn of Fury*, London: Andre Deutsch, 1983.

David Hirst and Irene Beeson, *Sadat*, London: Faber and Faber, 1981.

Derek Hopwood, *Egypt: Politics and Society 1945–1981*, London: George Allen & Unwin, 1982.

Shawky F. Karas, *The Copts Since the Arab Invasion*, New Jersey: ACA, 1985.

Gilles Kepel, *The Prophet and the Pharaoh*, London: Al Saqi Books, 1985.

Ninan Koshy, *Religious Freedom in a Changing World*, Geneva: WCC, 1992.

Ministry of Information, Arab Republic of Egypt, *Meeting by President Mohamed Anwar El Sadat with the Moslem and Christian Religious Leaders*, Cairo, 8 February 1977, State Information Service, Cairo, 1978

Gwendolen A. Plumley, *A Nubian Diary*, Cambridge University Library, 1977.

Jehan Sadat, *A Woman of Egypt*, London: Hodder and Stoughton, 1987.

Helen Watson, *Women in the City of the Dead*, London: Hurst, 1992.

John Watson, *The Exiled Pope*, London: The Tablet, 1982.

——, *Church of the Martyrs*, Copts (Christians of Egypt), London, 1982.

——, *Prisoner of Conscience; Christian Patriarch*, Medan Books, 1984.

Chapter 8   *Thinking with the Church*

Martin Bernal, *Black Athena; the Afroasiatic Roots of Classical Civilisation*, London: FAB, 1987.

Raymond E. Brown, *Death of the Messiah*, London: Geoffrey Chapman, 1994.

Henry Chadwick, *The Early Church*, Middlesex: Penguin, 1967.

Kenneth Cragg, *The Arab Christian*, Kentucky: John Knox Press, 1991.

——, *Troubled by Truth*, Durham: Pentland, 1992.

J. Dominic Crossan, *The Historical Jesus*, Edinburgh: T&T Clark, 1991.

Bishop Gregorious, *The Christological Teaching of the Non-Chalcedonian Churches*, Cairo, 1961.

——, ed. *St. Mark and the Coptic Church*, Cairo: Patriarchal Publishing, 1968.

Henry Hill, ed. *Light from the East*, Toronto: Anglican Book Centre, 1988.

L. Hodgson, *For Faith and Freedom*, Oxford, 1955.

Fayek Matta Ishak, *Overall perspectives on the Works of Fr. Matthew the Poor*, Ontario: Coptologia Publications, 1998.

Tadros Malaty, *Introduction to the Coptic Orthodox Church*, Ontario: Coptic Church Publications, 1987.

——, *Christology according to the Non-Chalcedonian Orthodox Churches*, Sporting Alexandria: St. George Coptic Orthodox Church, 1986.

Y. Masriya, *Une minorite chretienne: Les Coptes en Egypte*, Geneva, 1973.

Iris Habib El Masri, *The Story of the Copts*, Cairo: Middle Eastern Council of Churches, 1978.

Matthew the Poor, *The Communion of Love*, Crestwood, NY: SVS Press, 1984.

Frank McLynn, *Burton: Snow Upon the Desert*, London: John Murray, 1990.

Otto Meinardus, *Christian Egypt, Faith and Life*, Cairo: American University Press, 1970.

Salama Musa, *The Education of Salama Musa*, trans. L. O. Schuman, Leiden: E.J. Brill, 1961.

C. E. Padwick, *Temple Gairdner of Cairo*, London: SPCK, 1929.

Birger A. Pearson and James E. Goehring, eds., *The Roots of Egyptian Christianity*, Philadelphia: Fortress Press, 1986.

Wolfram Reiss, *Erneuerung in der Koptisch-Orthodoxen Kirche*, Hamburg: Lit Verlag, 1998.

Pope Shenoudah, *Die Natur Christi*, Taunus: Flacius Verlag, 1990.

Hany N.Takla: various papers from St. Shenouda the Archimandrite Coptic Society, 1701 South Wooster, Los Angeles, CA 90035, USA.

Matthias Wahba, *The Doctrine of Sanctification in St. Athanasius' Paschal Letters*, Rhode Island, 1988.

John Watson, *Tadros Yacoub Malaty*, Copotologia, vol. X, 1989, Toronto, Canada 1989.

Frances Young, *From Nicaea to Chalcedon*, London : SCM Press, 1983.

Chapter 9   *Conclusion: Era of the Martyrs*

Imad Boles, ed. *The Coptic Voice*, Bedford, UK from 1998.

C. E. Bosworth, *The Islamic Dynasties*, Edinburgh: Edinburgh University Press, 1967.

Numerous papers and reports from: *Egyptian Organization for Human Rights*, Giza, Cairo: Mohandessin.

Robin Lane Fox, *Pagans and Christians*, Harmondsworth: Penguin, 1988.

C. Wilfred Griggs, *Early Egyptian Christianity*, Leiden: Brill, 1991.

Paul Marshall, *Their Blood Cries Out: The Untold Story of Persecution Against Christians in the Modern World*, Dallas: Word Publishing, 1997.

Nina Shea, *In the Lion's Den*, Nashville, Tennessee: Boardman and Holman, 1997.

Herbert Schlossberg, *A Fragrance of Oppression: The Church and its persecutors*, Wheaton Illinois: Crossway, 1991.

Rodolph Yanney, Coptic New Martyrs, *Coptic Church Review*, vol. 14, no. 4., Lebanon, Pennsylvania, 1984.

Bat Ye'or, *The Dhimmi: Jews and Christians under Islam*, London and Toronto: Associated University Presses, 1985.

——, *The Decline of Eastern Christianity Under Islam: From Jihad to Dhimmitude*, New Jersey: Associated University Press, 1996.

Index of Names and Subjects

Abaluya, 75
Abba, term defined, 20; used of Desert
    Fathers, 20, 39, 27–8; used of Abba
    Justus, 21–7 passim, 149, 154, 156;
    used of Kyrillos VI, 48, 52, 57–8, 62;
    used of Shenouda III, 70; used of
    Johannes XIX, 71; used of Al-Masudi,
    50; used of Antony the Great, 25
Abbasiya, 9, 66, 100
Abd al-Malik al-Masudi *Abouna* (Arabic,
    Father), 50
Abd al-Masih El-Israeli, 130
Abd al-Masih ibn Salib el-Baramousi
    Abouna, 50
Abd al-Masih Abouna, *el Habashi* (Arabic,
    the Ethiopian) thirty-five years as
    hermit, 15; Matta El Meskeen and, 18;
    meets Kyrillos VI, 51; monastic tradi-
    tion dependent upon, 54; influence in
    Church, 65
Abd al-Rahman, Sheikh, 115
Abdel Messih, Yassa Dr (1898–1959)
    Director of the Coptic Museum, 124
Abdou Yusuf, Yusuf, Abouna, 74
Abilius, 3rd Coptic Patriarch (d. 95),
    44
Abu El Sefein, the Monastery of St.
    Mercurios, 41
Abu Maqar, 17; *see* Macarius, Monastery
    of St.
Abuna, Ethiopian term for Chief Bishop,
    55
Abu Quorqas, 149
Abyssinia, 55; *see* Ethiopia
ACA, *see* American Coptic Association
Adad, Ephraim (d. 1897), 131
Addis Ababa Conference (1965), 57–8
Africa, 1
Agape meal at St. Macarius, 18; at Duena,
    147
AIDS, 128

Aigyptos (Greek, Egypt), Aigyptios
    (Egyptian), 7
Akamba, 75
Al Ahali (Arabic lit. The Relatives), news-
    paper, 110
Al Ahram ("The Pyramids"), 6, Papal elec-
    tion in 1971, 46; reports apparitions at
    Zeitoun, 63; *majlis milli*, elections, 69;
    see also Heikal, Mohammed
Al Ahrar (Arabic lit. The Freemen), news-
    paper, 68
Al-Akhbar, 110
Algeria, 23
Al Kiraza (Arabic lit. Proclamation or
    preaching), Coptic Orthodox weekly,
    edited by Patriarch, 67
Al-Antuni, Maximus, Abouna; *see*
    Maximus al-Antuni
Al-Azhar, the Islamic University in Cairo,
    principal Islamic centre, 7, brought
    under government control, 95, 106;
    foundation in 972 in Cairo, 119
Al-Bahnassa, Site of Shrine of St. George,
    143
Al-Baramus, Deir, Monastery of the
    Romans, 14–15, 41, 49, 50–1, 74
Alexander the Great (356–323 BCE), 1
Alexandria 9–10, 15, 21, 49, 71, 93, 116,
    119–120, 122, 134, 140, 142, 150, 153–4
Al-Gemaat el-Islamiya (Arabic, the Islamic
    Group), 148–9
Al-Hakim (996–1021), Fatimid Caliph,
    144, 148, 154
Al-Karmah (Arabic, The Vine), 133
Al-Kharrat, Edwar (b. 1926), 70, 161
Allah (Arabic God, lit. *the* God), 128
Allenby, Edmund, 1st Viscount, Field
    Marshall (1861–1936), 1
Al-Muharraq, Monastery, 13–14, 20, 31,
    146, 148
Al-Qiddis Athanasius ar-Rasuli (1981), book

by Matta El Meskeen, 123
Al-Wasiti, Ghazi (fl. 1292), 145
Al-Watani, Egyptian/Coptic weekly
  paper, 10
American Aid, 116
American Bible Society, 129
American Coptic Association (ACA),
  104–8 passim, 113–16 passim
Amgaad, widow of the martyr Abouna
  Rueiss, 146, 148
Amnesty International, 115
Anaphora (Greek lit. offering. Central
  Eucharistic prayer), 37
Anawati, George, 9
Anderson, Norman, 161
Andreos, Amba, Bishop of Abu Tieg,
  Abouna Angelos El Amba Bishoi, 146
Anglican(s) 9; and arrest of Shenouda,
  109–10, 113, 121; dialogue with the
  Copts (1990), 128; Lambeth
  Conference (1988), 136–9, 141
Annianus, 2nd Coptic Patriarch, (d. 83) 44
anno martyrii (Latin,in the year of the
  martyrs), 144
Anthony, Metropolitan of Sourozh, 33
Antioch, 2, 112
Antonious Es-Souriani, 65; *see* Shenouda
Antonious Marcos, Coptic Bishop for
  Africa biog. Summary of, 74, 83;
  Mark of Scetis appeals to, 88; meets
  Mubarak, 115, 161
Antony the Great, Monastery of, 19–20,
  22–4 passim, 29, 41, 149
Antony the Great, Saint, father of monas-
  ticism, (*c.*251–356), 11, 19–20, 153
Antony, the life of, 19, 25, 153, 160
apocatastasis (Greek, doctrine that all free
  moral creatures will receive the grace
  of salvation), 122
Apologetics, as feature of Coptic thought
  122–3; in Shenouda's thought, 132
apophatic (Greek), 139
Arabic, 5, 8, and Islam, 10, 30, 34; in the
  Liturgy, 38, 80; 38, 79, translation of
  English Theology, 121; 123–4,
  becomes language of Coptic
  theology, 127; terms shared with
  Islam and ensuing debates, 128, 131;
  Bibles in, 129; Matthew Henry in, 129,
  146
Ard El Golf, Heliopolis, St. Mary's Coptic
  Church, iconography in, 42
Armana, 6
Armenia, 57, 126, 139
Arsenius, Abba (5th Century), 28
artophorion (Greek lit. bread basket, box
  for communion of the sick), 36

Asceticism in life of Abd al-Masih, 15; in
  Wadi Rayan, 16; and Antony the
  Great, 19; in Abba Justus, 20, 22–7
  passim; and Kyrillos VI, 49, 51, 53; of
  Sarabamoun, 50; and Mark of Scetis,
  80, 123
Asia, 1
Ascott, Dr Jackie, Iconographer, 160
As-Surian, Deir, Monastery of the Syrians,
  14
Assyrian Church of the East, the, 2
Assyut in 1854, 8; Al-Muharraq
  monastery, 13; Abba Justus born in,
  20; icons destroyed in, 40; Shenouda
  born in, 64; Metropolitan Mikhail and
  dangers of, 103, 117; Fr. Rueiss born
  in, 146; terrorist activity in, 148; 154
Aswan Dam, 155
Athanasius, Amba, Bishop; *see* under
  Beni Suef
Athanasius, Saint (296–373), 11, 19, 73,
  120, 153
Athenogoras, Ecumenical Patriarch,
  Eastern Orthodox, 48
Atiya, Aziz Suryal, Professor, writer and
  academic, 3, 11–12, 124, 159
Atta, Azer Yussef, 49, 154; *see*, Kyrillos VI,
  Coptic Patriarch
Attalla, Waheeb, 99; *see* Gregorios, Bishop
  for Higher Studies.
Attar, Farid ud-Din (*c.*1120–1220), 1
Avicenna 1; *see* Ibn Sina
Awlad, Elias, 146
Ayyubid, Islamic Dynasty (1169–1252),
  131, 154
Aziz, Ibrahim, Abouna, 86, 91, 108
Aziz, Sa'ad, 100; *see* Samuel, Amba,
  Bishop of Social, ecumenical and
  foreign affairs

Bandung Conference, the (1955), 46
Banha, 64
Bar-Lev Line, Sinai, site in October War
  (1973), 106, 155
Barmen, the Theological Declaration of,
  (May 1934), 93
Bat Ye'or, 163
Bawit, icon and monastery, 41
Begin, Menachim, Prime Minister of
  Israel, 106
Bellaire, Texas, 84–5, 89
Bellow, Saul, novelist, 99, 162
Ben-Gurion, David Prime Minister of
  Israel (1886–1973), 1
Benha Kaliobia, 15
Beni Suef, Bishop & Metropolitan
  Athanasius of, biographical note

concerning, 99, 107, 109, 117, 133, 159
Bernal, Martin, 140, 162
Betts, Robert Brenton, 162
Bilqas, Site of Shrine of St. Demyana, 143
Bimen, Amba, Bishop, of Malawi (b. 1935) Kamal Habib, biog. summary, 103–4
Bishoi, Deir Anba, Monastery of St. Bishoi, 14–15, 17, 73, 88, 104
Bishoi, Metropolitan, of Damietta, Thoma El-Suriani, 138–9
Bishoi, Saint (fl. 390), 15
Bishop for Africa, Coptic; *see* Antonious Marcos
Black Athena, 140
Black Theology, 134–5
Blackman, Winifred S., 159
Blake, Eugene Carson, 48
Blom von Assendelft J., 79
Bohairic, Lower, Northern, Egyptian dialect of Coptic Language, 9, 37, 50, 158
Boles, Imad, 163
Bonhoeffer, Dietrich, German Pastor, (1906–45), 72, 98
Book of Common Prayer, the (1662), 39
Book of Hours, the, horologion/agbeya, 12, 26, 161
Bosworth, C. E., 163
Botros, Nosshi A., Dr Director of Cairo Centre of Patristic Studies from 1982, 124
Boulad, Henri SJ, 9, 159
Boutros, Guirgis (1892–1967), Abouna, 64
Boutros-Ghali, Boutros, UN Secretary General, 12, 47, 108–16 passim, 159
British Museum, the, 1
British Library, the, 160
Brown, Raymond E., 141, 162
Bulgakov, Sergei (1871–1944) Russian Orthodox priest and theologian, 121
Bulus, Bulus, Abouna, 101
Bureau of Public Affairs, USA, Department of State (1982 census), 11
Burton, Richard, Sir (1829–90), explorer, linguist, polymath, 126
Butt, Gerald, 106, 162

Caesar, Gaius Julius (*c*.102–44 BCE), 1
Cairo, Protestant churches in, 7; 11, 13–15 passim; 21, *zebaleen* in, 31–2; pollution in, 68; 73–4, 88, 100–1, 104; funeral of Sadat in, 106, 111, 116, 121; Patristic Centre in, 124, 154; *see also* Old Cairo and Abbasiya
Cairo, University of, 15, 64, 99–100, 124, 130

Calvin, John (1509–64) theologian & Reformer, 132
Camp David (1979), 74, 106, 156
Canberra, 106
Canepa, Bernard (Bishop Athanasios of France), 79
Canons, the laws of the Church, 87–8, 114
Cappadocia, 16
Carrington, Peter, Lord 106
Carter, B. L., 159
Carter, Howard, 154
Carter, Jimmy, President USA, 106, 162
Cassian, John (*c*.360–435), 73
cataphatic, 139
Census (1960) Egyptian, 11
Central Committee, WCC; *see* World Council of Churches
Chadwick, Henry, 122, 162
Chaillot, Christine, 160
Chalcedon, the Council of (451), 9–10, 154
Champollion, Jean-François (1790–1832), 154
Charles, Prince of Wales; at Sadat's funeral, 106
Chatwin, Bruce, 61
Cheops, Khufu, 6, 153
Chester Beatty Library, the, Dublin, 2
Chevillat, Alain and Evelyne, 160
Cheysson, Claude, 107
Chicago, Judy artist, and, 5, 159; *see* Dinner Party
Chitty, Derwas, Revd. Dr (d. 1971), 14, 160
Christian Peace Conference, 101
Christodoulos (1047–77) Coptic patriarch, 39, 131, 154
Christology, 10–11, 81, 120, 126–7, 134, 136
Christology of the non-Chalcedonian churches (Sporting, Alexandria, 1986) book by Tadros Y. Malaty, 134
Chronology, a Coptic, 153–6
chronos (Greek, chronological time) 30–1
Clement, Saint of Alexandria, philosopher (*c*.150–215), 11, 19, 153
Clericalising, in Coptic Theology, 124
Clinical Pastoral Education, 82–3
Columbia, University NY, USA, 106
Comparative Theology (Cairo, 1988), book by Pope Shenouda, 132
Concise Oxford Dictionary (1994), 5
Conference of the Birds, the, Mantiq Ut-tair (*c*.1170), 1
Constantinople, Council of (381), 126
Constitution (1956), 61; (1964), 95, 99, 155
Copt definition, 5–7 passim
Copte, French, 7; *see* Copt
Coptic Calendar, 142, 153
Coptic Catholic Church, 8

Coptic Church as a church of Erudition and Theology, the (Ottawa, 1986), book by Tadros Y. Malaty, 134
Coptic Church Review; *see* Yanney
Coptic Language, the, 5, 20, 26, 30, 37
Coptic monasticism, 14–31 passim
Coptic Music, 37–8
Coptic Orthodox Church, in Middle East, 2–4; historical origins, 10–11; revival in, 12, 17–18, 20; liturgy in 34–9 passim; iconography of, 39–43 passim; concept of Church in, 44; missiology 72–3; in USA, 85; Theology in, 120–41 passim; martyrdom of, 142–5, future of, 149
Coptology, term, 3; introduced into English, 12
corban (Hebrew lit. gift, the Bread of the Eucharist), 49
Council of Florence, the (1438–45), 8
Courtyard of the House of the Coptic Patriarch, painting, (1864), 70: *see also* Lewis, J. F.
Cragg, Kenneth, Arabist and Orientalist, sometime Anglican Bishop in Egypt, 5, 10, 162
Cromer, Lord, UK Consul in Egypt (1883–1906), 7
Cross and Crescent logo, 66
Crossan, Dominic, 141, 162
Cultural Action for Freedom, 32 ; *see also* Freire, Paulo
Cyril, Saint, theologian, "the pillar of Orthodoxy" (d. 444), 11, 37, 120, 153

Damanhur, 49, 64
Dar al-Qibt (Arabic, home of the Copts), 7, 80
Dar-Es-Salaam, Tanzania, 74
Dayan, Moshe (1915–81), 1
Death of Jesus, the, Newsweek magazine article (1994), 141
Decalogue, 78
Decree, the Presidential, No. 493 (1981), 98
Demyana, Saint, *Sitt Dimyana*, 142
Deputy Prime Minister of Egypt, the, Kamal Hassan Ali (1982), 108
Desanti, D., 161
Desert a City, the, 15, 160
Desert Fathers, the, 14, 17–18, 20–1; and fasting, 24; and silence, 27; and labour, 28, 30
D'Estaing, Giscard, President of the French Republic, 106
development, as theological concept, 128
dhimmi (Arabic, subject peoples under Islam, Jews and Christians who pay a

faith tax called *jizya*, symbolising subjection), 56, 145
Diaconate of the *Rif*, countryside, the, 101
Diaspora, 5, 17, 56, 79–80; debate concerning term, 85–6; 91, 99, 106, 125
Didascalia (text, *c*.150), 129
Didaskaleion, the, Catechetical school in Alexandria (*c*.170), 11, 119, 122, 141
Didymus, the Blind, Coptic Saint, theologian (*c*.313–98), 11
Dinner Party, the, multi-media artwork (1979), 5; *see* Judy Chicago
Diocletian, Roman Emperor (fl. 303), 142, 148, 153
Dioscorus, Bishop, 129
Dioscorus, Coptic Pope & Saint (d. 454) Feast day Tut 7 in Coptic Calendar September 17, 11
Divine Liturgy, the, of Saint Basil the Great, 33–8 passim; 83, 146, 160
Divinity of Christ, the (Melbourne, 1980), book by Pope Shenouda, 132
Doctrine of Sanctification (1988); *see* Wahba, Matthias
Doorn-Harder, Pieternella van, 31, 68, 159–60
Drew University, Madison, New Jersey USA, 82
Duena, 146–8 passim
Dutch Reformed Church, 74
Dyson, Freeman, 10
Dzelska, Maria, 159

Easter; "banning" by Shenouda (1980), 96–7
Ecumenical Council and the Ministry of Peter, the (thesis by Mark of Scetis), 82
Egypt, 2
Egyptian Army, victory in Yom Kippur war, 94; and Sadat, 107
Egypt Today, English language, semi-official paper, 69
Egyptian Church Struggle, the, (1981–5), 3, 93 ff.
Egyptian elections (1984), 116
Egyptian, Human Rights Centre, 3, 148, 163
El-Berba, 146
Elections; *see* Egyptian elections, Patriarchal elections, *majlis milli*
El-Gohari brothers, Ibrahim and Girguis Iconographers, 41
Eliot, T. S., 13
Elissar, Eliahu ben, Israeli Ambassador to Egypt, 94
El-Khair ibn at-Taiyib Abul, 131
El-Mahgoub, Rifaat, 116

El-Nekheila, 146
Emmanuelle, Sister, 160
Encyclopaedia, Catholic, 158
Encyclopaedia, the Coptic, 12, 159
Endtime, the, 21; see also Parousia
Entebbe Raid (1976), 78
Ephesus, Council of (431), 126, 153
Ephraim, the Syrian, Saint (c.306–73), 15
Eritrea 58
Ethiopia 57–8, 73, 139
Ethiopian Orthodox Church, the imperial
    lions of, 48; 55–8 passim; special place
    of, 58, 74; see also Hailie Selassie
Eucharist 34–8 passim; see Divine Liturgy
    of St. Basil the Great
Eugenides, Jeffrey, 5–6
Euphrates, the River, 1
Europe, 1
Eusebius (c.260–340) Early Church histo-
    rian 2, 142
Eustathius the Greek, al Rumi,
    Iconographer, 41
Evagrius the Solitary (c.346–99) 42, 66
Evdokimov, Paul (1901–70) Russian
    Orthodox theologian 40, 42, 121, 160
Exeter, University of, 12
Existentialism, 134–5
Ezbat al-Akbat, 149

Fakher, Raafat, Khalil, 146–7; see Rueiss,
    Father
Fanous, Isaac, Professor, Master of Coptic
    Iconography, 40–3 passim, 149
Farag, Antonious, Abouna, 86
Fasting, 24; as imitatio Christi, 25; in life of
    Abba Justus, 22–5 passim; criticised,
    124
Father Mark of Scetis early life, 75–6; his
    family, 76–8; relationship with Amba
    Samuel, 77; in Egypt, 78–80; in
    Greece, 80; in the UK, 81; in the USA,
    78, 82–91; murdered 89–91, 108; see
    also Theology, Egyptian Church
    Struggle
Fatimid, Islamic Dynasty (969–1170), 144,
    154
Fayek, Ashraf, Iconographer, 42
Fayoum; portraits and zeballen children,
    32; monastic site, 51
FBI, Federal Bureau of Investigation, 90
feddans (Arabic, acres of land), 59
Feminism, 65, 134
Fertile Crescent, the, Crescent of agricul-
    tural land from the Arab Gulf to the
    Nile Valley, 1–2
Fifth Assembly of WCC (Nairobi 1975),
    131; see World Council of Churches

Florence, Council of (1438–45), 8
Foda, Farag, 66
fool baladi sa'idi (Arabic, white beans), 24
Fool, a, for Christ, Abba Justus as, 29–30;
    St. Rueiss as, 147
Ford, Gerald, President USA, 106
Fortescue, Adrian, 159
Foyer Internationale des Etudiants, 40
France, 1, 29, 40
Free Officers' Organisation (1952) coup
    by, 46
Freetown, Sierra Leone, 74
French, 82
Freire, Paulo, 32, 160

Gabriel, Coptic Pope (1130–44), 143
Gairdner, W. H. Temple (1873–1928), 121,
Gayed, Nazir, 155; see Shenouda III
Gebel al-Guyushi, 51; see also Mokkatam
    Hills
Gebel el-Tarif, 10
George, Saint, Anba Guirgis, 142–3
Gerspach, M., 160
Gharbiyah, 49
Gilgamesh, the Epic of (c. the third millen-
    nium BCE), 1
Giza, 133
Golding, William, 13
Government Committee, 86; see Papal
    Committee
Graf, K. H. (1815–69) theologian, 130
Gray, Michael, 90–1
Great Pyramid, 6, 153; see Cheops
Greece, 80
Greeks, 1
Greek Orthodox Church; see Melkite
Gregg, Robert C., 160
Gregorios, Amba, Bishop of Higher
    Education, 62, 86, 88; biog. summary
    99–100, 117, 130, 133, 162
Griggs, C. Wilfred, 163
Guirguis, Fouad, 162
Guirgis, Anba; see George

Habib, Gabriel, Dr, General Secretary of
    the Middle East Council of Churches
    (1983), 112–13
Habib, Guirgis, (1876–1951) founder of
    Sunday School Movement, 133
Habib, El-Masri, Iris; see under Iris Habib
    El-Masri
Habib, Kamal; see Amba Bimen of Malawi
Habib, Samuel, Dr, 113
Hafiz, Mohamed, General, 115
Hague, the, Capital of the Netherlands, 6
haikal (Arabic, poss. from Syriac, temple),
    sanctuary and altar, 34

Hailie Selassie, Emperor of Ethiopia relations with Kyrillos VI, 48, 54, 56–7; assassinated, 58

Hak-Ka-Ptah (Egyptian, hieratic: the house of the temple of the spirit of Ptah), 7

Hall Patrick, Theodore, 159

hamal (Arabic lit. Lamb), loaf chosen at the Eucharist, 35–6

Hamayouni Decree, Ottoman (1856), 67

Haroun al-Rashid, the Caliph (786–809), 1

Harries, Richard, Anglican Bishop of Oxford, 138

headship, a Pauline theological concept, 137

Heikal, Mohammed, 46, 54, 62, 162

Helwan, 50, 53

Henein, Antonious, Abouna, 86, 91, 108

Henry, Matthew (1662–1714) Puritan-Protestant biblical exegete, 129

Heraclas, Coptic Pope, (232), 11

Hermit Antony the Great as, 11, 19; Matta El Meskeen as, 16; major aspect of religious life, 18; El Habashi as, 18; Paul of Thebes as, 20, 27; Shenouda and eremitic life, 65, 71; Mark of Scetis as hermit, 80

hieroglyphics, 9

Hill, Henry, 162

History of Eastern Christianity, the, 12

Hitler, Adolf, Reich Chancellor and Führer (1889–1945), 98

Hodgson, L., Professor, 126, 162

Holy Cross Seminary, Boston USA, 83

Holy Family, the, 13–14, 63

Holy Myron, the, 41

Holy Synod, the, 45, 47, 56, 118

Holy Trinity, the, 22, 26, 35

Homosexuality, 65, 128, 138

Hondelink, H., 160

Hopwood, Derek, 162

Horner, G. Editor of Coptic NT., 121

Houston, Texas, 84–91 passim, 108, 151–2

Hypatia (d. 415) Alexandrine philosopher, 5, 122, 159

Ibn Kaldun Abd-ar-Rahman (1332–1406), 1

Ibn Naqqash (d. 1362), 145

Ibn Raga, Al-Wadi (10th cent.), 130

Ibn Sina, Abu Ali al-Husayn, 1; *see also* Avicenna (980–1037)

Ibrahim the Scribe, El Nasikh, Iconographer, 41

Ibrahim, Fouad N., 159

Icons 39–43 passim, 149, 160–1

Icons the (Alexandria, 1970), book by

Tadros Y. Malaty, 134

Ignatius of Antioch, Saint (d. *c.*107), 44

Ignatius Yacub, Mar, the Third, Syrian Patriarch, 58

Ikhshidid, Islamic Dynasty (935–69), 144

Iman (Arabic, faith), 128

Iman Secondary School , Shoubra, 64

Immaculate Conception, RC doctrine (1854), rejected by Orthodox, 131

Incoherence of the Philosophers, the, Tahafut al-falasifa (*c.*1021), 1

Indian Orthodox, 57, 139

Infitah (Arabic, opening, Sadat economic policy), 94

Injil (Arabic, Gospel), 128

Institute of St. Sergius, Paris, 40

Internet sites, 157–8

Introduction to the Coptic Orthodox Church (Ottawa, 1987), book by Tadros Y. Malaty, 134

Ireland, 29

Iris Habib El Masri (1918–94) Coptic historian and author, 120, 124, 163

Isaac of Nineveh; *see* Mar Ishaq al-Suryani, St. Isaac the Syrian, 50, 91–2

Ishak, Fayek M., 12, 161–2

Ishaq al-Bishoi, Abouna, 73

Isidore of Pelusia, Abba (*c.*350), 27

Iskander, Yussef, 154; *see* Matta El Meskeen

Islam, 1, 7, 35, 46–7, 52; the religion of Egyptian State, 61, 66, 95–6, 105, 117

Islam and Coptic theology, 128, 130–1; 132, 144–5

Islamophobia, 149

Isra'iliyun, 131

Israel, 1, 109

jahilliyah (Arabic, time of ignorance, i.e. period in Arabia before Muhammad), 95

Jehovah's Witnesses, 132

Jerusalem, 94

jizya (Arabic, poll tax), 145

Johannes, Bishop of Gharbia and Tanta (d. 1987), 98–9, 133

Johannesburg, 73

John Kame, Saint (died *c.*859), Feast day Kiahk 25 in Coptic calendar, January 3rd, 80

John of Damascus, Saint (*c.*655–750), 39

John the Short, Saint (*c.*339–409) Feast day Baba 20 in Coptic calendar, October 30th, 16

John XIX, Coptic Patriarch (reigned 1928–42), 50, 71

John XXIII (1881–1963) Catholic Pope, 9

Johnston, Francis, 161
Joseph of Arimathea, 35
Joshua, 1
Jordan, River, 35
Judaism, 1, 130
Justus, Abba of Saint Antony (1910–76), 20–31 passim, 149, 154–6, 160

kairos (Greek, time), 30; in teaching of Abba Justus, 31
Kamel, Bishoi, Ishak, Abouna (1931–79) Coptic Orthodox priest and author, 142, 149–50
Kamel, Maurad, Dr (1907–75), 124, 130, 161
Kamil, Jill, 159
Kannisat al-Zabbalin (Arabic, church of the garbage collectors), 100
Karas, Shawky, Professor, President ACA; biog. summary, 105, 162
Kennedy Onassis, Jackie, 106
Kenosis (Greek, self-emptying; theological concept), 22
Kenya, 74–6 passim
Kepel, Gilles, 162
kharaj (Arabic, land tax imposed on Dhimmi), 145
Khomeini, Ayatollah Ruhollah, the (1902–89), 1, 105
khouria, also *khourieh* (Arabic – in some dialects), 135
Kikuyu, 75
Kimbangu, 75
Kingsmead College, Selly Oak, Birmingham, 81
kitab (Arabic, Book), 128, 130
"Kittel", theological word book of the NT, ed. Gerhard Kittel (1888–1948), 130
König, Franz, Cardinal, RC; meeting with Shenouda, 110–11
Kontolglou, Photis (1895–1965) Greek Iconographer, 42
Kopte, German; *see* Copt
Koshy, Ninan, Dr (WCC official 1982), 111–12, 162
Kurds, 66
Kyrillos IV, Coptic Pope, (reigned 1854–61) "The Reformer" justifies Iconoclasm, 39–40; 129, 133, 154
Kyrillos VI, Coptic Pope, 15, daily celebration of Liturgy, 34, 45, iconography of, 48; early life, 49; monastic life, 49–51; as hermit, 50–1, 54–5; his attitude to the Eucharist, 54–5; at the old windmill, 51; election as Pope, 52; his tomb a place of pilgrimage, 143; at return of St. Mark's relics, 54; and the

Ethiopian Church, 55–8 passim; relations with *majlis milli*, 59; relations with Nasser, 60–1; apparitions at Zeitoun and K., 62–4; 67, 73, 77, 99, 143, 154–5

Labour, monastic, 16
Lakehead, University of, Canada, 12
Lambdin, Thomas O., 159
Lambeth Conference (1988), 136–9 passim
Lane Fox, Robin, 163
Langen, Linda, 41; *see* Hondelink, 160
Latourette, K. S., 161
Lebanon, 1, 9, 112
Leclercq, Jean, 160
Leeder, S. H., 159
Leo the Third, Byzantine Emperor (c.717–41), 39
Leonard, Graham, sometime Bishop of London; visit to Egypt, 113–14
Lewis, John Frederick (1805–75), artist, 70
Liberation Theology, 134–5
Library of Congress, USA, 12
Library of the Fathers, the, 121; *see* E. B. Pusey
Life of Solitude in Saint Isaac the Syrian, the, Book by Pope Shenouda (1963), 123
Liturgy, 18, 25, 34–8 passim; *see also* Divine Liturgy of St. Basil the Great
Liverpool, University of, 12
Logos (Greek, Word), 120, 136
Longinus, 73
Lossky, Vladimir (1903–58) Russian Orthodox theologian, 121
Louvre Museum Bawit icon in, 40
Luther, Martin (1483–1546) theologian and Reformer, 132
Luo, 75

Macarius, Saint, the Great (c.300–90), 14
Macarius, Monastery of Saint, 14–18 passim; 31, 39, 97, 103, 121, 123, 149; *see also Abu Makar*
MacCoull, Dr L. S. B., papyrologist, 10, 159
Maghrib, 23
Mahfouz, Naguib, 135
Mahgoub, Rifaat El, Speaker of Egyptian parliament, 116
Majlis Milli (Arabic: Community Council) defined, 45; established, 47; relations with Kyrillos VI, 59–60; relations with Shenouda the Third, 69
Makari as-Suriani 77; *see* Samuel, Amba, Bishop of Social, ecumenical and foreign affairs
Makarios, Father; *see* Samuel, Amba

Malaty, Tadros Yacoub, 134–6 passim, 162
Mamluk, Islamic Dynasty (1250–1517), 1, 144, 154
Manasseh, Qummus, the (d. 1930) Coptic theologian, 120
Mansfield, Peter, 161
Mansur, Abu, 144
Maqaddimah, the, Kitab al-Ibar (c.1381), 1
Mar Ishaq Al-Suryani 50 ; *see also* St. Isaac of Nineveh, and Isaac the Syrian (7th cent.)
Marahrens, August, Bishop of Hanover, Germany (forcibly retired, April 1947), 98
Marcos el-Askiti, Abouna, 3, 75, 86, 88, 91; *see* Father Mark of Scetis
Marion County, Texas, 90
Mariout Desert, the photograph of Kyrillos VI in, 48; Kyrillos VI wishes to establish shrine in, 51; Kyrillos VI remains moved to, 143; UNESCO declares a site of universal value, 156
Mark, Saint, the Evangelist and Apostle of Egypt founder of Alexandrine church, 2; First patriarch in Egypt, 11; 44, 52; return of his relics to Egypt, 54, 72, 78
Markos, Metropolitan of Toulon, 79; *see* Blom v. Assendelft
Marqus Al-Antuni, the silent (14th cent.), 26
Marriage, African family tradition, 76–8 passim; Copts obtain dissolution from Syrian Orthodox, 58; Nasser strips Community Council of jurisdiction over marriage and divorce, 59; Egyptian family law and Coptic marriage, 105; inter-faith marriage, 113; Orthodox priestly marriage, 135; Demyana and arranged marriage, 143; Fr. Rueiss married, 146
Marshall, Paul, 163
Martyr (martyrdom) of St. Mark, 2; Al-Muharraq the site of recent, 14; and Antony the Great, 25; icon of, 42; Shenouda and martyrdom of office, 71–2; and Mark of Scetis, 86; of three saints, 142–3; era of martyrs begins, 144; of Fr. Rueiss, 146–8
Marxism, 134
Mary, the Blessed Virgin, 2, 13, 63; *see* Theotokos
Mashkur, Abu, 144
Masriya Y., 163
Matta El-Meskeen, Matthew the Poor Man, early life, 15; in Wadi Rayan, 15–16; publishes St. Mark monthly,

17; reforms Macarius monastery, 16–18; 31, 62; *Time* magazine interview, 97, 103; relations with Sadat, 102–3; relations with Anglicans, 109, 114; and Eastern Orthodox theology, 121; Commentary on *Orthodox life of prayer*, 123; Commentary on St. John, 124; on the Ordination of Women, 138, 149, 154, 157
matushka (Russian, the wife of an Orthodox priest), 135
Maurice, Saint, 72
Maximus, Al-Antuni, 26, 160
Mayo, semi-official newspaper, 96
McLynn, Frank, 163
MECC, Middle East Council of Churches; *see* Habib, Gabriel
Mediterranean Sea, the, 1, 13
Meinardus, Otto F. A., 39, 51; contribution to Coptic Studies, 120–1; 157, 159–60, 163
Melkite (Emperor's Men, Byzantine Christians), 9, 144
Memphis, 7
Merton, Thomas, Father, OCSO (1915–68), 22, 51
Mengistu, Hailie Mariam, Marxist dictator, 58
miaphysite, 127
Miftah, Butrus (d. 1875), Patristic scholar, 123
Mikhail, Kyriakos, 161
Mikhail, Metropolitan, of Assyut, 103, 117
Mina al-Muttawahad El-Baramusi ; *see* Kyrillos, Coptic Patriarch
Mina el-Makari, Amba, Metropolitan of Girga, 44
Mina, Saint, *Abu Mina*, 51, 142–3
Minya, 149
Moftah, Ragheb, Professor of Music, 37–8
Mokkatam Hills, the, 31–2
Monasteries; *see* Al-Baramus; Al-Muharraq; Antony the Great, Monastery of; Bishoi, Deir Anba, Monastery; Macarius, Monastery of; Samuel Al-Qalamun, Monastery of; St. Shenouda the Archimandrite, Monastery; Syrians, Monastery of; Paul of Thebes, monastery of *monophysism* (Greek, of one nature), 126
monophysite (Greek, adherent of One nature doctrine), 10, 126, 140
Montreal, 9
Moses, 1, 32
Moses the Black (died c.395), Coptic Saint, Feast day Paouna 24 in the Coptic calendar, July 1st, 16

Mubarak, Hosni, President of Egypt, 67, 107; in Kenya, 115; 156
Muhammad, 1
Muhammad Ali Pasha, (*c*.1769–1849) The Founder of Modern Egypt, 145, 154
mulukhiyyah (Arabic, leafy summer vegetable in Egypt), 24
Musa, Salâma (1887–1958), 140, 163
Muslim Brotherhood, the, 61

Nag Hammadi codices, 10
Naguib Shah-hat, 154; *see* Justus, Abba of Saint Antony
Nairobi, 74
Nairuz, Hanna, lawyer, 113
Naomi (deaconess), 75
Naoum, Nabil, 161
Napoleon Bonaparte, the First, Emperor of the French (1769–1821), 1, 154
Nasser, Gamal Abd el, President of Egypt (1918–70), 1; at Bandung, 46; attends return of St. Mark's relics to Egypt; relations with Kyrillos VI, 59–61, 74, 155
National Assembly, 95, 105
National Democratic Party; relations with monastery of St. Macarius, 17
Nature of Christ, the book by Pope Shenouda (Ontario, 1988), 132
Nazianzen, St. Gregory of (*c*.330–90), "the theologian", 37
Nefertiti, Nofret Ete, 6
Neill, Stephen, 161
New York Times, 94
Newlandsmith, Ernest, British musicologist, 38
Newsweek, USA magazine, 140
Nicaea, First Council (325), 11, 126
Nicaea, the Second Council of (787), 41
Nicodemus, 35
Nile Delta, 2, 13
Nile, the River, 1, 28
Nixon, Richard, President USA, 106
Norfolk, Lord; *see* Norwich, John Julius, historian
Norwegian aid, 32
Norwich, John Julius, Lord, 39, 161
Nostra Aetate, Vatican Declaration (1965), 131
Nubia, 73
Numeri, President of the Sudan, 106
Nuns, 31, 68, 160

odium theologicum, mutual hatred amongst theologians, 133
Oglesby, D. L., Detective, 90
Old Cairo, 51–2

Ordination of Women, 128, 135–8 passim
Organisation of African Independent Churches, the, (1978), 74
Oriental Orthodox Churches, the, 2, 57–8, 63, 109, 126,139
Oriental Studies, the Dominican Institute of, 9
Origen (*c*.185–543) theologian, 11, 121–2, 126
Orthodox life of prayer, the (*Hayat as-Salat al-Orthodoksia*) book by Matta El Meskeen (1952), 17, 123
Ostrich eggs, 34
Ottoman Empire, the (1282–1924), 1, 49, 64
Our Lady of Zeitoun; *see* Zeitoun.
Ouspensky, Leonid (1902–87), 40–2, 161
Overlook Hospital, Summit, New Jersey, 82
Oxford Movement, 121

Pachomius, Saint (*c*.290–346), 14
Padwick, Constance E., 163
Palestine, 1–2
Palmer, Andrew, Dr, SOAS, 160
Pantaenus (died *c*.190) Founder of Alexandrine Catechetical School, 11, 119, 153
Papa Abba (Coptic/Greek, father of the fathers, patriarchal title): usage explained, 44
Papal Committee: appointed by Sadat, 97, 108, 110; appointed by Shenouda, 69; *see also* Government Committee
Papyri, 2, 10
Paris, University of, 12
paten, 36
Parousia (Greek), 129; *see* Endtime
Patriarchal election, the (1959), 45, and Apostolic practice in Acts, 52, 155; (1971) 44–5, 155
Paul, Saint, of Thebes (died *c*.340), 19; monastery of, 20
Pearson, Birger A., 163
Pedagogy of the Oppressed; *see* Freire, Paulo
Pentapolis, 72
Peter, Coptic Patriarch (d. 311), 143
Pharaonism, 6
Philokalia (Greek. Lit. "love of beauty", primary Orthodox text: pub. 1782), 40, 42,161
philosophia perennis, 122
Philosophical Theology, 135
Philotheus Ibrahim (d. 1904) Patristic scholar, 123, 131, 133
Pimen, Saint (died *c*.451) Feast day 9 September, 16

Plato (428–348 BCE), philosopher, 119–20
Plumley, Gweldolen A., 162
Plumley, Jack, the Reverend, Professor of Egyptology, Cambridge, 98
Poemen, Abba, The shepherd(*c.*450), 24
Poverty 22; in Abba Justus, 23–4
presbytera (Greek, the wife of an Orthodox priest), 135
Prestige, G. L., 122
Prince of Wales's Institute, London, now the Prince's Trust, 42
Princeton University, 100
Pro Oriente, 110
prospherine (Greek, lit. a taking of food, cloth on the altar), 36
Protestants in Egypt, 7–8
Purgatory, 131
Pusey, E. B. (1800–82) Anglican theologian, 121

Qaddafi, 104
Qalalah mountains, the, 19
Qur'an, the Holy Book of Islam, 1, 67, 128, 130
qur'anising the Bible, 128
Qutb, Said, 95, 115

Radio Damascus, 106
Ramadan, ninth month of Islamic calendar, month of the annual fast, 128
rasul (Arabic, Apostle/Messenger), 123
Red Sea, the, 19
Reformed Church, Hungary, 101
Reiss, Wolfram, Pfarrer Dr Theol., 133, 163
Release of the Spirit, the, book by Pope Shenouda (1957), 123
Religious News Service from the Arab World (RNSAW), 158
Rene, Dr Stephane, Iconographer, 42, 161
Return to God (Cairo, 1989), book by Pope Shenouda, 132
Revolution, the Egyptian Republican, (1952), 46
RNSAW; *see* Religious News Service from the Arab World
Robertson, Marian, 161
Rock of Sarabamoun, the, 50
ROCOR, Russian Orthodox Church Outside Russia, 83
Rofail, Farag, 160
Roman Catholic Church: the response to apparitions at Zeitoun, 63; 79
Royal College of Art, the, 42, 161
Royal Irish Academy, the, 73
Roycroft, David, British Civil servant, 113

Roz El Youssef (Arabic name of founder and first publisher) newspaper, 68–70
Rublev, Saint, Andre (*c.*1370–1430), 42
Rueiss, Father, parish priest of Duena, 146–8 passim
Rueiss, Saint (d. 1401), 147
Runcie, Robert, Archbishop of Canterbury, 109, 113
Russia, 29
Russian Orthodox Church, 101
Rutgers, University, 106

Sadat, Anwar, President of Egypt: gives land to Macarius monastery, 16; and election of Shenouda, 46, 48; issues Decree 493 (1981), 94; economic policy, 94; visit to Jerusalem, 95–6, 99; role in Church Struggle, 99; assassination (October 1981), 85, 106, 155–6
Sadat, Jehan, Mrs, 62, 162
Sadel, Maurice, 70
Sadek, Maximos Ibrahim, Hegoumenos, 88, 107–8
Sahidic, Upper, Southern, Egyptian dialect of Coptic Language, 10, 50
Salah al-Din Al-Ayyubi, Saladin (1137–93), 1, 144
Salvation: the Orthodox Concept (New Jersey, 1977), book by Pope Shenouda, 132
Samuel al-Qalamun, Saint, monastery of, 15, 51
Samuel, Amba, Bishop of Social, ecumenical and foreign affairs, 62, 85; biog. summary, 100–2, 129; and Zionism, 131, 145
Saulchoir, Dominican centre near Paris, 9
Sarkissian, Karekin, 161
Sarubin, Mikhail, (d. 1918), 120
Sawirus al-Gamali, Boutros, 131
Scattolin, G., 160
Scetis; *see* Wadi Natroun
Scharoubim, G. R., 108
Schlossberg, Herbert, 163
Schmidt, Helmut, German Chancellor, 106
Scofield Bible, the, 129
Seal of the martyrs; *see* Peter, Coptic Patriarch
Second Vatican Council, the, 9, 78
Secret Service, Egyptian, 89
Severus ibn al-Muqaffa, Coptic bishop (10th cent.), 44
Sharia, Islamic law based upon the Qur'an, 67, 105, 113, 116
Shaw, George Bernard (1856–1950) playwright, 140
Shea, Nina, 163

Shenouda III, His Holiness Pope, Coptic
    Patriarch, born. 1923, Nazir Gayed,
    11, 15, 45, 62; early life, 64; monastic
    life, 65; place in public life, 66;
    confrontation with Sadat, 67, 94–106
    passim; editor of *Al Kiraza*, 67–8;
    difficulties with *majlis milli*, 69; in
    Zaire, 75; election, 80; involvement
    with Mark of Scetis, 80, 85–6, 88, 91,
    93; under house arrest, 106–16;
    ecumenical meetings, 109–15; and
    Christology, 127 ff.; banning
    pilgrimage to Jerusalem, 131; early
    books, 123; some theological writ-
    ings, 132–3; message to Lambeth
    (1988), 137, 151–2, 155–6, 163
Shepherd of Hermas, Patristic text,
    (*c.*1150), 129
She-re Maria, Coptic Hymn, 38
Shoubra, 133
Shoucri, Mounir, Dr (1908–90), 124
Sicard, Claude, Fr. SJ (1677–1726), 154
Sidarouss, Fadel, 68
Sidfa, 146
Sidhom, Mansour, 87
Sierra Leone, 74
Silence, 26, 27–8, 30
Simaika, Marqus, 6
Sinai, Egyptian Peninsula, 62
Six-Day War (1967), 62, 131, 155
Smith, Eli (1801–57), Bible translator, 129
Smith, Robert L., Judge, 86, 88–9
Sohag, 50
Sons of the pharaohs, 7
South Africa, the Republic of, 73
spadikon (Greek, Lit. To draw off, configu-
    ration of eucharistic bread), 35
Sphinx, the, *Abu Hol* (Arabic, the father of
    terror), 6
Spong, Jack, Bishop of Newark, NJ, USA,
    138–9
Spurgeon, Charles Haddon (1834–92)
    Preacher, 130
Sri Lanka, 73
St.. Vladimir's Seminary, Crestwood,
    New York, 83
St. Moritz, Swiss Winter sports centre, 72
St. Mark monthly periodical, 17, 123, 157,
    160
St. Petersburg, Russia, 60
St. Shenouda the Archimandrite,
    Monastery, 50
Stephen, Saint, the Protomartyr, icon by
    Isaac Fanous, 42
Story of the Copts, book by Iris Habib el-
    Masri, 120, 163
Suez Canal, 46, 62, 154–5

Sulayman the Magnificent , Ottoman
    Caliph (1520–66), 144
Sunday School movement, the, 69, 133
Sunna, Muslim Tradition, secondary
    source after the Qur'an for Islamic
    Law, 105
Switzerland, 72
Syria, 1–2, 29
Syrian Orthodox, 15, 50, 57–8, 139
Syrians, Monastery of, 14–15, 65, 77, 80,
    98, 100
Syriac, 50

Tablet, the, Catholic international weekly
    paper, 101, 162
Tadros, Abouna, 49
tailasana (Arabic, an amice), 36
Takla, Hany, Dr, President Coptic Society
    LA California USA, 125, 157, 163
Tales from One Thousand and One Nights:
    Baghdad (Arabic trans. *c.*850), 1
Tamburlaine,"Lame Timur" (1336–1405),
    1
tarboosh, (Arabic), *fez* (Turk.) conical head-
    dress; worn by Kyrillos VI, 49; worn
    by Shenouda III, 64
TAV, *see* Today's Arabic Version of the
    Bible
Tertullian , Quintus Septimius Florens,
    (*c.*160–225) African Church Father,
    142
Texas, 84–91, passim, 108, 151–2
Theban Legion, the, 72–3
Theological Word Book of the NT; *see* Kittel
Theology, 22, 63–5, in the life of Mark of
    Scetis, 77, 79, 82, 87–8, 91; and Coptic
    history, 119–22 passim; and
    Apologetics, 122; Historical
    Theology, 123; clericalising Theology
    in Egypt, 124–6 passim; Biblicism in,
    129–30; Coptic Theology and Israel,
    130–1; polemics in, 131–3; and the
    ordination of women, 137–9; method-
    ology, 139; the future of, 141
Theonas (d. 300), 16th Coptic Patriarch, 45
Theophilos, Patriarch-Catholicos of
    Ethiopia (martyred 1979), 57
Theophilus Es-Souriani, Amba, 65
theosis (Greek, deification, sanctification
    and divinisation), 81, 123
Theotokos (Greek, the God-bearer, Mother
    of God), 38–9; theological importance
    of, 63; 79, 120
Thomas Cook and Son (Egypt) Ltd, 49
Tigris, the River, 1
Till, Walter, 99
Time, US Magazine, 97, 106

To Jerusalem and Back, book by Saul
    Bellow, 99
Today's Arabic Version, of the Bible
    (TAV), 129
Toukh El-Nassarah, 49
Trade Centre, NY, 115
Trisagion, the, 35
Tulunid, Islamic Dynasty (868–905), 144
Turabuha Za'faran (Arabic, City of
    Saffron), 70; *see* Al-Kharrat, E.
Turkey, 46
Tutankhamen, Tut Ank Amun, 6, 154–5

Uganda, 76–8 passim
Umayyad Dynasty (661–750), 144
UNESCO (United Nations Educational,
    Scientific and Cultural Organisation),
    156
United Press International (UPI), 90
USSR, 57
Utah, University of, 12

Valley of the Kings, the, 6, 155
Van Dyck, Cornelius (1818–95) Bible
    translator, 129
Vatican, the, 2, 110; *see* Second Vatican
    Council
Vatikiotis, P. J., Professor, SOAS, London
    University, 96, 161
Viaud, Gerard, 161
Victor, the Church of Saint, Gizah, 39
Virgin Suicides, The (1993), 5; *see*
    Eugenides, Jeffrey
Vita Antonii, 19; *see* Antony, Vivian, life of,
    Tim, 125
Vogt, Kari, Professor, Oslo University, 159

Wadi Arabah, 19, 27–8
Wadi El-Rayan, 15, 17–18
Wadi Natroun, 14, 17–18, 28, 80, 153
Wafd Party, the, *Al-wafd al-Misri* (Arabic,
    Egyptian Delegation), 60–1
Wahba, Matthias, Abouna, priest-theolo-
    gian, 123, 163
Wakin, Edward, 53, 145, 161
Wanyama, Raphael, 3, 75–8 passim; *see*
    Father Mark of Scetis
wapfs (Arabic) Endowments and trusts,
    59–60
Ward, Benedicta, Sister, SLG, 160
Washington, 9, 101

Watson, Helen, 162
Watson, John, 160–3
WCC; *see* World Council of Churches
Weir, Michael, Sir, British Ambassador in
    Egypt (1983), 113
Wellhausen, Julius (1844–1918) theolo-
    gian, 130
Wesley, Charles (1707–88) Methodist
    founder and poet, 81
Westcott, B. F. (1825–1901), Anglican
    scholar and Bishop of Durham, 124
Womack, Max, 90
Women priests; *see* Ordination of Women
Woodward, Kenneth L., 141
World Council of Churches, 40, 75, 81, 99,
    109, 111–12, 117, 120, 131
World Service, the, of the BBC, 96, 107,
    111–12, 156

Yacoub, Magdi Habib, Professor Sir,
    surgeon, 12
Yamagata, Takao, 16, 160
Yanney, Rodolph, Dr, and Coptic Church
    Review, 125, 157, 160, 163
Yazid the Second, Caliph, 39
Yemen, *Arabia Felix*, 73
Yohanna the Armenian, Iconographer, 41
Yom Kippur War, 94
Young, Frances, 163
Youssef, N., 160

za'im al-umma (Arabic title, the
    outstanding national leader, applied
    to Zaghlul, 61
Zaghlul, Sa'ad, 61
Zaire, 74
Zambia, 75
Zarabi Dir ul-Mahraf, 20
Zawiya al Hamra, 98
Zebaleen, garbage collectors in Cairo,
    31–2
Zeitoun, apparitions (1968–71), 52, 62, 78,
    155
Zeno, 120
Zimbabwe, 75
Zionism, 46
Zurich, 73

Index of Biblical References

Genesis
14:18   28
48:13ff.   35

Exodus
12:5   35
12: 14–20   28
25: 30   28

Isaiah
19:19   13

Matthew
2: 13–23   13
6: 28   23
8:20   23
19:21   19

Mark
1:15   30
8: 14–20   29
14:17–31   29

Luke
20:34–36   13

John
6: 35–40   29
10:11   52
20: 12   36

Acts
1:26   52

Romans
12:2   19

1 Corinthians
2:9   37

Revelation
8:1   26